D1065426

En témoignage de religieuse gratitude —

Soeur Marie Agnès de Rome

29 janvier, 1946

THE SOCIAL THOUGHT OF FRENCH CANADA AS REFLECTED IN THE SEMAINE SOCIALE

This dissertation was conducted under the direction of Professor Paul Hanly Furfey, Ph.D., as Major Professor, and was approved by Reverend Bernard G. Mulvaney, C.S.V., Ph.D., and Right Reverend Donald A. MacLean, Ph.D.

THE CATHOLIC UNIVERSITY OF AMERICA

VOL. NO. 18

The Social Thought of French Canada as Reflected in the Semaine Sociale

BY

SISTER MARIE AGNES OF ROME GAUDREAU, M.Ed.
OF THE
SISTERS OF THE PRESENTATION OF MARY
NASHUA, NEW HAMPSHIRE

A DISSERTATION
SUBMITTED TO THE FACULTY OF THE SCHOOL OF SOCIAL SCIENCE OF THE CATHOLIC UNIVERSITY OF AMERICA IN PARTIAL FULFILLMENT OF THE REQUIREMENTS FOR THE DEGREE OF DOCTOR OF PHILOSOPHY

THE CATHOLIC UNIVERSITY OF AMERICA PRESS
WASHINGTON, D. C.
1946

MURRAY & HEISTER
WASHINGTON, D. C.
PRINTED BY
TIMES AND NEWS PUBLISHING CO.
GETTYSBURG, PA., U. S. A.

To a Trinity of Benefactors
Sister Marie Madeleine of Jesus, Dean of Rivier College
Dr. Gladys Sellew
F. T.

TABLE OF CONTENTS

TABLE OF CONTENTS (Continued)

TABLE OF CONTENTS (Continued)

TABLE OF CONTENTS (Continued)

PREFACE

This dissertation aims to point out the social teaching of the French Canadian elite as found in the courses and conferences of the Semaine Sociale of Canada.

The Semaine Sociale is an "ambulatory university" which on its annual tour to various cities purports to spread the social doctrine of the Church to the French Canadian elite. The courses given and the conferences made are then published as the Proceedings of the Semaine Sociale.[1] Although these are entitled *Semaine sociale du Canada,* the writer is mainly concerned with the French Canadian groups of the Province of Quebec. Exception, however, is made for Ottawa where the Semaine Sociale held its study week on three different occasions. The isolated French Canadian groups outside of Quebec have peculiar problems and disheartening complications occasioned by their distance and isolation from their own kind. As the vast majority of the French Canadians live in the Old Province of Quebec, we may say that Quebec is "French Canada," that is, the stronghold of the whole race.

In 1877 appeared the *Essai sur le droit social chrétien* by Father L. P. Paquin, O.M.I., the first book in social sciences written in French Canada. Other works have appeared subsequently but the volumes of the Semaine Sociale seem to be the most comprehensive source for the social and philosophical thought of French Canada. To one unacquainted with conditions in French Canada, the Proceedings of the Semaine Sociale lose much of their flavor and meaning, for the courses and conferences are specifically directed to French Canadians forming an intimate group cognizant of their domestic and provincial problems. The foreign reader will miss the allusions to existing laws and conditions, to previous discussions, and to anonymous individuals who have played a part in social movements.

Because of this handicap, various other source materials in the form of tracts, brochures, the weekly *L'Ordre Nouveau,* the offi-

[1] The Annual Proceedings of the Semaine Sociale du Canada will be cited as *S. s. du Canada.*

cial organ of the Semaine Sociale from 1936-40, and the learned monthly periodical *Relations* from 1940 on, were indispensable.[2] Among other valuable sources of information were the numerous interviews with the President and the members of the General Commission of the Semaine Sociale residing in Montreal and Quebec City, and other prominent speakers of the Semaine Sociale. For the unfailing courtesy shown, prompt assistance and useful information given by eminent bishops, rectors, provincials, a patriotic Chief Justice, an outstanding Senator, capable professors, conscientious lawyers, prominent industrialists, enterprising union leaders and social workers, the writer is extremely grateful. Without the assistance and advice of Father Archambault, S.J., President of the Semaine Sociale, who, with never failing generosity initiated a chain of interviews and furnished prompt and detailed answers to many letters and valuable source material, this study might never have reached completion.

The writer wishes to express her gratitude to Reverend Professor Paul Hanly Furfey, who suggested the subject of this dissertation and directed its development with scholarly, encouraging advice and kindly interest. She also acknowledges the generous assistance and valuable suggestions received in the preparation of the manuscript from the readers, Reverend Bernard G. Mulvaney, C.S.V., and Right Reverend Monsignor Donald A. McLean. She is, moreover, grateful to her superiors and members of her Community for the opportunity of pursuing studies at the Catholic University of America. For the various kindnesses received from the staff of the Laval University Library, that of the Bibliothèque Saint-Sulpice, that of the Municipal Library, both in Montreal, the writer expresses her sincere thanks.

---

[2] All are published by the Ecole Sociale Populaire, a center for the diffusion of sound doctrine and of social action: Secrétariat des Semaines Sociales du Canada, Ecole Sociale Populaire, 1961, rue Rachel Est, Montréal.

CHAPTER I

Some Social Movements in French Canada Before the Semaine Sociale

Catholic social action in French Canada existed long before these three words were invented to designate it. At the turn of the century we find traces of its manifestations which furnished Miss Marie-Claire Daveluy, as early as 1923, enough material to make a study on the social spirit of the women of Ville-Marie.[1] Under its various forms this Catholic social action is an indication of the spirit of charity which in French Canada as elsewhere animates all the followers of the gospel and of the teachings of the Catholic Church. Expressive of Catholic social thought, it can best be understood by a brief description of a few of the social movements which preceded the establishment of the Study Weeks in French Canada.

The *Societé Saint-Jean-Baptiste* of Montreal was founded in 1834, a very critical period in the history of Canada. It aimed at grouping the French Canadians to safeguard their religious and national interests. Originally, the members of the society attempted to gain political rights. Today they strive to preserve the customs and traditions of their country, to foster the settlement of new lands, to impart a liking for farm work, to keep the French language free from anglicisms, to encourage education and professional organizations, to render public morals wholesome. In short, the society aims to make the French Canadians a better people.[2]

The extensive emigration either to other countries or to Canadian cities awakened the Clergy to action. In 1848, a Society of Colonization was founded in Quebec by Bishop Signay. Bishop Turgeon, his coadjutor, was named director. In Montreal, Msgr. Bourget followed a similar policy. In his pastoral letter dated June 17,

---

[1] *La Bonne Parole,* June, 1923, pp. 6-8.

[2] Adélard Dugré, *La Paroisse au Canada-français* (Montréal: Ecole Sociale Populaire, 1927), pp. 52-53.

1848, he points out the double advantage of such a society, namely, help the colonists to establish themselves on good soil and enable them to practice their religion.[3]

Founded in 1876, in Montreal, the *Société des Artisans Canadiens-français* was also a beneficent undertaking. Besides providing for the temporal welfare of its members by insuring them against illness or death, it helped in parish work and participated in religious demonstrations.[4]

A *patronage* for the protection of young girls and women laborers was established in Quebec by the Saint Vincent de Paul Society as early as 1880.[5] A similar settlement was the *Foyer* for young girls. This institution was founded in 1903 by Father Henri Gauthier, S.S. The story of the sufferings and misery of two young girls in particular gave rise to this benevolent institution.[6]

On the eighth of December, 1900, the first cooperative organization in French Canada was founded by Alphonse Desjardins at Levis. It took the form of a People's Bank known as *Caisse populaire Desjardins*. It was a saving and credit cooperative and to this day it lives up to its motto: "Everyone for all, all for everyone."[7] There has been an extensive development of *Caisse populaire* throughout the Province.

Indicative too of a sense of social duty is the *Association Catholique de la Jeunesse Canadienne-française* founded in 1904 by Father Samuel Bellavance, S.J., and organized on the model of the *Association Catholique de la Jeunesse* of France. Its aim was to prepare youth for the defense of their religion and their country. The means employed to form this elite were piety, study, and action.[8] Affiliated to this association was the *Groupe Pie X*, a study club for young men. Founded in 1907, it had for director the founder of the *Association Catholique de la Jeunesse Canadienne-française*. The members of the *Groupe Pie X* were always active

[3] S. s. du Canada, Rimouski, 1933, pp. 258-259.

[4] Dugré, *op. cit.*, pp. 53-54.

[5] Personal communication of Mr. Arthur Saint-Pierre, September 28, 1944.

[6] S. s. du Canada, Montréal, 1920, p. 126.

[7] S. s. du Canada, Saint-Hyacinthe, 1937, pp. 178, 248.

[8] S. Bellavance, *La Formation d'apôtres sociaux par l'A.C.J.C.* (Montréal: Ecole Sociale Populaire, 1915), pp. 4, 12.

and cooperative in all works of charity and at religious ceremonies.[9]

Another important undertaking was the founding of the *Société d'Economie sociale et politique* in Quebec in 1905. It endeavored to study labor questions and to present literature on such problems. Its president, Joseph Evariste Prince, and Father Stanislas Alfred Lortie were active and devoted members. Archbishop Paul-Eugène Roy praised the zeal of Father Lortie in an article entitled *A Pioneer of Catholic Social Action,* calling him the *Apostle of laborers.* The society prospered for a few years and then disappeared.[10]

Two years later, 1907, the *Action sociale catholique* was established in Quebec under the direction of Father Paul-Eugène Roy. As the name implies, it is an institution of action rather than of study. Nevertheless, its teaching program is most interesting. To develop a Catholic sense, to form a Catholic social conscience, to study social questions, to make known Catholic life in general were some of its main objectives. Its program of action consisted in religious, moral, benevolent associations, labor unions and organizations of an economic nature. It achieved remarkable success through the efforts of the Catholic press which it sponsored in its battle against alcoholism, and in the inspiration it gave the working classes to form Catholic syndicates.[11]

That same year, 1907, the first Canadian Catholic syndicate (trade union), the *Fédération ouvrière de Chicoutimi,* was regularly and definitely organized in Chicoutimi under its Vicar General, Msgr. Lapointe.[12] Trois-Rivières had its *Corporation Ouvrière Catholique* in 1913. In 1915 with much ado and great difficulties the *Union Catholique des Ouvriers Mineurs de Thetford* was established. Similar unions were formed in Quebec and Hull in 1915, in Lauzon, Montreal, Levis, and Asbestos in 1918, in Lachine,

---

[9] Dugré, *op. cit.,* p. 43.

[10] Personal communication of Father J. P. Archambault, September 26, 1944 and Sister M. Amadeus Welton, *Monseigneur Paul-Eugène Roy* (Québec: Les Editions de l'Action Catholique, 1941), p. 150.

[11] A fine summary of the progress of the *Action Sociale Catholique* in Quebec may be found in Sister M. Amadeus Welton, *Monseigneur Paul-Eugène Roy,* pp. 29-173.

[12] S. s. du Canada, Québec, 1921, p. 87.

Sherbrooke, Saint-Hyacinthe and Granby in 1919. That same year Sherbrooke and Hull had their women syndicates.[13]

To foster and spread these unions, Father E. Hébert founded in Montreal the *Cercle Léon XIII* in June, 1918. The main objective of this study club was the formation of a labor elite who would then be efficient enough to direct the Catholic Labor movement. Its study program consisted in sociological works, in writings which aimed to give a knowledge of international unions from different points of view and a labor chronicle bearing on the principal labor events which took place during the week in Europe, America and in Canada. Mr. F. Roberge was the first president of the *Cercle Léon XIII*. As a result of the work of this Study Club many Catholic syndicates were founded to the advantage of the workers and of society in general.[14]

While the Clergy, the elite and the laborers themselves were active in propagating Christian principles based on the Social Encyclicals and the teachings of the Church, the Catholic Canadian women were also contributing to the betterment of society by their social action as members of the *Fédération Nationale de Saint-Jean-Baptiste*. Mrs. Béique and Mrs. Gérin-Lajoie were the initiators of this movement in 1907.[15] The Federation created a press organ *La Bonne Parole,* which related the activities of its members. It also formed study circles, such as the *Cercle Jeanne-Mance* founded in 1913,[16] which were centers of instruction and of spiritual and intellectual development, destined to complete family education and to prepare young ladies to accomplish effectively their role of mothers. Professional associations, within the Federation, saw to their moral security and to hygienic conditions. *La*

---

[13] S. s. du Canada, Montréal, 1920, pp. 134, 135, 299 and Gérard Tremblay, *L'Organisation ouvrière catholique au Canada* (Montréal: Ecole Sociale Populaire, 1922), p. 4.

[14] The number and names of the various Catholic syndicates in French Canada may be found in Tremblay, *L'Organisation ouvrière catholique au Canada,* pp. 17-25.

[15] Interview with Mother Gérin-Lajoie, July 11, 1944. Mother Gérin-Lajoie is the foundress of the Order of the Sisters du Bon Conseil, which is a community of social workers founded in 1926. Mrs. Gérin-Lajoie is Mother Gérin-Lajoie's mother.

[16] Dugré, *op. cit.,* p. 40.

Société des Ouvrières Catholiques, as an institution of preservation and instruction, occupied the workers of all ages in useful and charitable labor. *L'Enseignement ménager paroissial* for both married and unmarried women and *Le Comité des Aides maternelles,* which had a bureau for the placement of young girls who wished to help future mothers, were also functions of the Federation.[17] In short, this group of social workers was influential in preventing the establishment of new taverns, in obtaining the recognition of their rights, and in bettering their working conditions. One of their activities was the visiting of poor people in their homes. A record of each person visited was kept and monographs written.[18]

In 1912 the *Assistance maternelle* was founded to help poor mothers in their homes before and after the birth of a child. The mothers were entitled without charge to a doctor's visits, a nurse's care, remedies, clothing, bed linen, food, milk and heat. One regulation stated that food must be given during the ten consecutive days following the birth of the child.[19]

The *Cercle Jeanne d'Arc* had a feature all its own. Founded in 1915 in Montreal, it had as its first president and foundress Miss Laetitia Desaulnier.[20] It enlisted principally members of the higher class of the French Canadian society. It purported to foster the culture received in the convents by stressing literature, history, music, and the study of contemporary problems.[21] During the same year another type of study clubs, modeled on the groupings of the Belgian women, appeared as the *Cercle de Fermières.* As the name implies, it is an agricultural association known in the English-speaking provinces as Women's Institute. The activities of this institute are intellectual, moral and professional.[22] Founded

---

[17] *La Bonne Parole,* Mai 1933, pp. 2-3.

[18] Interview with Mother Gérin-Lajoie, July 11, 1944. The latter studied at the New York School of Social Work in order to become acquainted with the techniques of present-day social workers of the United States.

[19] Dugré, *op. cit.,* p. 34.

[20] Personal communication of Mr. Arthur Saint-Pierre, September 26, 1944. Miss Desaulniers is now Mr. Saint-Pierre's wife.

[21] Arthur Saint-Pierre, *Questions et oeuvres sociales de chez nous* (Montréal: L'Ecole Sociale Populaire, 1914), p. 90.

[22] Personal communication of Mr. Arthur Saint-Pierre, September 26, 1944.

in February 1915, in Chicoutimi, a number of women and young girls, most of them former pupils of the Domestic Science School of the Ursulines of Roberval, or members of rural families, started to study a program of action and to enact a constitution which has since been amended as new needs arose. It was evident that these women shared Max Turmann's belief that "where woman is there is the home"; and as land is intimately associated with the French Canadian home it became imperative to offer women an outlet to their social propensities more seducive and less arduous than that which was often presented them.[23]

The year 1911 saw the appearance of the first center for social research in the Province of Quebec: the *Ecole Sociale Populaire* founded by Father Hudon, S.J. and his collaborators in Montreal and based on the *Action Populaire de Reims*. It consisted of four committees: a committee of organization, a committee of studies, a committee of propaganda and a committee of finance. Doctor Gauvreau was its first president and Mr. Arthur Saint-Pierre, its secretary until 1914.[24] Its periodicals, conferences, special courses and monthly pamphlets, with a circulation of 30,000 to 40,000, constitute a rich doctrinal collection of French Canadian social documents, one of inestimable value as contributors of unusual competence wrote on current subjects. After World War I, due to a lack of homogeneous grouping, the activities of the School were restricted to the publication of its pamphlets.[25]

At this time, the two great Catholic universities, Laval and Montreal, each possessed a chair of Political Economy, held by Mr. Joseph Evarest Prince and Mr. Edouard Montpetit respectively. Their teaching directed a good number of young men in the study of social problems.

Again, the *Cercle d'étude sacerdotal du diocèse de Montréal* was a gathering of priests for the purpose of studying economic and social problems. Sponsored at first by Msgr. Gauthier, it gradually ceased to exist. In 1918, a similar social study club was active at the Grand Séminaire in Montreal.[26]

---

[23] S. s. du Canada, Saint-Hyacinthe, 1928, p. 177.

[24] Tremblay, *op. cit.*, p. 11.

[25] Joseph-Papin Archambault, *Esquisses sociales* (Montréal: Librairie d'Action Canadienne-française, Ltée, 1930), pp. 124-125.

[26] Personal communication of Father Archambault, September 26, 1944, and of Father Jean-Baptiste Desrosiers, September 27, 1944.

The French-speaking population was not alone active in social movements during the first two decades of the century. Although the English-speaking minority encountered unimagined obstacles and set-backs, it nevertheless achieved remarkable success, especially in the organization of the Catholic Social Service Guild.

The inspiration for the foundation of this Guild was drawn from the work in England of the late Father Charles Dominic Plater, S.J., the originator of the English *Catholic Social Guild,* and in particular from his booklet, *Catholic Social Work in Germany.* In French Canada the Guild was founded in 1915, incorporated in 1919, and designed under Father William Hingston's initiative to give regular social service to those needing it. A group of volunteers, with Lady Hingston as leader and a Jesuit Father as moderator, formed a Ladies' Committee, who under a Board of Directors, chiefly male members, organized various works of charity for English-speaking Catholics.

Some of the chief responsibilities assumed by the Guild are: the prompt and thorough investigation of all reported cases in English-speaking Catholic sectors; reference of these cases to proper institutions or agencies; the maintenance of complete records of such cases; the giving of necessary cooperation as far as possible in bringing the problems involved to a satisfactory solution.

Among the early social workers we find Miss Lily Barry, a lay apostle, who has given her whole time without remuneration over a period of several decades to Catholic Social work. In this she has made not only a great pecuniary sacrifice, but also the sacrifice of her literary gifts and her ambitions in the fields of literature and painting.

Today the Loyola School of Sociology and Social Service is an outgrowth of the Guild's need for expertly trained social workers. The formal organization of the School was arranged by Father Hingston, Mothers Saint Anne-Marie, Saint Eliza of the Congregation of Notre Dame and Miss Lily Barry during a meeting at Notre Dame de la Garde in August 1920. The result of this innovation was a fair enrollment of students on a paying basis.

It is interesting to note that this school, with the exception possibly of Toronto University's course in Social Service, was the first to be established in Canada. The course was a two-year one comprising nine prescribed subjects: Ethics, Mental Hygiene, Social and Economic History, Statistics, Community Health, Salesmanship, Social Economics, Field Work and Hospital Social Service. One feature of the course was the insistence on sound principles of ethics. The course was wholly original and designed to meet the particular needs of the English-speaking people. The school is affiliated to the University of Montreal and the first diplomas actually issued by the University as an autonomous institution, were conferred upon the graduates of the Loyola School of Sociology.[27]

Significant is the friendly and helpful cooperation which the social workers of this School met at every turn from other social agencies, first and chiefly from the good Sisters, who gave institutional care to children recommended to them, notably in the boarding schools of the Sisters of the Presentation,[28] of the Municipal Assistance, the Hospitals, the Montreal Convalescent Home, Saint Vincent de Paul Society, and the non-Catholic bureaus with whom the social workers have been brought in contact. Most of the members, being bi-lingual, are constantly requested for community services.

The influential part which the journals and publications played in the study and diffusion of social questions must also be mentioned. First in importance is *L'Action Catholique,* followed closely in the order of influence by *le Devoir* and the *Revue Trimestrielle.*[29]

The French Canadian universities, too, contributed to spread social thought and the social doctrine of the Church. Laval, founded in 1852 by the Seminary of Quebec, received a pontifical brief which granted the Archbishop of Quebec the authority to confer degrees in theology to the ecclesiastical students of the

---

[27] Personal communication of Father William H. Hingston, S.J., October 27, 1944, and of Miss Lily E. J. Barry, November 12, 1944. The latter is Honorary Secretary-Treasurer of the Catholic Social Service Guild.

[28] Personal communication of Miss Madeleine Sheridan, September 26, 1944. The latter is still an active member of the Catholic Social Service Guild.

[29] Archambault, *Pour un catholicisme conquérant* (Montréal: Ecole Sociale Populaire, 1933), p. 79.

University. Only in 1876 did Laval University receive its pontifical charter from Rome. That same year, this University established a branch in Montreal to favor the students of that region. In 1920, the Legislature of the Province of Quebec granted civil recognition to this institution of Montreal.[30] These two universities have been active in propagating social doctrine in their social philosophy and ethics courses. These universities will be discussed further in the chapter on Education.

The Saint Vincent de Paul Society appeared early in the history of French Canada. The first conference, called *Conférence Notre-Dame,* was held in Quebec on November 12, 1846 in the Saint Louis Chapel of the Cathedral, under Dr. Painchaud, assisted by Father Baillargeon, pastor of the Cathedral of that city. In less than a year, eight such conferences were organized by the same benevolent leader. In August, 1847, Dr. Painchaud sent a report to Paris asking that the nine conferences recently founded be joined to the French groupings.[31] The chapter on the Church will include a study of this important organization.

Social science in French Canada remained now to be elaborated under the inspiration of the Holy Ghost who vivifies all action; it remained to be disseminated among the elite and the Canadian people. Soon after World War I, a group of French Canadians, sometimes called "social Catholics" attempted under the inspiration of Father Joseph-Papin Archambault, S.J., to spread Catholic sociology by means of Study Weeks called the *Semaine Sociale.* There follows in the next chapter the genesis of this institution.

---

[30] *Annuaire général de l'Université Laval pour l'année académique 1943-1944* (Québec: L'Action Catholique, 1943), p. 13.

[31] Personal communication of Father Emile Cloutier, February 6, 1945.

CHAPTER II

Notes on the History of the Semaine Sociale

The Semaine Sociale is defined by its founder and current President, Father J.-P. Archambault, S.J., as an ambulatory institution of Catholic sociology, having for its express purpose the spreading of a social doctrine based on the gospels and the teachings of the Church. The members of the General Commission of the Semaine Sociale plan a social program which is concerned not only with the economic conditions of French Canada, but also with the application of the doctrine of the Church to these conditions.[1] Hence, the Semaine Sociale is, as it were, the "loudspeaker of the Vatican."[2]

In 1929, Msgr. Amédée Gosselin, Rector of Laval University, spoke of the Semaine Sociale as an extension of University work, offering opportunity for the application of principles, discussed in academic circles, to the requirements of the social milieu and the different classes of the French Canadian population.[3] Wilfrid Guérin in his "Impression of the Semaine Sociale" of 1930 called it "a reservoir of truth."[4] It has been variously defined as an economic assembly of the French Canadian people;[5] as a school, —a prolific school of doctrine, of truth, of justice and of charity.[6] Cardinal Villeneuve adds that the Semaine Sociale is an institution of light, a kind of "saisissement de l'âme" which impels people to action.[7] It is, in truth, a teaching force, an institution of learning, in which literary devices are subordinated to thought. The Semaine Sociale uses science as a means, its principal end

---

[1] S. s. du Canada, Montréal, 1920, p. 14.

[2] S. s. du Canada, Chicoutimi, 1929, p. 15.

[3] S. s. du Canada, Québec, 1927, p. 409. In French Canada we do not find that stratification of classes as it exists in France.

[4] S. s. du Canada, Saint-Hyacinthe, 1928, p. 22.

[5] S. s. du Canada, Ottawa, 1931, p. 269.

[6] S. s. du Canada, Québec, 1941, p. 199.

[7] *Ibid.*, p. 259.

being to utilize this knowledge to enlighten, orient, and direct practical action. It has as its motto "Science for action."[8] In short, then, the Semaine Sociale consists of "gatherings of social-minded people for the purpose of studying in the light of Catholic doctrine the social problems of the hour."[9]

Msgr. Gibier's definition, though referring to the Semaine Sociale of France, is one of the best that we have, ". . . it is a temporary and ambulatory university which travels from year to year to our large cities of France, which studies present-day social problems and gives to its audience a theoretical and practical teaching directly orientated towards action."[10]

Again, Mr. Guy Vanier, Secretary of the Semaine Sociale of Canada, makes of the movement a "manifestation of ideas," a continuation of life.[11]

Since the first of their annual meetings, the French Canadian leaders of the Semaine Sociale unanimously have adopted as their general purpose the diffusion of the teaching of the Popes. Specifically, they are planning to instruct an enlightened elite that will then be able to form apostles and launch them into their social milieu with sound social ideas. His Eminence, Cardinal Villeneuve, denies that the Semaine Sociale is intended to form laborers and patrons, or even union leaders; rather is it bent on inoculating sociologists and professors with a sense of social values.[12]

This ambulatory university also aims to posit the principles which should govern social relations and to study existing social problems in the light of Catholic doctrine. In a word, the Semaine Sociale attempts to form, by an approach at once doctrinal and practical, an elite who will spread the knowledge of a Christian

---

[8] Hector Lalonde, "Chronique de l'A.C.J.C.," *Le Devoir,* Montréal, August 31, 1925, p. 4.

[9] *The Canadian Register,* Kingston, Ontario, September 18, 1943, p. 11.

[10] Joseph-Papin Archambault, *Esquisses sociales* (Montréal: Librairie d'Action Canadienne française, Ltée, 1930), p. 90: . . . "elle est une Université temporaire et ambulante qui se transporte d'année en année dans nos grandes villes de France, abordant l'étude des problèmes sociaux les plus actuels et donnant à son public d'auditeurs un enseignement théorique et pratique directement orienté vers l'action."

[11] Statement by Guy Vanier, personal interview, July 5, 1944.

[12] S. s. du Canada, Montréal, 1920, p. 210.

social doctrine, and thus bring about a revival of the Christian spirit in the customs, institutions, and laws of the French Canadian population.

As far back as 1920, the year of the inauguration of the Semaine Sociale in Canada, Msgr. Philippe Perrier, one of the founders of the Semaine Sociale and present Vicar General of Montreal, was very emphatic about spreading the social teachings of the Church. In an article published in *Le Devoir,* his words of reprobation to the French Canadians were striking: "Your country was hungry, and you gave it nothing to eat, it was thirsty and you gave it nothing to drink, it was stripped and you clothed it not, in chains, you delivered it not: I disown you, go."[13] In his opinion, the so-called study week aims at a just and possible adaptation of the doctrine of the Catholic Church to the varieties of needs of his fellow-countrymen as well as to the world at large. He wants the Semaine Sociale to voice these truths to all the deaf who shut their ears lest they be disturbed in their comfortable self-complacency. One's neighbor is not this or that individual; rather is he a collectivity, a class, a profession. And it is precisely as a class, that he is to benefit by all Christian work.[14]

The motto of the Semaine Sociale, "Science for Action," clearly expresses the aims enumerated above: learn not only to know but particularly to do, to act, to execute. His Eminence Cardinal Andrieux, Archbishop of Bordeaux, commenting in 1922 on the motto of the Semaine Sociale in France said, "I like this formula, 'Science for Action,' but it is interesting to note that science finds expression in action only through love." He then added, and significantly: "The solution of the social problem must be a work of love."[15]

---

[13] Philippe Perrier, "Idée sociale en marche," *Le Devoir,* Montréal, June 19, 1920, p. 1: "Ton pays a eu faim et tu ne lui as pas donné à manger; il a eu soif et tu ne lui as pas donné à boire; il était depouillé et tu ne l'as pas vêtu; enchainé, tu ne l'as pas délivré: je te renie, va-t'en."

[14] *Ibid.*

[15] S. s. du Canada, Saint-Hyacinthe, 1937, pp. 114-115: "J'aime cette formule, 'la science pour l'action,' mais il n'est pas sans intérêt de faire remarquer que la science ne passe à l'action que par l'amour," car, disait-il aussi, "la solution du problème social doit être une oeuvre d'amour."

The words of Father F. Goyer, S.S.S., to the disciples of the Semaine Sociale of Canada in 1941, add weight to the above confirmation, "You are working to re-Christianize society. Your ambulatory university sets out to inject into a world dying of languor, of extreme weariness, not the narcotics of moral ideologies but the saving tonic of evangelical teaching and of a social doctrine derived from Holy Scripture."[16]

The Semaine Sociale of Canada, as approved by the Bishops of the Province of Quebec, consists of a General Commission (commission générale) sometimes called the Permanent Committee (Comité permanent). At the present, there are thirty-six life members in this General Commission, although the number has not been fixed. They include His Eminence Cardinal Villeneuve, O.M.I., the Honorary President, Father Joseph-Papin Archambault, S.J., President, Mr. Guy Vanier, Secretary, and thirty-three members representing different dioceses and professions of the country. The members have no other obligation than to attend the Semaine Sociale and the two meetings of the General Commission. Now and then, however, they are expected to prepare, upon request, either a 'course' or a conference.[17] The General Commission meets twice a year. The first session takes place during the Semaine Sociale itself, generally in late summer, and the second in November.

The purpose of the first gathering is to choose the subject of the next session as well as the date and place of meeting.[18] Several subjects, bearing on contemporary problems, are proposed but never imposed by the General Commission.[19] The members make it a point to decide upon a definite, doctrinal subject, one that is determined by the circumstances and needs of the French Ca-

---

[16] S. s. du Canada, Québec, 1941, p. 216: "Vous travaillez à la rechristianisation de la societé. Votre 'Université ambulante' s'acharne à injecter au monde mourant de langueur, de lassitude extrême, non pas les stupéfiants des idéologies mortelles mais le tonique sauveur de l'enseignement évangélique et d'une, doctrine sociale, tirée des pages saintes."

[17] Interview with Maximilien Caron, August 22, 1944, at the University of Montreal.

[18] Statement of Father J. P. Archambault, personal interview, June 19, 1944, at the Ecole Sociale Populaire.

[19] Statement of Guy Vanier, personal interview, July 5, 1944.

nadians, and appropriate to the time and milieu.[20] Occasionally, during the course of this meeting, outstanding men, who have shown interest in social problems, and who are influential socially in some way or other, or who have made some contribution to society either by intellectual works or by organizing a Semaine Sociale in their respective cities, are elected as members of the General Commission.[21] It is thus that, in 1942, Mr. Jacques Cartier, active member of the Local Commission of Saint-Jean, was nominated for life; similarly, in 1943, Msgr. Léger of Valleyfield. Both elections were submitted to the approval of the Diocesan Bishop.

At the second meeting, held each year in November, at the Cercle Universitaire in Montreal, the members of the General Commission, who should, by then, have studied the program, discuss the subject proposed for the next session of the Semaine Sociale. Once a decision is reached, speakers who are chosen are specialists in the particular field. Members who are unable to attend this meeting send written suggestions. There are times when the meeting is not adjourned until after three or more hours of heated discussion.[22] Immediately thereafter, the program is submitted for approbation to the bishop of the diocese in which the Semaine Sociale is to be held.

A Local Committee also forms part of the organization of the Semaine Sociale. This is subdivided into a Reception Committee, a Propaganda Committee, and one on Finance. The first of these is charged with finding quarters for outsiders who plan to attend the annual meeting. It is the duty of the members of the Propaganda Committee to provide newspapers and periodicals with the details relative to the program, courses and conferences. The Finance Committee must see to the acquittal of all debts contracted by the organization. For this purpose the members solicit sub-

---

[20] Statement of Esdras Minville, personal interview, July 5, 1944, at the Ecole des Hautes Etudes Commerciales.

[21] Interview with Father Archambault, August 21, 1944, at the Ecole Sociale Populaire.

[22] Interview with Father Gaudrault, August 1, 1944. Regardless of the date chosen, this meeting is held at 7:00 p. m. and informal discussions go on during and after dinner.

scriptions that range from five to ten dollars. These funds help defray expenses incurred by the printing of the annual proceedings and various pamphlets and leaflets destined to publicize the movement.

In addition to the Local Committee, there is a permanent Secretariat, located at the Ecole Sociale Populaire of Montreal, whose members write and edit the communiqués to be sent to the printers.[23]

To turn to the specific method used by the Semaine Sociale: the disciples of this Institution claim that for a century sociologists and economists have been studying social problems with the spirit and method which apply to the natural sciences, convinced that observation and interpretation of facts are sufficient to arrive at desired solutions. But to the followers of the Semaine Sociale a million collected and classified facts do not tell what ought to be attacked, modified, remedied in order to solve a social problem.

The lecturers of the Semaine Sociale pay scrupulous attention to facts, never once neglecting economical, sociological, historical, geographical, judicial or psychological research. But they realize that man has the right and duty to use facts, to dominate realities and to make them serve his ends in accordance with his nature and destiny. Confronted with this moral and spiritual element inherent to social problems, a purely descriptive science remains ineffective. It observes the changes and conflicts of passions and interests but it possesses no tool to regulate these and to judge their morality.

French Canadians interested in the Semaine Sociale movement consider first the spiritual prerogatives of the human person and the moral ends of society. Then, after having investigated and examined pertinent scientific facts, the Semaine Sociale brings these facts into relations with Christian principles with a view to determining how the "what is" of a situation may be orientated towards the "what ought to be." Thus, the Semaine Sociale is not merely theoretical in outlook but truly practical. It offers modes

---

[23] Interview with Father Archambault, June 19, 1944, at the Ecole Sociale Populaire.

of action to its followers. It remains faithful to its motto, "Science for Action."[24]

Actually, the Semaine Sociale originated in Germany in 1893 under the name of "Practical Social Courses" (*Praktische Schulungskurse*) and as one of the projects of the Volkverein under Windthorst.[25] In France, in August, 1904, the institution changed its name and adapted its teaching to the needs of the French population of the period. It also underwent certain modifications in its organization.[26] At the beginning of the Twentieth Century, the religious situation became very critical in France. The State ordered the expulsion of religious orders and the separation of Church and State and the secularization of all schools. The socialists were on the alert during this difficult situation and seized the opportunity to sow the seed of their pernicious doctrines. It became imperative to instruct the French people on their individual and social duties and obligations. Sociologists feared lest this crisis menace the national and religious life of France, and so inaugurated the Semaine Sociale.[27]

The first Semaine Sociale of France was founded in 1905 by Marius Gonin, a worthy tertiary of Saint Francis. It grew out of Gonin's acquaintance with Léon Harmel of Val-des-Bois. Henri Lorin was its first President. Soon it became a national institution with annual sessions[28] and with study clubs which helped popularize the teaching of the 'Study Weeks.' Founded in Lyons, the Semaine Sociale soon made its round of France. In Orleans, it met with brilliant success. The Dijon and Amiens sessions showed progress in the number of auditors as well as in the efficiency of their participating professors. Marseille, Bordeaux, Rouen, St.-Etienne-

---

[24] *L'Ordre Nouveau,* Montréal, September, 1938, p. 2, and *Le Richelieu,* Saint-Jean, September 17, 1942, pp. 10-11: *L'Ordre Nouveau,* a weekly publication, was the official organ of the Semaine sociale of Canada from 1936 to 1940. It is now replaced by *Relations* in which a more comprehensive and scientific treatment of social and cultural problems is given.

[25] S. s. du Canada, Saint-Hyacinthe, 1928, p. 173.

[26] Max Turmann, *Le Développement du catholicisme social* (Paris: Félix Alcan et Guillaumin Réunis, 1909), pp. 328-329.

[27] "Tertiaries in Action," *Third Order Forum,* February 1, 1928, pp. 330-332.

[28] S. s. du Canada, Nicolet, 1940, p. 12.

Limoges counted more than a thousand auditors. In 1913, it was decided at the Versailles meeting to devote the entire week to the discussion of a single subject only. After World War I, late Professor Eugène Duthoit of Lille University, became President, Henri Lorin having died in 1915. Metz, Caen, Toulouse, Strasbourg, and other cities, each in turn, held the annual meeting with ever-increasing success.[29]

Holland, in 1906, was the first country to imitate France. The history of the Semaine Sociale of Holland is divided into two periods. The first comprises seven national meetings held before and one held after World War I. The second period starts in 1925. Due to the efforts of Msgr. Poels, a former Professor of the Catholic University of America, diocesan meetings were held each year in different cities. This new approach was regarded as very successful.

In 1907, Spain held its first Study Week in Valence. Five annual meetings followed, but political intrigues brought a halt of twenty-one years. Sessions were held, however, in Madrid in 1933, and in Saragossa in 1934. Both were successful. The same year, Pistoia saw its first Italian Study Week. Since then, twenty sessions have been held.

In 1908, the Catholic Belgians inaugurated their two Study Weeks, one for the Flemish, the other for the French population. These were regularly held in Louvain. During one of these weeks, labor questions were studied; the other week was devoted to rural problems. The founder of these Study Weeks was Father Rutten, O.P.

The following year, 1909, Poland had its Study Week. In 1910, Switzerland had its session in Fribourg. Many other countries have also held similar Study Weeks: Lithuania, Austria, Czechoslovakia, Yugoslavia, and England. The institution crossed the oceans and met with success in Uruguay, Chile, Argentina, and Rhodesia.[30]

Without doubt, outside of France, it is in Canada that the institution of the Semaine Sociale has seen its greatest develop-

---

[29] *Le Richelieu,* Saint-Jean, September 17, 1942, p. 10.

[30] *Ibid.,* p. 10, and *Les Semaines sociales* (Montréal: Secrétariat de l'Ecole Sociale Populaire, 1920), No. 87, p. 2.

ment. We are told that on a certain night four persons chanced to meet in one of the rectories of the city of Montreal. They were: a pastor, Father Philippe Perrier, experienced in the handling of current social problems; a lawyer, Mr. Guy Vanier, a man of culture and a great devotee of worthy causes; a journalist, Mr. Omer Héroux, later editor-in-chief of *Le Devoir,* open-minded and intelligent; and a Jesuit, Father Joseph-Papin Archambault,[31] the learned, tenacious, devoted, energetic, and apostolic sociologist, who in the opinion of a large body of French Canadians is the very soul of the Semaine Sociale of Canada. Around this little coterie the Semaine Sociale of Canada was founded.

Inaugurated in Montreal in 1920, modeled on the Semaine Sociale of France, patronized, encouraged, and blessed by the episcopacy, the Semaine Sociale was introduced into French Canada by Father Archambault with the collaboration of priests and laymen. At the very outset, it won the praiseworthy and unanimous approbation of the French Canadian episcopacy and of Pope Benedict XV himself.[32] Its first patron and protector, Archbishop Bruchesi, addressed the audience at the opening session.

Since 1920, this ambulatory university has been going from city to city, from one French Canadian center to another, to carry the "torch of truth." Montreal, Quebec, and Ottawa benefited of its sessions on three different occasions; Sherbrooke, Saint-Hyacinthe, and Trois-Rivières, twice; Chicoutimi, Rimouski, Joliette, Nicolet, Saint-Jean, and Salaberry-de-Valleyfield, once. In 1926, 1930, and 1934, which were election years, the Semaine Sociale was cancelled. Likewise in 1939, and for a very obvious reason: it had previously been decided to discuss the subject *Peace.*[33]

The first Semaine Sociale took place from June 21 to 25. The next eleven sessions were held in August. During the years 1935-37, the Semaine Sociale met in July, and since 1938, in September,

---

[31] Joseph-Papin Archambault, *Pour un catholicisme conquérant* (Montréal: Ecole Sociale Populaire, 1933), pp. 83-84.

[32] The brief of Pope Benedict XV, which was sent to the Secretary of the Semaine sociale, Mr. Guy Vanier, may be found in the first volume of the Semaine sociale of Canada, Montréal, 1920, pp. viii-xix, together with the other letters of approbation from the bishops of the various dioceses.

[33] Interview with Father Archambault, August 21, 1944, at the Ecole Sociale Populaire.

that is, after the opening of the Universities and Seminaries to favor attendance of the students, as they are regarded as the future elite of French-Canadian society.

It had been the custom formerly to open the Semaine Sociale on a Monday with a Pontifical Mass officiated by the Apostolic Delegate. It was also customary, for the bishop of the diocese to welcome the members of the assembly and at the same time to expound some point of doctrine. Thence, the auditors proceeded to the hall designated for the courses. The Representative of the Pope next delivered an allocution and the President of the Semaine Sociale then took the stand. At this point, Father Archambault would state the motives for the choice of the subject to be studied in the course of the week, and the reason for the choice of the city. Three courses were given daily. Evenings were taken up either by conferences or by what the members chose to call "manifestations ouvrières." Again, on a determined night, a religious ceremony would take place in a church as a special feature of the French Canadian Study Week. The meeting would close on Friday night.

This was the procedure of the Semaine Sociale of Canada until 1931, at which time the "week" was reduced to four days. In 1933 and during the years which followed until 1940, the Semaine Sociale opened its program on Sunday night instead of Monday morning, and closed on Friday night. World War II caused a notable reduction in the number of days allotted to Study Week discussions. In 1940, the annual meeting was held over a week-end, favoring those laymen who could not leave their business affairs on weekdays. Since that date, the Semaine Sociale of Canada has been taking place over week-ends only.

During the first years, a nominal fee of a dollar was charged for attendance at all of the sessions of the Semaine Sociale and fifty cents for any one session. We find evidence of this procedure as late as 1927: the Quebec daily, *L'Action Catholique* reports in that year that anyone can get for the small sum of one dollar an incomparable food for the intellect which will fortify him against many moral dangers.[34] Today, admission is free at all times for both men and women.

---

[34] *L'Action Catholique,* Québec, August 27, 1927, p. 5.

As stated above, the Semaine Sociale was founded to propagate the social doctrine of the Church. This task it can best accomplish by appealing to the social teachings of the Popes. Hence, it devoted its first session to the Encyclical *Rerum novarum,* the workingmen's catechism as Archbishop Bruchési called it, its eleventh to the Encyclical *Quadragesimo anno,* veritable synthesis of the principles of Catholic Sociology, its sixteenth to *Divini Redemptoris,* a defense of natural and Christian rights denied and combatted by the Communists, and the intervening sessions to particular subjects from any one of these encyclicals. Thus, the doctrine which the Semaine Sociale has elaborated is a doctrine of peace, of justice, and of liberty, based on the immutable natural law. Insistence on moral principles outlined in the encyclicals is basic.[35] In the words of Father Archambault, no important reform is possible if it does not rest on sound principles. To move the will to action, he goes on to say, it is necessary first to enlighten the mind. Thus, it is imperative to cultivate a sense of social responsibility in French Canada where a profound individualism had been at work undermining society and despoiling its best qualities. That is why the study and dissemination of the doctrine contained in the social encyclicals is so urged as a duty incumbent upon all French Canadians. The teaching of the Semaine Sociale is essentially doctrinal while at the same time having a practical purpose. The Semaine Sociale tackles contemporary problems, considers them in the milieu where they exist, and seeks immediate and practical solutions.

Meeting annually, always under the same general direction and with the same aim, it has developed particular characteristics. In the first place, one finds everywhere evidence of intense intellectual activity. The Semaine Sociale teaches in an official manner. It assumes the form of lectures commonly found in universities. The professor goes to the rostrum and gives his course. The speaker does not end with the expression of a wish or a hope. He is there to expound social doctrine. Each course begins and ends with a prayer.

A second characteristic of this institution is the charming family spirit which exists between auditors and professors. It has

[35] Archambault, *Esquisses sociales, op. cit.,* pp. 174-176.

fostered a facile interchange of views on many problems. Should anyone wish to interview a professor after the courses, he is given every opportunity to do so.

Again, the Semaine Sociale is not a place for the dilettante. It is not study for the mere pleasure of studying or even to enrich the mind with sterile knowledge. It is study for action.

Incidentally, the Semaine Sociale of Canada resembles that of France. Father Archambault, who established the Semaine Sociale in Canada, attended the Semaine Sociale of France in 1913, admired it, and carefully copied most of its features. For example, both publish annual proceedings.

One important difference is that in France the audience is much larger.[36] This can be readily explained by the fact that French Canadians must travel over greater distances to attend the sessions. People living, let us say, in Gaspesie find it difficult to attend a Study Week in Ottawa.[37] Attendance in Canada, however, may at times reach a thousand or more.

In Canada, there are no public meals following the courses. But there is a workingman's demonstration (manifestation ouvrière) a popular meeting, entirely devoted to the study of labor unions or Catholic syndicates. This usually takes place in a public park or in a large hall. In connection with this innovation, there are sightseeing tours including visits to some of the industrial plants. In 1925, the assembly of Trois-Rivières visited the Shawinigan Water and Power Plant, the Saint-Maurice Paper Industry, and the Wabasso Cotton Company.[38]

Mother M. Saint Honoré, Counsellor General of the Sisters of the Presentation of Mary and for more than fifteen years a resident of France, notes another important difference in the teachings of the Semaine Sociale in the two countries. In France, the sole concern is the social question and religion, while in Canada, the groups are interested, besides the social question, in problems of language and nationality as well as religion.[39]

---

[36] Interview with Father Gauthier, C.S.V., September 27, 1944, at the Ecole Hippolyte of Montréal.

[37] Interview with Father Lévesque, O.P., September 18, 1944, at Laval University, Québec.

[38] *Le Devoir,* Montréal, August 14, 1925, p. 1.

[39] Interview with Mother M. Saint Honoré, September 25, 1944, in Marieville, Canada.

Closely allied to the characteristics of the Semaine Sociale is the all-important matter of its influence on the French Canadian population. In order to detect this influence it is necessary to study the efforts made by the members to diffuse their doctrine and to listen to what people in general say the influence has been.

Summaries of the courses and conferences, articles on the doctrine of the Semaine Sociale or on the weekly program are sure to be found in the important daily newspapers of French Canada, namely: *L'Action Catholique* of Quebec and *Le Droit* of Ottawa,[40] both of these official papers of the Catholic Church; *Le Devoir, La Presse, La Tribune,* the *Montreal Daily Star;* the weekly *Canadian Register,* formerly called the *Montreal Beacon*[41] and finally the weekly *L'Ordre Nouveau,* official organ of the Semaine Sociale from 1936 until 1940. Relative to this last periodical, many testimonials have been received certifying that this weekly enlightened the mind, fortified convictions, exposed errors, and spread truth.[42] The foreign press has added its word of praise. The *Social Justice Review* of July-August, 1942, contains an article on the Study Week of Canada by Father Joseph H. Ledit, S.J. In the same year, Father Lafarge writes at some length in *America* on Catholic Action and Henri Franchet has an appreciation in particular of the eleventh Semaine Sociale of Canada in the *Chronique sociale de France.*[43] What is more significant: in 1938, Radio-Canada broadcasted the courses and conferences of the Semaine Sociale of Sherbrooke and again in 1941, the Study week of Quebec.[44]

There is no doubt, then, that the Semaine Sociale is what the French call a "semeur d'idées." The principles spread by the

---

[40] At the first session of the Semaine sociale in Montréal in 1920, Charles Gauthier, Thomas Poulin, and J. Edmond Cloutier, reporters for *Le Droit* attended each meeting and sent daily a complete and detailed rendering of the courses and conferences. *Le Droit,* Ottawa, June 21, 1920, p. 3.

[41] Interview with Guy Vanier, July 5, 1944.

[42] *L'Ordre Nouveau,* Montréal, November 20, 1940, p. 1.

[43] Interview with Father Archambault, August 21, 1944, at the Ecole Sociale Populaire.

[44] Richard Arès, "La Semaine sociale de Sherbrooke," *L'Ordre Nouveau,* October 5, 1938, p. 2, and Omer Héroux, "A Propos de la Semaine sociale de Québec," *Le Devoir,* September 18, 1941, p. 1.

Semaine Sociale inevitably, though at times imperceptibly, inspire the social leaders and the legislators of the Province of Quebec. A certain similarity has been claimed between the demands made by leading politicians and the solutions proposed by the Semaine Sociale: an indication of the latter's social influence.

That the Semaine Sociale contributed more than any other institution to spread the knowledge of the social doctrine of the Church in French Canada is the belief of Mr. Esdras Minville and Professor Edouard Montpetit, Director of the School of Social Science at the University of Montreal. Mr. Antonio Perreault claims the influence to be indirect rather than direct. Mr. Maximilien Caron and Mr. Omer Héroux believe that it is imperceptible, while Mr. Guy Vanier is of the opinion that the Semaine Sociale fosters research and directs public opinion. Senator Léon-Mercier Gouin and Father Gauthier state that the main influence is exerted via the press, and Msgr. Gagnon and Msgr. Maurault via published volumes. The Semaine Sociale of Rimouski—the latter city is an agricultural center—was influential, claims Father Gaudrault, primarily because it reached its milieu directly. It is the elite that we reach, says Father Marchand; on the other hand, Msgr. Maurault believes that this influence is not particularly great since the number of elite is rather limited.

The size of the audience attending the Semaine Sociale is still another index of their influence. Early in the history of the Semaine Sociale, the number of auditors was very small. According to Father Gauthier, there were some twenty-five persons in attendance at one of the afternoon sessions held in Montreal in 1923. At night, however, the group had reached eight hundred. Later, in 1940, to be exact, Nicolet counted 1,000 present, and Saint-Jean as many in 1942. In small cities, the audience is relatively greater. In Saint-Hyacinthe the audience comprised mainly members of religious orders.[45] At the Ottawa, 1944 meetings, which the writer attended, the total number of persons in attendance reached 1,000.

Mr. Oscar Gatineau, one of the speakers at the Semaine Sociale of Saint-Hyacinthe in 1928 and Secretary of l'*Union Catholique des Cultivateurs,* in his course on *Le Crédit rural* claims that "the

---

[45] Interview with Father Lévesque, September 18, 1944, at Laval University.

agricultural class will always be the first one of all the popular classes to follow the beautiful path which the Semaine Sociale of Canada is tracing to our French Canadian people."[46]

Senator Léon-Mercier Gouin, one of the pioneers of the Semaine Sociale of Canada, maintains that he has derived from these assemblies the most consoling intellectual delights. Each year he has returned from these fraternal meetings with the feeling of having enriched himself spiritually and morally.[47]

Finally, in the words of His Eminence Cardinal Villeneuve, Archbishop of Quebec, a national renovation possibly may be accomplished by the Semaine Sociale.

> No one can measure the incommensurable value of this institution for our national renovation . . .

and adds:

> Continue, Gentlemen, to voice your lessons of order and equity. At first, we felt that you were in the clouds, in abstractions, that your studies did not aim at practical problems. You are now in the concrete, and still we do not come to you in large numbers. But you will none the less succeed. Little by little, the French people will be penetrated with a deeper sense of social reforms. We shall have leaders who will be seized by the flash of your teachings, of their evident good sense, of their practical import. The day is near at hand, when your dogmas will have their daily application in your economic life.[48]

---

[46] S. s. du Canada, Saint-Hyacinthe, 1928, p. 214: ". . . la classe agricole sera toujours la première de toutes les classes populaires à suivre la belle voie que les Semaines sociales du Canada tracent à notre peuple canadien-français."

[47] Léon Mercier-Gouin, "Appel d'un Laïc," *L'Ordre Nouveau,* Montréal, September 20, 1938, p. 2.

[48] "La Portée des Semaines sociales," *L'Ordre Nouveau,* Montréal, August 5 and 20, 1937, p. 1: "Personne ne peut encore mesurer la portée incommensurable, pour notre rénovation nationale de cette institution," et son encouragement final: "Continuez, Messieurs les semainiers, criez partout vos leçons d'ordre et d'équité. D'abord, on soutenait que vous étiez dans les nuages et les abstractions, que vos études ne visaient à rien de pratique. Maintenant, vous êtes dans le concret, et on ne vient pas beaucoup plus vous entendre. Mais vous aboutirez quand même. Peu à peu le peuple est pénétré

It may be noted, incidentally, that if the Semaine Sociale at first met with opposition, nevertheless its work was not without bearing fruit in the course of time. Cardinal Villeneuve admits that though the Semaine Sociale did not interest the public in general, it did form the minds of the people and influence public opinion. And now, by means of the Catholic press which is ever and ever more powerful, the social theories studied at these meetings have become better known. Even political programs have come to admit the necessity of Christian morality, and if politicians speak as they do, it is evident that something has been changed in their opinion.[49] For example, serious efforts have been made to better the lot of the proletariat in the Province of Quebec. Little by little a more humane legislation is being enacted. Some measures were directly inspired by the principles found in the encyclicals and whose justice and opportunity the professors of the Semaine Sociale have repeatedly proved.[50]

Archbishop Charbonneau of Montreal, at the twentieth session of the Semaine Sociale in Valleyfield, asked his audience to calculate if possible what the work of these years represent in the spread of sane ideas, in the orientation of public opinion towards a more just conception of the social order. In fact, this ambulatory university has contributed to eradicate social abuses and to bring about beneficent reforms. But that was not all. In 1933, the members of the General Commission of the Semaine Sociale published a brilliant declaration on the social problems then discussed which produced happy results, and in 1937 one on the autonomy of the Provinces. In 1943, a declaration entitled, *Pour un ordre meilleur*, appeared. It is a remarkable synthesis of the Catholic doctrine on the restoration of society. The declaration establishes the principles which must direct the restorers of the society of to-morrow if they wish to succeed and a few of the most urgent applications of a practical order form the third part

d'un sentiment plus social. Des groupes se forment qui exigeront des réformes urgentes. Des chefs paraissent qui seront saisis de la fulgurance de vos enseignements, de leur bon sens manifeste, de leur côté pratique. En tout cas, le jour s'annonce où vos thèses auront leur influence quotidienne dans notre vie économique."

[49] S. s. du Canada, Trois-Rivières, 1936, p. 340.

[50] S. s. du Canada, Montréal, 1932, p. 370.

of the declaration.[51] Besides, the compilation of the courses and conferences of the Semaine Sociale constitute a vast source of information for all social apostles. That it has familiarized a great number with the social teaching of the Church has been affirmed by the episcopacy in a collective letter dated May, 1941.[52]

That the Semaine Sociale stimulates the zeal of Catholics and directs it resolutely towards an activity distinctly social was the sincere belief of Archbishop Gauthier. It furnishes the man of action, who has not leisure for extensive studies, safe principles capable of directing him in the solution of his economic and social problems.[53] Likewise, the Apostolic Delegate, Archbishop Cassulo claimed to have positive proof of the great results derived for the Church and for society from these courses.[54]

To be more specific: the Semaine Sociale has met with enough success to become a permanent institution. At the Ottawa gathering of 1931, Archbishop Forbes announced that, as a direct result of its teaching, the University of Ottawa was to inaugurate a course in sociology.[55] After the 1936 Semaine Sociale of Trois-Rivières devoted to the study of the Professional Organization, there appeared cooperative activities of various kinds and attempts at corporative organization. Similarly, after the Semaine Sociale of Saint-Hyacinthe in 1937, there was a magnificent increase of cooperative organizations in Quebec and in the *Union des Cultivateurs Catholiques.*[56]

Less precise as to date and time are the campaigns that the Semaine Sociale has stimulated: one in favor of the keeping of the Lord's day, another in favor of the reduction of income tax for large families.[57] The Semaine Sociale also promoted the syndical movement[58] and on April 10 and 11, 1944 organized a

---

[51] S. s. du Canada, Salaberry-de-Valleyfield, 1943, pp. 26-27.

[52] *Ibid.*, pp. 33-34.

[53] S. s. du Canada, Montréal, 1932, pp. 9-10.

[54] S. s. du Canada, Chicoutimi, 1929, p. 12.

[55] S. s. du Canada, Ottawa, 1931, p. 337.

[56] Jacques Cousineau, "Carrefour social," *L'Ordre Nouveau,* Montréal, October 5, 1940, p. 1.

[57] Hermas Bastien, "Le Père Papin Archambault," *L'Action Française,* Montréal, XII (November, 1924), 271.

[58] Interview with Msgr. Perrier, September 2, 1944.

Congress of colonization.[59] In 1943, the Semaine Sociale on Temperance is said to have influenced public opinion considerably.[60]

In short, the solutions proposed by the professors of the Semaine Sociale for the various social problems form a coherent and positive program of the traditions and customs to be maintained and the reforms to be accomplished in the life of the French Canadian family and nation.

As regards the recognition given the Semaine Sociale, people from all classes of French Canadian society have shown their appreciation either orally or in writing, through the press or by actual attendance at the meetings.

The Popes too have been favorable to this ambulatory university. In France, Pius X defended the institution when it was attacked by suspicious persons. In 1920, Benedict XV addressed a letter to the Secretary, Mr. Guy Vanier, which contained an apostolic benediction and expressed appreciation for the newly-conceived project.[61]

The next year Cardinal Bégin of Quebec received the following cable from Cardinal Gasparri:

> Rome, August 31, 1921
>
> Cardinal Bégin, Quebec,
>
> Holy Father accepts filial homage of the participants of the second Canadian Semaine Sociale under presidency of your Eminence, gathered to study Catholic professional organization. Happy to send requested Apostolic Benediction.
>
> Cardinal Gasparri[62]

---

[59] Interview with Maximilien Caron, August 22, 1944, at the University of Montreal.

[60] Interview with Edouard Montpetit, September 20, 1944, at the University of Montreal.

[61] S. s. du Canada, Montréal, 1920, p. VIII.

[62] S. s. du Canada, Québec, 1921, p. XIII: Rome, August 31, 1921
Cardinal Bégin, Québec,
Saint-Père, agréant filial hommage des participants à deuxième Semaine sociale Canada, sous présidence votre Eminence, réunis pour étudier organisation professionnelle catholique, envoie de tout coeur bénédiction apostolique implorée.
Cardinal Gasparri

In like manner, Pope Pius XI encouraged the Semaine Sociale of Canada as early as 1922. For the closing session of the Study Week of Ottawa, a cable was received which read as follows:

> R. P. Archambault, S.J.
> Montreal, Canada,
> Important occasion Semaine Sociale, Ottawa, His Holiness heartily sends Apostolic Benediction, with paternal wishes for complete success of endeavors in noble country.
>
> Cardinal Gasparri[63]

Again, at the 1929 Popular Assembly in Chicoutimi where the audience numbered some two thousand or more, the Apostolic Delegate read a similar telegram from His Holiness Pope Pius XI.[64]

Moreover, His Eminence Cardinal Villeneuve is the patron and protector of the Semaine Sociale of Canada and its Honorary President. The Representative of the Pope, Apostolic Delegate Cassulo, was a friend of the Semaine Sociale. On one occasion, Bishop Decelles of Saint-Hyacinthe is reported to have said: "If Saint Paul were living now, he would be a very fervent friend of the Semaine Sociale and most probably a constant victim of Reverend Father Archambault." The present Apostolic Delegate Ildebrando Antoniutti has been a regular attendant at its sessions. Bishop Larocque called it a timely institution, necessary to offset ignorance of social principles; one which should regulate the existence of the family, of the profession, and of society.

The encouragement which the laity gave to the Semaine Sociale is also noteworthy in many instances. Mr. Lucien Borne, Mayor of Quebec, claims that the Semaine Sociale has been steadily gaining

---

[63] "Sa Sainteté Pie XI bénit la Semaine sociale d'Ottawa," *Le Droit*, Ottawa, September 5, 1922, p. 3:

> R. P. Archambault, s.j.
> Montréal, Canada
> Occasion importante Semaine sociale, Ottawa, Sa Sainteté envoie de tout coeur bénédiction apostolique, formant voeux paternels plein succès travaux dans noble pays.
>
> Cardinal Gasparri

[64] S. s. du Canada, Chicoutimi, 1929, p. 274.

in importance. Mr. J. E. Perrault, prominent lawyer of Montreal, extends congratulations for its excellent work. Henri Franchet, a distinguished French sociologist, stated in 1933 that the social directions of the Church have never been explained with such clearness and eloquence. Numerous are the public men who have expressed gratitude to the Semaine Sociale for the work it accomplished. These sincere expressions represent the testimony of the entire nation. Even outsiders recognize the value of the social doctrine of these Study Weeks. Bishop Lamarche tells how great leaders who analyzed complacently its works welcomed these Catholic social gatherings as eminently constructive and influential. At times, these leaders have asked for representatives of these groups to appear in their councils. At the 1944 session, Mr. Stanley Lewis, Mayor of Ottawa, a non-Catholic, commended the teaching body of the ambulatory university for coming to his city; and getting into the spirit of the institution, he ended by saying, "Look to Almighty God for guidance and leadership."

The notable persons attending the sessions of the Semaine Sociale are still another index of the appreciation extended to them. In 1933, an ever-increasing interest in the gathering was shown by the presence of such eminent figures as: Cardinal Villeneuve, His Excellency Msgr. Cassulo, Apostolic Delegate, six members of the episcopacy, the Honorable Maurice Dupré, the Honorable Ernest Lapointe, the Honorable Adélard Godbout, Maurice Duplessis, the present Prime Minister of the Province of Quebec, many deputies, a large number of clergymen, and a crowd of distinguished laymen belonging to all the classes of society.[65]

In Montreal in 1932, the attendance was not less imposing. Three archbishops, five bishops, two ministers of state, many ecclesiastical and civil dignitaries,—prelates, provincials, magistrates, deputies—representatives of the principal Catholic and national associations of French Canada, even foreigners like Henri Boissard, the Vice-Superior General of the Order of Saint-Sulpice and Mathew Fortier, Dean of the Department of Sociology of Fordham University were present.[66] Msgr. McLean of Catholic

---

[65] Eugène L'Heureux, "La Semaine du bon sens," *L'Action Catholique*, Québec, August 22, 1933, p. 4.

[66] Joseph-Papin Archambault, "La Semaine sociale de Montréal," *Le Devoir*, Montréal, September 7, 1932, p. 1.

University, distinguished Professor of Philosophy, attended the 1936 and 1942 sessions of the Semaine Sociale and Father LaFarge, Director of the Interracial Review, was present in 1937.

To summarize, the Semaine Sociale received episcopal approval at the very outset. Its beginnings were humble but on reaching maturity it won proper and widespread admiration and recognition. Its outstanding leaders, its founders in particular, were largely responsible for its success. *Rerum novarum,* in 1891, came as a ray of light on ill-prepared ground, but by 1920 its doctrine had become a source of life, suited to the humble laborer and proud demagogue as well. The Semaine Sociale aims to explain principles which will govern social relations, to impose duties, to note limits; in a word, to direct the social thought of French Canada. Today it has become a permanent institution and a hope for the future. From its ranks have come men who are today prominent in the nation's judiciary councils and Church leaders: three bishops and a Cardinal.

To understand the social thought of French Canada as reflected in the Semaine Sociale, it seems expedient to make a brief study of the members of its General Commission. They constitute its brain-power and an acquaintance with each member, as representative of his special group, may be helpful to evaluate the significance of the institution itself in the life and traditions of the French Canadians.

CHAPTER III

Outstanding Leaders of the Semaine Sociale

The social thought of a people is made clearer by a knowledge of the outstanding individuals who contributed more or less to its formulation. Very important, then, for the purpose of our study is an acquaintance with the members of the General Commission of the Semaine Sociale, constituted not by a "closed" group but representing rather the various professions and different regions of French Canada. Information on the different members of the General Commission of the Semaine Sociale was obtained either through personal communication, interviews, questionnaires, or from biographical data graciously furnished to the writer. References are to published works only.

The founders of the Semaine Sociale will be given first consideration. This will be followed by an account of its Honorary President, Cardinal Villeneuve. The members of the clergy, the University group, and prominent laymen of the General Commission will then be mentioned not only as individuals but as representatives of the social thought of their respective groups.

Born in 1880, Father Joseph-Papin Archambault, S.J., received his education at the College Sainte-Marie in Montreal. In 1897 he entered the novitiate of the Society of Jesus and in 1912 received Holy Orders. In 1909, he was instrumental in instituting in French Canada the movement known as "the layman's retreat." The young Jesuit then spent a year abroad. Upon his return he was successively assigned the charge of Villa Saint-Martin and Villa Manrèse in Quebec, remaining seven years at each post. In 1912, in collaboration with Dr. Joseph Gauvreau, he founded the *Ligue des Droits du français*. In 1925, with Msgr. Lapointe, he founded the *Ligue du dimanche*. In 1929 he became Director of the Ecole Sociale Populaire. The first Catholic hour in Canada is due to the initiative of this energetic man. Similarly, the Ecole de formation sociale of Vandreuil owes its beginnings in 1932 to him.

In addition, Father Archambault at various intervals gave courses in Catholic Action at Laval University, at the Scholasticat de l'Immaculée-Conception and at the Institut pédagogique. In 1940 he gave a course on *Directives pontificales* at the Social Science School of the University of Montreal. Besides the many articles in periodicals and journals, he has published some sixty books or pamphlets treating of religious or social topics. Worthy of mention are: *Les Retraites fermées* (1915), *Le Devoir professional* (1928), *Restauration de l'ordre social* (1932), *Action catholique d'après les directives pontificales* (1938), *Les Objectifs de l'action catholique* (1940), *De Rome à Montreal* (1942), and *Pour un ordre meilleur* (1944).

Truly an apostle with broad-minded vision, he believes in the spread of Catholic thought in his country. It is with this in mind that he founded in 1920 the institution of the Semaine Sociale. Propagator of Catholic sociology in the Province of Quebec,[1] endowed with a brilliant intellect and a marvelous activity,[2] he exercises a social apostolate[3] in voicing the conditions affecting the family, a problem which he considers most serious in French Canada, and in rendering incalculable services to the national cause.[4] A born leader, he manages to give direction unostentatiously, a point which made Mr. Ernest Lapointe exclaim, "Father Archambault is the only dictator whom I am happy to obey."[5] Like Mr. Omer Héroux, Msgr. Lafortune in referring to Father Archambault's tenacity says: "We can not refuse this learned sociologist the least request because he knows so well how to ask."[6] His casual, modest bearing in no way betrays the responsibilities which bear heavily upon him.[7]

---

[1] Hermas Bastien, "Le Père Papin Archambault," *Action française,* XII (November, 1924), 271.

[2] Ferdinand Bélanger, "La Semaine sociale," *L'Action catholique,* August, 1924, p. 3.

[3] S. s. du Canada, Saint-Hyacinthe, 1937, p. 9.

[4] S. s. du Canada, Trois-Rivières, 1936, p. 283.

[5] S. s. du Canada, Rimouski, 1933, p. 322.

[6] S. s. du Canada, Nicolet, 1940, p. 226.

[7] Edouard Lavergne, "Semaine sociale," *L'Action catholique,* September, 1923, p. 3.

Moreover, he manifests a "fanatical loyalty," in the expression of Dr. Furfey, to all that the Holy Fathers have to say. His is an entire intellectual submission to the words of the Popes. At the 1935 meeting of the Semaine Sociale, Bishop Papineau, after thanking and congratulating Father Archambault for the inauguration of so many Catholic movements in the Province of Quebec, ended by saying that the following statement addressed to one of the greatest defenders of the Church applies well to him, "Never did the Greeks and the Romans love the fatherland as Athanasius loved the Church."[8] No less impressive is Cardinal Villeneuve's appreciation of this worthy prelate's notable works.

> Thirty years have passed and the Reverend Father Archambault . . . sees his labor take on year after year a scope and a force that we dared not at first surmise. The good which resulted and which will arise is enormous,—were it only to have opened a rostrum to reflective and Christian sociologists, thus enabling them to contradict the aphorisms of adventurous sociologists and the "pronunciamentos" of industrial, political and labor paragons of which the press bring us too often the equivocal and imprudent formulas.[9]

Like Father Archambault, Guy Vanier, one of the founders of the Semaine Sociale and its first secretary, born on December 22, 1888, studied at the Collège Sainte-Marie and received the bachelor's degree with high honors in 1908. He then specialized in law at the University of Montreal receiving his licentiate in 1912 and later becoming Professor of Social Economy, Private Finance, and Commercial Law at the School of Social Science. Not content

---

[8] S. s. du Canada, Joliette, 1935, p. 324.

[9] S. s. du Canada, Saint-Hyacinthe, 1937, p. 318: "Trente ans ont passé, et le R. P. Archambault . . . voit son labeur prendre d'année en année un essor et une force qu'on n'eût point soupçonner. Le bien qui en est resulté et qui en surgira est immense. Ne fut-ce que d'avoir ouvert une tribune aux sociologues réfléchis et chrétiens pour les mettre en état de contredire les aphorismes des sociologues d'aventure et les pronunciamentos de certains parangons industrials, politiques et ouvriers, dont la presse nous rapporte trop fréquemment les équivoques et imprudentes formules."

to be an efficient professor, a charming companion, and an enlightened Christian,[10] he takes active part in patriotic and social movements of all kinds. At one time he was President of the *Association Catholique de la Jeunesse Canadienne-française* and later of the *Société Saint-Jean-Baptiste* of Montreal. At present, Mr. Vanier is Director of Studies at the School of Social Science at the University of Montreal and now and then serves as advocate in lawsuits. He does not divorce the ideal from the practical. Tall and elegant of stature, he appears to his students and friends, a man of great natural enthusiasm, exercising over them a beneficial ascendency.

Remarkable is Guy Vanier's distinct and attractive personality. In the field of politics he deliberately kept himself aloof; he would not be polluted by its intrigues. He preferred national and social action.[11] This took the form of French Language campaigns. "Formerly," he tells us, "we were unable to get a telephone number when we requested it in French. We insisted." The result was that the *Société Saint-Jean-Baptiste* attached French signs to telephone apparatus; this procedure proved satisfactory in every way. Again, the Secretary of the Semaine Sociale actually insisted on the maintenance of religious traditions, not only for their intrinsic value but because they are closely associated to national traditions. He also recommends the singing of French songs as a means of maintaining the happy disposition peculiar to the French Canadian.[12] He claims that the greatest social problem in French Canada is the condition which takes women out of their legitimate sphere, the home. According to him, this situation is against Christian morality. He has twice given conferences at the Semaine Sociale.

The ascendency, which Mr. Vanier enjoyed over his students, Msgr. Perrier, Vicar General of Montreal, possessed abundantly as a professor, pastor and educator. Born in March, 1870 in Saint Valentin, county of Saint-Jean, Msgr. Perrier studied at the Sem-

---

[10] Paul Dulac, *Silhouettes d'aujourd'hui* (Montréal: Le Devoir, 1927), p. 56.

[11] Robert Rumilly, *Chefs de file* (Montréal: Les Editions du Zodiaque, 1934), p. 257.

[12] *Ibid.*, pp. 262-263.

inary of Montreal where he was ordained in 1896. Professor for two years, student in Rome three more years, and again Professor at the Seminary of Montreal for another two years, he was then named Vice-Chancellor of the Archdiocese of Montreal. In 1906 he became Supervisor of the Catholic Schools of Montreal where his reputation in sizing up educational matters gained momentum, and thence Professor of Ecclesiastical Law at the University of Montreal.

As pastor of Saint-Lambert for three years and of Saint-Enfant-Jésus in Montreal for six additional years, he was a model of piety and of zeal, while at the same time noted for his doctrinal teaching and wonderful administrative powers. As General Chaplain of the Saint Vincent de Paul Society for the diocese of Montreal, he has actively participated in the social and national life of the French Canadians by his advice, speeches and clear perception of the serious problems of the day,[13] most serious of which, in his opinion, is the reintegration of women and young girls in the home. In 1932, this valiant pastor abandoned parish work for the teaching of Moral Theology at the Scholasticate of the Clerics of Saint-Viator in Joliette. Four years later he returned to Montreal to become Chaplain of the House of Sainte-Thérèse and in 1940 became Vicar General of the diocese of Montreal and shortly after was named Protonotary Apostolic.

That the Semaine Sociale was founded in Msgr. Perrier's rectory of Saint-Enfant-Jésus' parish and with his collaboration, is interesting to those concerned with our study. He is considered one of the founders of this institution and lived up to its motto, "Science for action." On six different occasions he gave courses at the Semaine Sociale. We find him voicing his disapproval of bad example and scandal; he is in the first rank with those who endeavor to purify the mores of the Montreal population, to prevent license and debauchery from invading certain sections of the city and degrading public conscience. In like fashion he is preoccupied about the future of the French Canadians in large cities, about the numerous repercussions of intense urban life on the home and other domestic institutions. For the homeless for whom

---

[13] S. s. du Canada, Trois-Rivières, 1936, p. 318.

he has particular affection and toward whom he manifests the solicitude of a father and apostle, he created societies.[14]

In a very different atmosphere, and with different weapons does Omer Héroux share in the great movement of "Science for action." He, too, is a founder of the ambulatory university. When asked for biographical notes, he replied abruptly: "It is all very simple: I was born and will be sixty-eight soon." Born on the eighth of September, 1876 in Saint-Maurice de Champlain, diocese of Trois-Rivières, he studied first with the Brothers of Yamachiche and then at the Seminary of Trois-Rivières from 1887 to 1895. Thenceforth, he chose journalism as his life career. First he was connected with the *Trifluvien* of Trois-Rivières; in 1900 with the *Journal* of Montreal; and in 1903 with *La Patrie*. At last, in 1905 Mr. Héroux saw the realization of his life-dream—Catholic journalism. In Quebec, he gave his talent to Mr. Jules Paul Tardivel, the Louis Veuillot of Canada, in the daily *Vérité*. Upon the death of Mr. Tardivel, one of whose daughters he had married, Mr. Héroux became Director of this paper. Two years later he was collaborating in *L'Action Sociale* now *L'Action Catholique*. In 1909, he returned to Montreal for the founding of *Le Devoir* by Mr. Henri Bourassa. At present, Mr. Héroux is editor-in-chief of this newspaper.

Those who read any of his editorials will quickly realize that he is not a "conformist." The most violent campaign of insults levelled against him and his political views have been to no avail. He rises above all suspicions and reproaches. He fights for truth, the common good and advancement of his compatriots,[15] and claims that the problem of the family in French Canada demands greatest consideration.

Omer Héroux is particularly interested in French groups outside of Quebec: Acadians, Western Canadians and the Franco-Americans. He has contributed to many religious national and social programs in his own country, and as a consequence of his activity is looked upon at home and abroad as a man of distinction with the gifts of honesty and courage, a clear judgment, the

---

[14] Dulac, *op. cit.*, pp. 142-144.

[15] *Le Droit*, Ottawa, July 21, 1936, p. 3.

courtesy of a polemicist, who would rather conquer by power of reasoning than by force of invection.[16]

While Omer Héroux waged war against abuses by his writings alone, Cardinal Villeneuve, Honorary President of the Semaine Sociale and a pioneer of the institution, resorted to both written and verbal instruction. Born in Montreal, November 2, 1883, Cardinal Jean-Marie Rodrigue Villeneuve, O.M.I., Archbishop of Quebec, studied at Plessis School and at Mont Saint-Louis in Montreal. At the age of seventeen he entered the Novitiate of the Oblate Fathers of Mary Immaculate at Ville LaSalle. From there he went to Saint Joseph's Scholasticate in Ottawa to study philosophy and theology. He made his profession on September 8, 1903 and was ordained to the priesthood by Bishop Duhamel in the Cathedral of Ottawa on May 25, 1907. He was then assigned to the faculty of Saint Joseph's Scholasticate at the University of Ottawa. Professor for twenty-three years, besides shouldering the burden of arduous duties in the classroom, he took an active part in the cultural and spiritual life of the University. From 1920-1930 he served as Superior of the Scholasticate and was appointed Dean of the Department of Theology and Ecclesiastical Law of the University of Ottawa.[17]

It was during these years that Father Villeneuve communicated to his pupils his profound doctrine. By turns, Professor of Philosophy, Liturgy, Canon Law and Moral Theology, he was always an attractive teacher;[18] his was an "Aristotelian brain" at the service of a soul lightly platonic.[19]

Father Villeneuve was nominated Bishop of the new diocese of Gravelbourg in Saskatchewan on July 3, 1930. Consecrated on September 11, in the Ottawa Basilica by Archbishop Forbes, he took possession of his Espiscopal See on September 14.[20] He soon became known as the Bishop of Catholic Action. His first pastoral letter was a bold program calling for the cooperation of religious and civil power and all classes of the laity, especially the university

[16] *Ibid.*

[17] *Les Biographies françaises d'Amérique* (Montréal: Les Journalistes associés, 1942), p. 12.

[18] *L'Action canadienne-française,* November, 1928, p. 304.

[19] "Le Père Rodrigue Villeneuve," *L'Action française,* July, 1925, p. 20.

[20] *Les Biographies françaises d'Amérique, op. cit.,* p. 12.

and professional class in Catholic Action.[21] The thoroughness with which he organized the new diocese, even to the establishment of a *Grand Séminaire* attracted the attention of the Holy See. Fifteen months after his first consecration he was promoted as Archbishop of Quebec. In March 1933, he was created Cardinal-Priest with the title Saint Mary of the Angels.

As Archbishop of Quebec, Cardinal Villeneuve has been in the fullest sense of the term, the spiritual leader of the French Canadians endeavoring to harmonize the natural aspirations of his people with the best interests of the Dominion as a whole and the welfare of the entire Canadian Church.[22] He is also responsible for the Federation of the Associations of Catholic youth. He strengthened the organization of labor unions, energetically sponsored the work of closed retreats and encouraged the founding of schools of social studies. Moreover, he has undertaken the most intrepid crusade in favor of the Catholic press, so well represented in Quebec by *L'Action Catholique.* His intense interest in missionary work has been noteworthy. The Vicariate of Basutoland entrusted to the Canadian Oblates constitutes another initiative of His Eminence.[23]

Among Cardinal Villeneuve's principal works are: *La Grève et l'enseignement catholique* (1921), *La Justice* (1934), *Directives sociales aux jeunes* (1935), *La Crise du droit de propriété et ses remèdes* (1935), *Devoir et pratique du patriotisme* (1935), *Le Mariage* (1936), *Le Cinéma, périls et réaction* (1937), and *Le Fait français en Amérique* (1938).[24] He has appeared on the rostrum of the Semaine Sociale thirteen times.

His whole life has been filled with religious, social, and national activity. As a religious he remains grateful to the Congregation that formed him; as an apostle he has a keen intuition into present-day problems; as pastor he is indifferent to none of the needs of his flock: such is the Cardinal of the Canadian Church,[25] the Representative of the Oblate Fathers in the Sacred College.

---

[21] *La Croix,* Paris, March 6, 1933.

[22] *Oblate World,* Buffalo, November, 1939, p. 5.

[23] *La Croix, op. cit.*

[24] *Les Biographies française d'Amérique, op. cit.,* p. 13.

[25] *Le Patriote,* Gravelbourg, March 1, 1933.

Another pioneer of the Semaine Sociale is His Excellency Msgr. Ross, first Bishop of Gaspé. He was born on March 6, 1869 in Grosses-Roches, pursued his classical studies at the Seminary of Quebec and completed his theology at the Seminary of Rimouski. In 1894 he was ordained by Bishop Blais. From 1892 to 1896 he was appointed Secretary to the Bishop of Rimouski. Thence, he was successively appointed to three different parishes. In 1904 he studied in Rome and received the title of Doctor in Canon Law. Two years later he returned to be named Principal of the Normal School of Rimouski, a position he held for seventeen years. It is in this capacity that he contributed valuable material in the line of education. In 1915 appeared his *Manuel de pédagogie* with a circulation of 30,000; in 1920, *Questions scolaires.*[26]

His contributions in the field of sociology are also notable. As Bishop he actively promotes cooperation movements in his diocese; the Syndicate of *Pêcheurs-Unis de Québec* has resulted from this initiative. At one time he also organized a colonization movement using as a password, "Let us organize." His pastoral letter dated March 20, 1944 on *Devoir social* is a masterly synthesis of the principles of Catholic social science, of the present organization of society, of the false systems which pretend to correct the defects of this organization, and of the remedies presented by the Church as the only ones capable of bettering present conditions.[27]

One of Bishop Ross' methods of solving social problems in French Canada is by the enactment of more humane social legislation. The control of industry and natural resources by trusts is, in his opinion, still too extensive. As a result of the abuses of capitalism, farms are deserted, births limited, and doors thrown wide open to socialistic and communistic propaganda. Cooperation in industry on the other hand, would bring a solution to economic difficulties by the Christian spirit of fraternity which it sponsors.

His Excellency Msgr. Desranleau, Bishop of Sherbrooke, is also an early and faithful collaborator of the Semaine Sociale. Since

---

[26] J. B. A. Allaire, *Dictionnaire biographique du Clergé canadien-français* (Saint-Hyacinthe: Imprimerie du Courrier de Saint-Hyacinthe, 1935), XVI, p. 482.

[27] Francois-Xavier Ross, *Lettre pastorale sur le devoir social,* March 20, 1944, p. 347, No. 20.

its founding he has missed only one session,[28] and has addressed the audience three times. Bishop Desranleau, a native of Saint-Sebastian, was born April 3, 1882. He studied successively at the Seminaries of Saint-Hyacinthe and Montreal. Ordained in 1909, he became a Professor of Philosophy at Saint-Hyacinthe, a curate at the Cathedral of the same city, and then was sent to Rome to study. He returned, after three years, with a Doctorate in Philosophy, and again was curate at the Cathedral from 1915 to 1931. He became Chancellor and General Secretary of the diocese of Saint-Hyacinthe, and its Vicar General from 1926-1931.[29]

Bishop Desranleau was at one time a regular contributor to the *Canada français,* the *Revue nationale* and the *Revue dominicaine.* He also sponsored Catholic syndicates, *caisses populaires,* and specialized movements of Catholic Action. He advocates a better distribution of wealth by the destruction of monopolies. Significant are Father Archambault's words addressed to His Excellency at the sixteenth session of the Semaine Sociale:

> Member of our General Commission since its inauguration, speaker at many of our sessions, organizer of the Social Week of Saint-Hyacinthe in 1928, Your Excellency was one of the best workers of our institution, one of the principal authors of its success.[30]

The most amiable speaker of the Semaine Sociale and member of the General Commission in 1923, His Excellency Msgr. Courchesne, Bishop of Rimouski since 1928, is remarkable by the solidity of his doctrine, his virile and dynamic character.[31] Born on September 13, 1880 in Saint Thomas de Pierreville, he studied at the Seminary of Nicolet where he was ordained in 1904. Thence

[28] Richard Arès, "Impressions d'un semainier," *L'Ordre Nouveau,* October 5, 1938, p. 2.

[29] Allaire, *op. cit.,* p. 249.

[30] S. s. du Canada, Sherbrooke, 1938, p. 24: "Membre de notre Commission générale depuis sa fondation, conférencier à plusieurs de nos sessions, organisateur de la Semaine de Saint-Hyacinthe en 1928, Votre Excellence fut l'un des meilleurs ouvriers de notre institution, l'un des principaux artisans de ses succès."

[31] Ferdinand Bélanger, "La Semaine sociale," *L'Action catholique,* August 12, 1925, p. 1.

he studied in Rome until 1910. Professor of Rhetoric in his Alma Mater, Principal of the Normal School of Nicolet and Professor of Pedagogy at the Normal School of Quebec from 1919-1928. In the last position he published his principal work *Nos Humanités* (1927),[32] revealing his vast erudition, sharp realism, lofty sentiments and ideas.[33] This work, which grew out of his various courses given at the Normal School of Laval University, deals with the methodology of secondary school teaching. His pastoral letters form three published volumes. He also contributed two tracts on temperance, numerous speeches and sermons; articles in *La Vie nouvelle,* in *L'Enseignement primaire* and in the *Revue dominicaine,*[34] and was heard on three different occasions at the gatherings of the Semaine Sociale.

His Excellency possesses a fine physiognomy in which one may discern gravity, gaiety, much wit and simplicity, together with a remarkable look of distinction. In this doctor, bishop, intellectual aristocrat, man of God, one looks into the "yeux les plus fins du monde." In less than the time required to say a rosary, he wins one's confidence and possesses the art of driving home with his winning smile, wise counsels, and important truths.[35]

Bishop Courchesne's chief interest is in the farmer, the most stable element of a given population, who, however, is in great need of social education. He advocates the organization of free professional unions in the form of cooperatives and professional organizations. As educator, he has prepared a sort of agricultural elite. Omer Héroux affirms this when he writes:

> The rural folk are not always fully aware that their new Bishop is one of them heart and soul; that he clings with every fiber of his being, with his every thought as well as with his whole heart to the old pioneer, "habitant"

---

[32] Allaire, *op. cit.* (Montréal: Imprimerie De LaSalle, 1930), V, pp. 232-233.

[33] *L'Action canadienne-française,* March, 1928, cited in *S. G. Mgr. Courchesne* (Montréal: L'Oeuvre des Tracts), p. 5.

[34] *La Vie Nouvelle,* April, 1928: *L'Enseignement primaire,* March, 1928; *Le Revue Dominicaine,* April, 1928; cited in *S. G. Mgr. Courchesne, ibid.,* pp. 9, 15, 16.

[35] *S. G. Mgr. Courchesne, op. cit.,* pp. 2-3.

> of our province; that one of his first dreams was to direct vocationally the best of his studies into the field of agriculture. . . .[36]

Although Msgr. Paul-Emile Léger was one of the last members to be inducted in the General Commission of the Semaine Sociale, he is by no means the least remarkable. Born in Valleyfield on April 26, 1904, he made his classical studies at the Seminaire de Sainte-Thérèse de Blainville and his theological studies at the Grand Séminaire, Montreal. He received the Bachelor's degree in Canon Law and the Licentiate in Theology at the University of Montreal and the Licentiate in Canon Law from the Catholic Institute of Paris. At present he is Vicar-General of the diocese of Valleyfield, pastor of its Cathedral and director of Catholic Action. In his opinion, the time is more than ripe when the natural resources of the Province of Quebec should be put at the service of the whole population; he finds no explanation of the present maldistribution of wealth in a country as rich in natural resources as his own. That the tubercular should lack care and that slums be the living quarters of a high percentage of the total population are beyond his grasp. For Msgr. Léger, the social question is not merely a matter of economics, as some politicians believe, but rather a matter for humane interpretation.

An early worker of the Semaine Sociale was Msgr. Eugène Lapointe. He was born on April 21, 1860 at La Malbaie and studied at the Seminary of Quebec where he received the degree of Bachelor of Arts. Ordained in 1891, he then completed his studies in Rome from 1891-1893 and was granted the degree of Doctor in Philosophy. Upon his return he became Professor of Philosophy and Sociology at the Seminary of Chicoutimi and successively occupied the position of director, superior and procurator. He is deeply concerned with labor problems. The economic question will be settled in French Canada by no other

[36] *Le Devoir,* February 3, 1928, cited in *S. G. Mgr. Courchesne, op. cit.,* p. 14: "La foule rurale sait probablement moins que son nouvel évêque est de coeur et d'âme l'un des siens, qu'il tient par toutes les fibres de son être, par sa pensée comme par son coeur, aux vieux fonds *habitant* de notre province, que l'un de ses premiers rêves a été de diriger vers l'agriculture une élite de ses élèves. . . ."

means, he claims, than by the cooperative movement; otherwise, "capitalism will swallow us up." In the line of literary contributions he has contributed many articles to journals and periodicals. He has also given many conferences and addresses on the social question and contributed three enlightening courses during the first three years of the Semaine Sociale. Although he states that he wrote "nothing for posterity, all for the present" no one ignores his monumental work in the founding of Catholic syndicates in Canada in 1907.

Msgr. Wilfrid Lebon, a disciple of the Semaine Sociale since 1935, was born on November 21, 1877 in Lévis, studied at the Collège de Sainte-Anne-de-la-Pocatière and at the Seminary of Quebec. In 1902 he was ordained by Cardinal Bégin. His years of teaching were interpolated with years of study abroad first in Rome then in Fribourg.[37] For ten years he was Professor of Sociology at Laval University. At present he is Superior of the classical college of Sainte-Anne-de-la-Pocatière, a constituent college of Laval University, of the Ecole Supérieure d'Agriculture and of the Ecole des Pêcheries, the latter having in Gaspesie an extension service similar to that of St. Francis Xavier University, Antigonish. He gave five courses at different meetings of the Semaine Sociale.

Canon J. A. Pellerin is a member of the General Commission of the Semaine Sociale since 1931. Born on September 22, 1880 in Princeville, he received his education from the Seminaries of Nicolet and Quebec. After a few years of ministry, he went to the Angelica University in Rome to study from 1911-1913 and received the Doctorate in the philosophy of Saint Thomas. He then taught Moral Philosophy at Nicolet for fifteen years and Moral Theology for seventeen additional years. Appointed Principal of the Normal School of this city in 1928, he remained at this post eleven years. In 1939 he was nominated pastor of Saint-Martyrs Canadiens in Victoriaville and since that time founded a new parish of 5,000 souls. Canon Pellerin claims that both labor and agriculture are questions of major consequence. Colonization in connection with the latter issue should be sponsored widely and

[37] Allaire, *op. cit.*, p. 292.

persistently. As for education, he believes that there are already too many who have a hand in its organization without having the required competence.

Father Joseph Gilles Marchand, O.M.I. and Father Pie-Marie Gaudrault, O.P., the present Provincials of their respective orders, were inducted as members of the General Commission of the Semaine Sociale in 1931. Father Marchand was born in Champlain on May 11, 1886. His education was received at the University of Ottawa and at the Pontifical Gregorian College in Rome where he made his profession in 1908 as a member of the Oblate Fathers. He returned with Doctorates in Philosophy and Theology. Thence he taught at the University of Ottawa from 1914 to 1930, became its Rector from 1930 to 1936 and then Provincial of his Order in Montreal.

He has contributed articles to the periodicals of the University of Ottawa and of the Oblate Missionaries of Mary Immaculate. He recommends a deeper study of the domestic question, in particular, of housing facilities for large families; living wages and family allowances for the normal establishment of the family; means of higher education for gifted children; the wholesomeness of reading and the press; the extinction of agents of corruption and the abolition of houses of prostitution by public authorities.

Father Pie-Marie Gaudrault, O.P., a native of Saint-Aubert, was born May 27, 1889, the second child of a family of nine. He studied first at the College of Sainte-Anne-de-la-Pocatière and then at the Seminary of Quebec receiving the degree of Bachelor of Arts in 1913. After entering the Dominican Order, he continued his studies in Rome at the Angelica and returned with a Master's degree in Theology. He was ordained on May 25, 1918. He taught dogma and philosophy fifteen years at the Convent of Study of the Dominicans in Ottawa. He was also at one time Professor at Laval University. In 1939 he was elected Provincial of his Order and reelected in 1943.

His reelection for a third term speaks in favor of Father Gaudrault's powers of administration. He has in truth accomplished important functions in his order and acquired degrees which prompts one to conclude that he was talented in every way. He is one of the founders of the *Institut d'Etudes medievales* of Montreal. As a member of the General Commission of the Semaine Sociale he has shown his interest in this institution by assiduous attendance at the various sessions. Although he finds little time outside his daily activities to consider social issues, he claims that the labor question and the agricultural problems are acute enough to demand careful consideration. He believes there are too many workingmen in cities in comparison with the number of agriculturists on the farms. He has long advocated a deliberate back-to-the-farm movement.

Pioneer work of a somewhat different character was done by two other clergymen of note in connection with the Semaine Sociale. Both have devoted time and energy to the study of social problems here and abroad. Both are in the strict sense of the words social workers. Father Leonidas Adam, pastor of Christ-Roi, Sherbrooke, was born in Saint-Mathias on June 5, 1886. He was educated at Saint-Charles Barromée Seminary in Sherbrooke; from the University of Louvain, he received a diploma in Social and Political Sciences, and from Laval University in Quebec, the degree of Master of Arts. He is also member of the *Société Historique* of Montreal and Sherbrooke.

For the twenty-fifth anniversary of the foundation of the A.C.J.C. in the diocese of Sherbrooke, he published in 1931 a pamphlet entitled *Aux Jeunes de chez nous.* Since 1917 he has contributed many articles,—most of them anonymous—in the *Messager de Saint-Michel* of Sherbrooke. On three different occasions he spoke at the Semaine Sociale.

From 1919 to 1925 he was the chaplain-founder of the Catholic and national syndicates in Sherbrooke and director of Catholic Social Action in the same diocese. At present, Father Adam is one of the directors of *La Régionale,* a consumers' cooperative. He is also diocesan chaplain of the *Cercles Lacordaire et Sainte-Jeanne d'Arc,* temperance societies, and of the *Canado-Americains,* According to him, cooperation in all its phases is the problem that demands the greatest attention and research in French Canada.

Father Emile Cloutier, a member of the General Commission of the Semaine Sociale since 1921, and pastor of Très-Saint-Sacrement in Trois-Rivières was born December 19, 1875, in Saint-

Prosper-de-Champlain. He studied at the Séminaire de Trois-Rivières, Laval University, where he received the degree of Bachelor of Arts and at the Apollinaire, Rome, where he received the Doctorate in Canon Law. He spent a year in sociological studies at Louvain University in Belgium.[38] From 1901 to 1904 he was Professor of Rhetoric at the Séminaire de Trois-Rivières and later Professor of Sociology at the Grand Séminaire.

He contributed six inspiring courses to the Semaine Sociale between the years 1921-1935. From 1908 to 1916 he was editor of the journal *Le Bien public* of Trois-Rivières, director of the diocesan social works, co-founder and chaplain of the Catholic labor syndicates and as pastor continued to be interested in social and labor questions proving it in words and deed. At present, he is member of the School Commission of Trois-Rivières.

Father Cloutier is a specialist in labor questions. He is the exponent of sound social doctrines and has been a leader in their application. He is aware of the difficulties of practical action on social grounds, but in the long run his fine personality and thoughtful kindness have obtained many of the desired results. Rather optimistic, he recommends the diffusion of the cooperative idea among common people of French Canada, with the view to keeping them from the grasp of economic dictatorship. This he aims to achieve through the professional organization of workingmen and agriculturists, that is, through the establishment of the corporative organization. Remarkable, he claims, is the progress that has been made within the past thirty or forty years in the establishments of *caisses populaires* and agricultural cooperatives of all sorts. He seems to think that this characteristic momentum may, without sufficient preparation, lead to failures. But that seems to be in his opinion "part of popular education," and so, "all is well!"

The next group of collaborators to the Semaine Sociale comprises University clergymen and laymen. Msgr. Cyrille Gagnon, Rector of Laval University and a pioneer of the Semaine Sociale, was born in Quebec on September 13, 1880. He received his classical education at the Seminary of Quebec and his theological

---

[38] *Ibid.* (Imprimerie du Devoir, 1911), III, p. 40.

training at the *Grand Séminaire* of the same city where he received the degree of Licentiate in Philosophy and Doctor in Theology. He was ordained by Bishop Bégin in 1906. The same year he was appointed Professor of Moral Theology at Laval University. Among the writings of Msgr. Gagnon we may note *Les Clubs neutres* (1925) and *Les Moines anglicans de Caldy* (1918). His is a familiar figure on the rostrum of the Semaine Sociale. In 1944 he discussed in a masterly fashion the *Rénovation spirituelle*. He still considers the question of the relation between capital and labor to be the most worthy of attention and solvable only by corporative organizations, which in his estimation are closely related to employee and employer unions. Thus, for him cooperation is an important factor in the social and economic restoration of the Province of Quebec.

The Rector of the University of Montreal, Msgr. Olivier Maurault, was also a pioneer of the Semaine Sociale. Born on January 1, 1886, and ordained to the priesthood in 1910, a Sulpician in 1911, after completing his education at the Collège de Montréal, the Seminary of Montreal and the Catholic Institute of Paris, Msgr. Maurault was appointed Professor at the Collège de Montréal from 1913 to 1915. He then served several parishes, first as curate of Saint-Jacques of Montreal, 1915-1926, then as pastor of Notre Dame from 1926-1929. For five years he was superior of the *Externat classique* of Saint Sulpice and since 1934 he has been the Rector of the University of Montreal. The titles and honors conferred upon him are too many to enumerate; the same holds true for his publications. Among the books published by Msgr. Maurault are *Marges d'Histoire* (1929-30), in three volumes, *La Paroisse* (1929), *Nos Messieurs* (1936), *Propos et Portraits* (1941), *Moisson de Ville-Marie* (1943), *and Aux Louisianais* (1943). Besides he contributed articles to the *Foyer, Revue Canadienne, L'Action Française, Revue Trimestrielle Canadienne,* the *Encyclopédie de la jeunesse* and others.[39]

Msgr. Maurault is particularly remarkable for his intellectual activity. He is interested in numerous fields: architecture, sculp-

[39] Raphael Ouimet, *Biographies canadiennes-françaises* (Montréal, 1926), p. 270.

ture, painting, music, poetry, literary criticism, archeology, history and sociology. Novelty attracts him; he is soon cognizant of new movements. Even hazardous enterprises appeal to him.[40] In his sermons he impresses, persuades, enlightens and convinces by a clear exposition of religious truths.[41]

Edouard Montpetit, Secretary General at the University of Montreal, and member of the General Commission of the Semaine Sociale since 1920, was born at Montmagny, September 26, 1881. After taking his B.A. at the College of Montreal he entered the University of Montreal where he received the degree of Licentiate in Law. Admitted to the bar in 1904, he practiced only twice. He then attended the Ecole libre des Sciences politiques in Paris from 1908 to 1910, and the College des Sciences sociales of the same city from 1910-1911. Successively Professor of Political Economy and of Roman Law, he was nominated to his present position in 1920. That same year he opened the Ecole des Sciences sociales, economiques et politiques at the University of Montreal. Mr. Montpetit is the author of many remarkable works, among which are: *Au Service de la tradition française* (1920), *Pour une doctrine* (1931), *Les Cordons de la bourse* (1935), *Le Front contre la vitre* (1936), *La Conquête économique* (1938), *Reflets d'Amérique* (1941), and his last one written in 1944, *Mes Mémoires.*

The activity of Mr. Montpetit is extensive and noteworthy. He holds notable positions in some ten different associations. He was sent as delegate of the French Canadian Government to various congresses abroad. In connection with one of these, the Apostolic Delegate remarked that it was "his triumphal mission to Europe."[42] In 1925 he gave a course of ten lectures on Canada at the Sorbonne and in 1928 at the University of Bruxelles. He also gave, under the auspices of the Clarence Webster Foundation, three conferences at Mount Allison University. As a lecturer, Mr. Montpetit has the power to captivate his listeners with amus-

---

[40] Henri d'Arles, "Un essayiste, M. Olivier Maurault," *L'Action française,* January, 1925, pp. 28-29.

[41] Dulac, *op. cit.,* p. 47.

[42] *La Presse,* Montréal, August 11, 1925, p. 9.

ing or ironic remarks. He learned from the French the art of communicating his knowledge,[43] remaining all the while deeply Canadian at heart.[44] He contributed five courses to the "ambulatory university."

Traditionally Catholic in thought and practice, Mr. Montpetit is deeply spiritual and supernatural in his teaching.[45] All his conclusions in matters of research are inspired by the doctrine of the Church. For him, there is a definite agreement between the spiritual interests of French Canada and its material interests, once these are well understood; between the science of economic and social facts and the traditional doctrine of the Church. "Here in Canada," he claims, "we have something which other countries have not." Sociology in his school is not considered a pure science; he tends to make it a practical science based on sound philosophy. He agrees with a good number of modern sociologists that the scientific study of social facts will coincide with the traditional doctrine of the Church.[46] He is truly a pioneer of the Social Sciences in French Canada, a true knight of French civilization, a gentleman and the perfect Canadian citizen.[47]

We find an associate of Mr. Montpetit at the University of Montreal in the person of Arthur Saint-Pierre, Director of the Research Center of the *Institut de Sociologie,* member of the General Commission of the Semaine Sociale since 1921, and seven times its speaker. Mr. St-Pierre was born in Walkerville, Ontario, September 30, 1885. When he was still young his family moved to Detroit, Michigan, where he attended a parochial school.

Ouimet speaks of Mr. St-Pierre as a self-made and well-read man. At the age of sixteen he wrote the woman's page in *La Patrie* and a few short literary compositions. At twenty-three he was contributing to the daily, *La Presse.* He was active in Study Circles of the *Association de la Jeunesse Canadienne-française,* in

---

[43] Edouard Lavergne, "Semaine sociale," *L'Action catholique,* August 31, 1923, p. 3.

[44] Dulac, *op. cit.,* p. 31.

[45] "Edouard Montpetit" *L'Action française,* November, 1923, p. 274.

[46] S. s. du Canada, 1928, pp. 277-278.

[47] Richard Arès, "L'heure des sciences sociales," *L'Ordre Nouveau,* January 5, 1936, p. 2.

the Leagues of the Sacred Heart, in the *Société Saint-Jean-Baptiste,* directing one of its periodicals *L'Oiseau Bleu,* and was Secretary of the *Ecole Sociale Populaire.* He promoted such projects as cooperatives, banks of savings and credit, and the Catholic professional organization in the Montreal region.[48] As early as 1914 he organized the Syndicate of Commerce and Industry, which at the time of World War I, had two hundred fifty members and a weekly, *La Vie professionelle.*[49]

Mr. Saint-Pierre, D.S.P., has published numerous works valuable from a sociological viewpoint: *Vers l'action* (1911), *L'Utopie socialiste* (1913), *Le Devoir social* (1914), *Questions et oeuvres sociales de chez-nous* (1914), *Le Comte Alberte de Mun* (1915), *La Question ouvrière du Canada* (1920), *Le Problème social* (1926), and is at present preparing a comprehensive study of the Franco-Americans sponsored by the Carnegie Endowment for International Peace. Professor of Applied Sociology and member of the Royal Society of Canada, he wins his students by his pleasant personality, his willingness to help and his wonderful urbanity. This able Professor realizes that the sociologist works on "living flesh." When reforms are to be effected, remedies must be chosen with an extreme prudence. This realization accounts for the extensive research done by this learned sociologist before he offers a solution to a particular problem. In his book, *Le Problème social,* he makes a few suggestions for the solution of the labor problem which he considers to be by far the most serious of all the social problems in French Canada.

Another pioneer of the Semaine Sociale, on six different occasions its speaker, is Antonio Perrault, prominent lawyer of Montreal. He was born in La Malbaie, September 15, 1880, and was educated at the Seminary of Quebec and at Laval University in Montreal. Mr. Perrault was appointed Professor of Law at the University of Montreal in 1912 and taught there thirty years while at the same time practicing law. In 1915 he became Doctor of Law, in February 1917, King's Counsellor, in June of the same year, member of the Royal Society of Canada, and in 1929

---

[48] Ouimet, *op. cit.,* p. 314.

[49] Gérard Tremblay, *L'Organisation ouvrière catholique du Canada,* p. 13.

member of the *Conseil de l'Instruction publique*. At present he is in a law partnership with his son Jacques. His contributions are extensive and numerous in both jurisprudence and sociology. He is president-director of the *Revue du Barreau* and from 1936 to 1940 published a *Traité de droit commercial* in three volumes. For forty years he has been contributing articles to various learned journals, periodicals, the Semaine Sociale, and publications of the Royal Society of Canada. Among his published pamphlets or articles bearing on sociology we may note: *Nos Oeuvres d'assistance* (1916), *L'Appel du devoir social* (1918), *Action sociale* (1920), *Le Nationalisme au Canada* (1924), *La Propriété littéraire et artistique* (1924), *L'Eucharistie et les classes dirigeantes* (1926), *A Propos de roman social; Jean Rivard et le Fils de l'esprit* (1944), and *Le Droit, soutien de l'ordre international* (1944).

Peculiar to Mr. Perrault's life is the fact that his profession did not handicap him in his public activities. He is at once professor, writer, speaker and apostle. To his peers he is a living demonstration of the truth that the social duties of a professional man are not incompatible with the exercise of that same profession; one can succeed in business, and at the same time contribute to social betterment by the good influence of Catholicism.[50] To the motto: "Probity, Learning, Independence," given by Mr. Chenu to the lawyers of Paris, Mr. Perrault added "Faith."[51]

Still another early collaborator of the Semaine Sociale is Léon-Mercier Gouin, senator since 1940. Born in Montreal, December 24, 1891, he was the son of Sir Lomer Gouin, former Premier of Quebec and of Elisa Mercier, daughter of Honorable Honoré Mercier, also former Premier of Quebec. He received his education from Collège Sainte-Marie where Father Archambault was his professor, Loyola College, Laval University, and Oxford University. At the 1944 meeting he stated, "I was born in Montreal, grew up in Quebec and matured in Ottawa!" He received the degree of Doctor in Law from the University of Montreal in

---

[50] S. s. du Canada, Québec, 1921, pp. 393-394.
[51] Dulac, *op. cit.*, p. 46.

1921. He attended an extension course in Political Economy at McGill University and was awarded various honors from different societies and institutions.

Senator Gouin is the author of *Hors commerce* (1920), *Le Droit commercial* (1924), which comprises two volumes, and *Industrial Legislation* (1937). For some years he was Professor at the Ecole des Hautes Etudes Commerciales and at the School of Social Sciences at the University of Montreal. At present he is titular professor at these schools, member of the Montreal and Canadian Bar Association, member of the Canadian Institute on Foreign Affairs, Vice-president of Canadian Institute on Economics and Politics, president of the Catholic Scouts of the Province of Quebec, and member of the Montreal Reform Club.

Mr. Gouin looks at life seriously.[52] Not only is he an eminent jurist, he is also the devoted servant, the sociologist, the fervent apostle of noble causes.[53] He is a familiar figure at the Semaine Sociale. On eleven different occasions he addressed the audience. Little wonder that the Apostolic Delegate on one occasion called him "the apostle of social questions."[54]

Doctor Albert Sormany, a member of the General Commission of the Semaine Sociale since 1928, was born in Lamèque, New Brunswick, August 21, 1885. He received his education from the Collège du Sacré-Coeur de Caraquet directed by the Eudistes Fathers and now called the Université du Sacré-Coeur de Bathurst. He pursued his medical studies at Laval University. From 1910 to 1928, Dr. Sormany practiced his profession. Since 1928 he has been in charge of the Department of X-Rays at the Hotel-Dieu de Saint-Basile. He was mayor of Edmundston for the years 1914 and 1915. He is connected with the School Commission of Edmundston, is president-general of the *Société Mutuelle d'Assomption* since 1927, and of the *Association Acadienne d'Education* since its foundation. Dr. Sormany has always taken an active part in the national and religious movements of Acadia. He is the most prominent member of the *Société d'Assomption,* the national so-

---

[52] *Ibid.,* p. 129.
[53] "Une heureuse nomination," *L'Ordre Nouveau,* November 20, 1940, p. 1.
[54] *La Presse,* Montréal, August 11, 1925, p. 9.

ciety of the Acadians. He received several honorary degrees, one a Doctorate in Social Sciences from Laval University.[55]

In this survey he is listed with University men because he is Professor of Anatomy, Physiology, and Diseases of the Nervous System at the Ecole des Gardes malades de l'Hotel-Dieu de Saint-Basile. He advocates the corporative movement as a solution of the labor question.

Esdras Minville, Director of the Ecole des Hautes Etudes Commerciales, was inducted as a member of the General Commission of the Semaine Sociale in 1933 and has given four excellent courses. He was born in Grande Vallée, November 7, 1896, and educated at the Boarding School of Saint-Laurent directed by the Christian Brothers, and finally at the school of which he is now Director and from which he received his Licentiate. In connection with the Commission Powell-Sirois he was asked to study labor unions and social institutions in the Province of Quebec. First as Professor at the Ecole des Hautes Etudes Commerciales and then as Director, he organized a Bureau of Scientific Research for the Province of Quebec.[56] This Bureau has contributed valuable voluminous works under the general titles of *Notre Milieu* (1942), *Montréal économique* (1943), and *Agriculture* (1943). These symposia are the work of specialists on the various topics studied.

Mr. Minville himself has many remarkable publications, among which only a few may be mentioned: *Instruction ou éducation* (1931), *L'Oeuvre de la colonization* (1933), *Comment établir l'organization corporative au Canada* (1936), *Invitation à l'étude* (1942), *La Force conquérante de la coopération* (1943). He has written a large number of articles for various periodicals, such as *l'Action française*, *Actualité économique*, of which he is one of the founders, and *l'Action nationale*. His studies, activities, teaching, collaboration and presidency of the *Ligue d'Action nationale* all aim to awaken in the French Canadians a keen sense of realities, to prompt them to utilize intelligently their material

---

[55] Les Biographies françaises d'Amérique, *op. cit.*, p. 512.
[56] *Ibid.*, p. 372.

wealth with a view to assuring their survival.[57] Although Mr. Minville is a young economist, he has already made an accurate estimate of the existing socio-economic problem in French Canada and has offered solutions in a pamphlet on the political measures needed and the economic and national value of colonization in French Canada. Intellectually outstanding and cultured, he is capable of proving, by historical and philosophical arguments, that the work of colonization is necessary and urgent in French Canada.[58]

Another University man, a lawyer, member of the General Commission of the Semaine Sociale since 1935, and speaker on five occasions, is Leo Pelland, who was born in Sainte-Elizabeth of Joliette, October 25, 1891. He received his education from the Seminary of Joliette and Laval University, and was successively granted the degree of Bachelor of Arts, Licentiate in Philosophy and in Law. In 1914 he was admitted to the bar. At present, in collaboration with Mr. Jean-Marie Guérard, he is editor of the *Revue du Droit;* a position he has held since its foundation in 1922. He became proprietor of this periodical upon the death of Mr. Eusèbe Billeau in 1939.[59] He was editor of *L'Action Catholique* from 1914 to 1919. In 1925, Mr. Pelland was appointed Professor at Laval University for introductory courses in the study of law and the history of law. He has prepared and published various studies of a juridico-sociological nature, one of which is *L'Action catholique et la politique.* Like Mr. Minville, he considers the problem of colonization a timely one and favors corporative reorganization of the economic and agricultural systems.

Another remarkable professor of the University of Montreal who became a member of the General Commission of the Semaine Sociale in 1937 is Maximilien Caron. Born in Valleyfield, July 16, 1901, he received his education at the college of Valleyfield,

---

[57] *L'Action nationale,* September, 1936, p. 24.

[58] Georges M. Bilodeau, "La grande question à l'étude," *Le Devoir,* July 18, 1933, p. 1.

[59] Pierre-Georges Roy, *Les Avocats de la région de Québec* (Lévis, 1936), p. 340.

the University of Montreal, the Ecole des Sciences politiques in Paris. He spent a few months in Burlington, Vermont, "to broaden his views," he claims, and learn the American way of life. In 1938 he was appointed Professor of Civil Law at the University of Montreal. He also teaches Roman Law and Commercial Law at the Ecole des Hautes Etudes Commerciales. As professor, Mr. Caron reveals remarkable aptitudes. His clearness of thought, his juridical sense, his concise and sure method of resting arguments on erudition and knowledge of facts assure him of that ascendancy possessed only by true professors and thus exert considerable influence even outside the University.[60]

President of the *Action Corporative,* Mr. Caron's interest in the professional question is always alive. He wrote in collaboration with several colleagues on the subject: *Vers un ordre nouveau par l'organization corporative* (1940); he is also the author of *L'Organisation corporative au service de la démocratie* (1942). Six times he took the stand at the rostrum of the Semaine Sociale.

Father Archambault when referring to Mr. Caron's collaboration on social questions at the 1943 meeting of the Semaine Sociale speaks of him as

> . . . one of those men who at present brings more honor to our nationality by his juridical sense of social responsibility, by the solidity of his convictions and the force and depth of his character. The Semaine sociale is happy to count him in its General Commission and among its most assiduous speakers.[61]

A similar appreciation would be to the point in the case of Alfred Charpentier, a pioneer of the Semaine Sociale, and president of the *Confédération des Travailleurs Catholiques du Canada* (C.T.C.C.). Born in Montreal, November 25, 1888, the eldest of a family of eighteen, he received a primary education

[60] "M. Maximilien Caron," *L'Action nationale,* September, 1938, p. 27.

[61] S. s. du Canada, Salaberry-de-Valleyfield, 1943, p. 16: ". . . . un des hommes qui font actuellement le plus d'honneur à notre nationalité par son sens juridique et social, par la solidité de ses convictions et la droiture de son caractère. Les Semaines sociales se réjouissent de le compter dans leur Commission générale et parmi leurs conférenciers les plus assidus."

in different Catholic schools of the Commission and at thirteen learned the bricklayer's trade. In that position he became a member of the International Union. In 1915 at twenty-six, he joined the Montreal Fire Department and remained at this work for twenty-five years. As a fireman, he devoted his leisure to the study of labor problems, so much so that his fellow-workers nicknamed him the "bourreau de travail." His interest centered chiefly on Catholic and national syndicates. With Father Edmour Hébert, he established the *Cercle Leon XIII* which is the first unit of Catholic and national syndicates in Montreal. In 1921, Mr. Charpentier contributed to the founding of the *Confédération des Travailleurs Catholiques* and became secretary of the new organization in 1922. A year later he attended courses in the Social Science School at the University of Montreal. Having completed his studies in 1925, he returned to the syndicate movement and became president of the Central Council in 1931 and of the C.T.C. in 1934. Mr. Charpentier has helped organize a great number of Catholic syndicates and has written several articles and pamphlets on labor questions in Canada,[62] such as *De l'Internationalisme au nationalisme* (1920), *L'Atelier syndical fermé* (1926). He was heard on six different occasions at the Semaine Sociale. He taught at the *Institut Pie XI* and published his courses in the periodical *Nos Cours.* Having grown up among workers and having himself worked and known from experience the hardships of the workingman, Mr. Charpentier is naturally prompted to sympathize with him. After winning his confidence and affection he succeeds in bringing about better conditions of work.

Another pioneer of the Semaine Sociale was Oscar Hamel, notary and banker. Born in Quebec, August 31, 1887, he received his education at the Seminary of Quebec and at Laval University and was graduated with the degrees of Bachelor of Literature and Licentiate in Law.

Mr. Hamel was secretary-general of the *Action sociale catholique,* and is now proprietor of this journal, which is one of the principal organs of the labor and employers' syndicates, of the *caisses populaires,* of cooperatives, of agriculture, and coloniza-

---

[62] "Biographie quotidienne," *Montréal-Matin,* September 9, 1941, p. 2.

tion. He favors the betterment of living conditions for the workingman and advocates the organization of cooperatives. Besides this, he has contributed a few tracts on Catholic youth, on religious communities and on the movies. In fact, he became president of the *Ligue du Cinema* when movie-censorship became expedient.

J. E. A. Dubuc, industrialist and deputy for twenty years, was still another pioneer of the Semaine Sociale. A native of Saint-Hugues, he was born on January 21, 1871, and followed a commercial course at the Séminaire de Saint-Charles Borromée in Sherbrooke. He was first employed as a clerk of the National Bank of that city. In 1892, he established a Branch of the National Bank in Chicoutimi. In 1897, he organized a pulp company in Chicoutimi, composed of French Canadians of the district of Quebec, whose capital of $50,000 at its outset rose eventually to $1,000,000. This initial success encouraged other amalgamations until the pulp industry in Canada became more important here than elsewhere the world over.[63]

To Mr. Dubuc, truly Christian employer that he is, the French Canadians owe a great deal. His Pulp and Paper Factories never operated on Sundays. When a correspondent from the United States asked Mr. Dubuc the reason for this attitude, the latter stated among other facts that uninterrupted work is a monstrous economic heresy, reducing man to the conditions of the beast; in short, it is a social crime.[64] Mr. Dubuc's interest in charitable, educational and Catholic social endeavors has been so intense that the Holy See in 1914 conferred upon him the title of Knight of the Order of Saint Gregory the Great.[65] As a far-sighted benevolent social leader, he expresses the hope that Quebec may never become an *Etat-Providence* but rather a colonizing country whose inhabitants live of and on the land.

Chenier Picard, notary, financier, and member of the General Commission of the Semaine Sociale since 1924, was born in Wotton, July 14, 1881. He studied at the Collège Sainte-Marie in

---

[63] *Biographie canadienne-française* (Ottawa: J. A. Fortier, 1920), p. 93.
[64] S. s. du Canada, Ottawa, 1922, p. 144.
[65] *Biographie canadienne-française, op. cit.*, p. 94.

Montreal, at the Séminaire de Saint-Charles Borromée in Sherbrooke and at Laval University. In 1907 he was a full-fledged notary, and since that date has been first and foremost a "professionel." However, he is ever devoted to the religious and charitable works of his diocese and gave much of his time and energy to the Semaine Sociale when this ambulatory university held its sessions in Sherbrooke. He considers the relations of capital and labor to be an important problem in French Canada and recommends the amelioration of the rural conditions of life to attract urban dwellers.

Albert Rioux, former president of the *Union Catholique des Cultivateurs* for four years and former *sous-ministre* of agriculture for three years, was inducted into the Semaine Sociale in 1933, and contributed three excellent courses. Born in Val-Brillant, March 10, 1899, he received his education from the Brothers at Sayabec, at the Seminary of Rimouski with the Jesuits and at the Ecole Supérieure d'Agriculture de Sainte-Anne-de-la-Pocatière. He is a Bachelor of Arts, a Bachelor in Agricultural Science, a Master of Arts and has a Licentiate in Agricultural Science from Laval University. *L'Electrification rurale de Québec* is the title of his dissertation for the degree of Doctor in Social, Political and Economic Sciences which he obtained from Laval University in 1942. A farmer in Sayabec from 1927 to 1932, he was elected Mayor of the village of Saindon in 1931. He was appointed librarian at the Ministry of Agriculture in 1939.[66] Mr. Rioux is the author of a number of pamphlets, *L'Enseignement agricole d'hiver, Le Programme de restoration sociale, La carrière agricole* among others. He is also a contributor to *Le Devoir, Terre de chez nous,* and *Relations.* At present he is director of the *Caisse populaire* of Saint-Romuald, founder-member of the Superior Council of Cooperation and president of the *Société d'Agriculture* of the county of Lévis.

As a remedy to the economic situation in the Province of Quebec he advocates a vast scheme of adult education for the majority of youth who have completed their primary studies, and this with a view to deriving a maximum yield from French Ca-

---

[66] *Les Biographies françaises d'Amérique, op. cit.,* p. 106.

nadian human capital. In his opinion, this is the most efficient means of bettering the material conditions in French Canada.

Although Jacques Cartier took his place in the ranks of the General Commission of the Semaine Sociale only in 1943, he is far from being last in point of achievement. A native of Saint-Jean, he was born in September 7, 1880, and studied successively at the Collège de Montreal, the Seminary and the University of Montreal. He is a *Licencié ès lettres* and in law. At present he is an eminent member of the bar, member of the Administrative Commission of the University of Montreal; also on the Executive Committee of the *Revue du Barreau,* ex-batonnier of the Richelieu bar, member of the Provincial Secretarial Office of Temperance, and Knight of Saint Sylvester. In 1940 at Saint-Jean at the *Journée catholique* (Catholic Day) he discussed *L'Eglise et le travail* and in 1942 at the Semaine sociale made a study of *La Valeur de la démocratie.*

Mr. Cartier is a man of action and a true Christian. As a member of the Saint Vincent de Paul Society, he has helped many an unfortunate. He is also an apostle of the French language. To better the economic situation of the Province of Quebec, he advocates a return to the land; first, by law of attenuation, in as much as possible, decreeing an exodus from the city or industrial center, where abnormal expansion—somewhat like the enormous head on the dwarfed body—tends to offset the equilibrium of the whole Province; secondly, by affording those who wish to return to the land after the war an opportunity to do so; and thirdly, by giving due consideration to the legitimate needs of industry and not abandoning it to disease or disorganization.

Another wise proposal made by Mr. Cartier is the creation of a central organism composed of a member of the General Commission of the Semaine Sociale, an officer of the Catholic syndicates, a director of the Ecole Sociale Populaire, a director of the *Union Catholique des Cultivateurs* and others, whose main objective would be to simplify and unify all the means of action and indicate the points of application for the social doctrine of the Church.

Among the eighteen living pioneers of the Semaine Sociale, Judge C. E. Dorion stands out as a veteran in social work, a renown speaker, a jurist of note and especially an eminent philosopher. Father Archambault speaks of him as "one of the most highly cultivated minds of French Canada with a fond attachment for the doctrine of the Church." Mr. Charles-Edouard Dorion was born in Quebec, November 16, 1860, was educated at the Seminary of Quebec and at Laval University receiving the degrees of Bachelor, Licentiate and Doctor in Law. Called to the bar of Quebec in 1884, he practiced until he was appointed to the King's Bench, July 1920. He retired in 1939.[67]

In 1898 Judge Dorion was appointed Professor of Civil Law and Dean of the Department of Law at Laval University. His ability in the field of social science and political economy is exceptional. At different meetings of the Semaine Sociale he gave nine enlightening courses. In addition to his vast juridical knowledge[68] he contributed pamphlets to the Ecole Sociale Populaire and wrote extensively on divorce and education.

The Honorable Thibaudeau Rinfret, Chief Justice of the Supreme Court of Canada since January 8, 1944, became a member of the General Commission of the Semaine Sociale in 1932. Born in Montreal, June 22, 1879, he pursued his academic studies at the Collège Sainte-Marie in Montreal receiving the degree of Bachelor of Arts and studied law at the University of Montreal receiving the title of Bachelor of Law. He also attended McGill University where he was granted the degree of Bachelor in Civil Law. Admitted to the bar of the Province of Quebec, he practiced his profession until 1922 when he was appointed to the Bench of the Superior Court of the Province of Quebec. In 1924 he was appointed Judge of the Supreme Court of Canada.

Chief Justice Rinfret was Professor in Comparative Law and the Law of Public Utilities at McGill University for ten years.

---

[67] B. M. Green, ed., *Who's Who in Canada,* 1940-41 (Toronto: International Press Limited), p. 534.

[68] Ferdinand Bélanger, "La Semaine sociale," *L'Action catholique,* Québec, August 14, 1924, p. 3.

Officer of the Legion of Honor of France,[69] he is at present director of the *Alliance Française d'Ottawa* and vice-president of the *Fédération de l'Alliance Française* in the United States and in Canada. He is also Honorary President of the Canadian Conference of French-speaking jurists for the Ottawa section.

He has written a few articles in newspapers and some of his addresses have been published in the following journals: *Revue de l'Université d'Ottawa, Revue du Droit,* and *Revue du Barreau.* From 1901-1910 he was a regular collaborator to the *Avenir du Nord,* a weekly published in Saint-Jerome, County of Terrebonne. Sure of judgment and clear in his thought, he is greatly interested in the doings of Canada's ambulatory institution. In 1944, he presided over the second popular meeting, presenting the famous orator, Mr. Felix Desrochers. Although he has been living in the Province of Ontario for twenty years, his interest in his native Province does not appear to dwindle. He remains a faithful defender of the French language and traditions.

Judge Léon Lajoie, a member of the General Commission of the Semaine Sociale in 1941, is a resident of Trois-Rivières. He was born on September 16, 1891, attended the Séminaire de Trois-Rivières, the Collège Sainte-Marie in Montreal and studied law at the University of Montreal. In 1916 he started to practice law; in 1926 he was elected *Conseil du Roi* and in 1940 was appointed judge. The following year he was elected President of the Trois-Rivières Council of the Saint Vincent de Paul Society. He is a member of the Committee for the *Ligue du dimanche* and at present president of a juridical military tribunal in Montreal. He is a model father of a large Christian family, devoting most of his time to his family and profession. Possessed of a wide culture, as a man of action, he would never divorce religion and supernatural needs from his profession and duties as head of a household. A daily communicant, the Eucharist for him is a compelling force.

---

[69] Ouimet, *Biographies canadiennes-françaises,* 1931-32, p. 470; *The Canadian Parliamentary Guide 1944* (Ottawa: Syndicats d'oeuvres sociales limitée), p. 651; and Pierre-Georges Roy, *Les Juges de la Province de Québec* (Québec: Service des Archives du Gouvernement de la Province, 1933), p. 463.

Of course, important and experienced as these persons are in public affairs and in the knowledge of social doctrine, it must not be inferred that they are the sole contributors to the movement. Each year at least twenty persons participate in diffusing the doctrine of the social encyclicals. Worthy of mention are Mother Gérin-Lajoie, foundress of the Institut de Notre Dame du Bon Conseil; Judge Arthur Laramée of the Juvenile Court, Father Léon Lebel, S.J., pioneer of the Family Allowance Program in French Canada; Father M. A. Lamarche, O.P., distinguished speaker, writer of note and director of the *Revue Dominicaine* from 1915-1940; Father Lorenzo Gauthier, C.S.V., an authority on communism and French Canadian social problems, well-known for his radio speeches; Father Georges H. Lévesque, O.P., director of the Social Science School of Laval University; Father Gonzalve Poulin, O.F.M., assistant-director of the same school, and Father Jean d'Auteuil Richard, director of *Relations* and leader in the fostering of housing projects.

As we examine the membership of the General Commission of the Semaine Sociale, we realize that this institution is not solely the work of the clergy: nineteen of its members are laymen, sixteen are clergymen. These together with the collaborators to the Semaine Sociale recognize that human happiness lies in knowledge for action. Therefore, they are instigators, endeavoring to form an active, conscientious, competent elite intent on an adequate application of Christian social doctrine; an ardent, disinterested elite that will preach action and love, combat indifference, negativism and hatred and thus bring about the necessary reforms of which French Canada is in need.

CHAPTER IV

THE SEMAINE SOCIALE AND THE CHURCH

The Semaine Sociale considers the Church to be the most important social institution and consequently has made the study of its social doctrine a primary duty. This chapter purports to state the definition, aim, rights and teachings of the Church, to indicate its traditional role in the economic and moral life of a people as these matters are presented by the Semaine Sociale. It will further discuss the significance of Sunday observance among French Canadians, the work of Catholic Action of the laity in cooperation with the hierarchy and the present condition of the Church in French Canada.

The Church is a society divine in its origin, supernatural in its faith and means of salvation, composed of baptized persons who profess the doctrine of Jesus-Christ and submit to legitimate authority, specifically in the person of the Holy Pontiff. To the Semaine Sociale the Church is a great civilizing force, the mother and guardian of intellectual advancement, the friend of all true progress.

Never once does the Semaine Sociale forget that the aim of the Catholic Church is the sanctification of its members, that Jesus-Christ, its founder, intended that His Church perpetuate His work. It is aware that a distinction was made by Christ Himself between the spiritual and the temporal power, between civil society and religious society, between what is due to God and what is due to Caesar. That is why the Semaine Sociale emphasizes that the Church is supranational, knows no boundaries, governs its faithful the entire world over—a position held by no other living society.

Bearing in mind that the preëminence and primacy of the ecclesiastical power was given to the Church by our Lord Himself, and that His Apostles filled with the Holy Ghost openly proclaimed that it is better to obey God than to obey men, Father Ferland compares the activities of the Church and State to two intercepting circles. The space circumscribed by each circle is divided into two parts: one belonging to each separately and the other being common to both. In the separate spaces each one is independent and sovereign, but in the part which is common to the two societies, reason and revelation command, order and peace require that one be subordinated to the other. The Church, he goes on to explain, received its monarchial form and constitution from Jesus-Christ Himself. Thus, should the State try to democratize the hierarchical organization of the Church because monarchies are outmoded, it would be taking upon itself to change the work of God, an act that is outright, culpable, odious presumption. Besides, Father Ferland asserts, it is in conformity with its constitution that the Church, to accomplish its mission of salvation, has the right to preach the gospel, to administer sacraments, to make laws and demand their observance, to judge and punish in religious matters, to acquire, possess and administer whatever material goods it needs for worship. The Church, as such, must supervise the Christian formation of youth, the sanctity of marriage and public morals. Even when, at one time or another, violence was used against the Church to force her to abdicate these rights, she never relinquished any of them, so essential are they to the carrying out of her divine mission.[1] Saint Paul, in chains, declared that "the word of God is not bound."[2]

Another right of the Church, upon which the Semaine Sociale insists, is its threefold immunity: local, real, and personal. This immunity is justified by the fact that ecclesiastical persons or things belong primarily to God, and as such, are not subject to the jurisdiction of civil society. This point the Semaine Sociale has maintained and repeatedly stressed. Local and personal immunity are well recognized in French Canada. Real immunity, however, does not exist throughout the entire Province of Quebec. In the opinion of the Semaine Sociale it could be maintained if people were properly educated as to its meaning and made aware of its obligation. The economy of religious communities in general, the simple standards of living of seminary professors and

---

[1] S. s. du Canada, Ottawa, 1931, pp. 118-124.

[2] 2 Tim. II 9.

parish priests, the poverty of religious houses, should reassure those who question the use that the Church makes of the money confided to her care.[3]

The next problem is, How does the Semaine Sociale interpret the Church's mission as teacher of all nations? Remembering that Scripture is open to all, that its pages abound in instructions on the social relations of men, the Semaine Sociale considers the Gospel in particular as of high social value and often looks to it for guidance. It is true that one does not find in Holy Scripture an explicit condemnation of the sweat-shop system, or the approval of collective conventions, or of popular banks, simply because the words of our Lord surpass all contingencies. They speak of no particular age, rather for all ages. They establish principles which may be applied according to circumstances and place.[4]

Another point: in French Canada the Church has jurisdiction over Christian marriages on the ground that for Christians there is no marriage without the sacrament. It is the Church which regulates its conditions and formalities, and pronounces on its validity. For a Catholic, only a sacramental marriage, administered according to the rites of the Church, creates a conjugal bond.[5]

As was mentioned previously, the French Canadians look upon the Church as the friend of all true progress. The Semaine Sociale recognizes that the Church esteems science, literature, and art, puts a price upon that precious freedom of her children and desires the happiness of all its faithful in justice, charity, and peace; in a word, it follows a middle course between contradictory errors. Because it is deeply human, the Church demands of individuals self-respect, sanctity, fortitude, generosity, and meekness. It requires that leaders become the servants of all, and subjects, submissive to authority. Life, a divine trust; authority, a public servant; obedience to legitimate authority—these are three notions

---

[3] S. s. du Canada, Trois-Rivières, 1925, pp. 319-326; and S. s. du Canada, Ottawa, 1931, p. 131.

[4] Archambault, *L'Eglise catholique et les devoirs du chrétien* (Montréal: Ecole Sociale Populaire, 1917), pp. 15, 21-23.

[5] S. s. du Canada, Ottawa, 1931, p. 150.

instilled by the Gospel at every turn, and on these notions all social life is based.[6]

Indeed, if the decalogue, as Father Mauger, O.P., calls it the "ancient Declaration of Rights of man," had been accepted by the pagan world, the social role of the Church in relation to slavery, to the family, to the workingmen would have been minimized. As early as 1920, the Semaine Sociale described the social and charitable role of the Church in the course of all the ages. In pagan society, slavery was a fundamental institution, sanctioned by law and morals. Certain men are born free, Aristotle had said, others are born in slavery; slavery is not only something useful to the slaves but just. Socrates, so great and upright, Xenophon, Socrates' echo, Plato, the most sublime of thinkers, the egoistic Epicureans, the rigid Stoics, never once attempted to do away with this inhuman institution. That reform was to be accomplished, slowly but surely, by the Church. First came a doctrine of equality and love. The Apostles of the Gentiles announced the new law, "There is neither Jew nor Greek; there is neither slave nor freeman; there is neither male nor female. For you are all one in Christ Jesus." Jesus Himself had said, "A new commandment I give you, that you love one another: that as I have loved you, you also love one another."

The next good turn of the Church, if we follow out the thought of the Semaine Sociale, was the renovation of the family. Woman regained her dignity, the child was given certain rights, and the family became the most fecund of social institutions. Centuries of trials and persecutions were necessary to accomplish this reform, but finally when the Roman empire bowed to the Cross, a change in the status of the family was possible, and with Constantine, laws were actually passed to insure the permanence of this reform.

Nor did the social accomplishment of the Church end there. For every monastery that was founded, for every cathedral that was built, for every trade that was organized, a hospital was established until the number of these institutions in the Church became an index of its extension and influence. During the eighteenth cen-

[6] S. s. du Canada, Chicoutimi, 1929, pp. 316-317.

tury, France alone possessed 20,000. Mr. Ladouceur does not fear to say that the existence of so many hospitals suffices to characterize Christian civilization and to separate it from pagan civilization. The archeologists or anthropologists of the future, who will study the remains of a Christian city will find not only forums, theaters, statues, columns, and temples, but monuments of zeal and charity in the form of leproseries, foundling homes, lazarettos, and hospitals.

In French Canada, according to the Semaine Sociale, these institutions of charity have extended their work so as to care for all the ills of society. They have reached a remarkable degree of perfection and specialization. Abandoned, illegitimate, and problem children, incurables, the lame, the cancerous, the aged, the wounded, the dying, the condemned, the poor, the unemployed, prisoners, sick workingmen, beggars, young girls without protection, all find their good Samaritan in some institution under the direction of the Catholic Church.[7]

This form of benevolence became insufficient when new economic problems appeared due to the introduction of machinery which revolutionized industry. Small factories gave way to large industries, hiring many workers. The relation of capital and labor then suffered a profound change. The Church has often been accused of being tardy in setting forth its social doctrine and lacking initiative. But, as early as 1840, eight years before socialism became the fashion, Frederic Ozanam, in one of his courses in jurisprudence, given at the University of Lyons, declared, the Semaine Sociale of 1936 reminds us, that it was the work of Christianity to proclaim, not only man's right to work, but his right to a just wage; that the laborer is not a tool to be exploited, but a human being to whom a living wage must be given; that conditions of work must be such that this human being will be able to live like a man, a citizen, the father of a family, a Christian. Ozanam even pointed to the injustice of private labor contracts and preferably advised collective contracts. Mention is also made, in the same issue of the Semaine Sociale, of how Msgr.

---

[7] S. s. du Canada, Montréal, 1920, pp. 149-160; and S. s. du Canada, Sherbrooke, 1938, pp. 363-372.

Ketteler, as early as 1848, borrowed the doctrine of Saint Thomas Aquinas to establish the claims of labor, which doctrine later became incorporated in the legislation of Germany. Similarly, in 1872, Count Albert de Mun and the Marquis de la Tour du Pin, two rich nobles of France, organized labor syndicates and forced the French Parliament to enact laws for the protection of workers.[8]

Finally, to denounce the unfortunate situation of the lower classes of society, Leo XIII in 1891, published his famous encyclical *Rerum novarum.* Another issue still of the Semaine Sociale reports on how, forty years later, Pius XI, under the inspiration of heaven, proposed the immutable principles of the Gospel as the solution of the solid economic problem. Indeed, the Church today has a social doctrine to offer, in which are expounded the necessity of inequalities and of suffering, the duties of the two classes of society, and the true use of riches.[9]

Judging from various utterances of the Semaine Sociale, the diffusion of this social doctrine is in the hands of the elite; and this elite for French Canada, at least, in the words of Mr. Edouard Montpetit, Secretary General of the University of Montreal and founder of its School of Social Science, consists of three classes: the clergy, the liberal professions and the bourgeoisie or the "élite paysanne."[10] Of these three groups, the functions of the clergy in parish work is probably the most important. Under the influence of the priest, the parishioner's soul rises above unworthy passions, the atmosphere of the home becomes purified and Christian civilization thereby preserves its ideals. Even the casual observer is aware that it is the parish that has made French Canada, saved it, and, in fact, is still perpetuating it. The parish is at the base of the French Canadian social organism. While promoting the economic well-being of the parishioners, it has helped the French people to rise above the materialistic attitude found in so many other countries. Mr. Henri Bourassa, an outstanding personality

---

[8] S. s. du Canada, Trois-Rivières, 1936, p. 346. A good summary of the projects undertaken in France for the benefits of the workingmen may be found in Semaine sociale du Canada, Sherbrooke, 1938, p. 376.

[9] S. s. du Canada, Montréal, 1920, p. 3.

[10] Interview with Mr. Edouard Montpetit, September 20, 1944, at the University of Montréal.

and famous journalist, wrote in the July 4, 1910, issue of *Le Devoir,*

> . . . the Canadian people will keep its faith, its language and its ethnic character only so long as the typical Canadian parish shall last with its familial and paternal pastor, its Church with silver belfry and its "banc d'oeuvre," its school and its convent, its parish hall, its Church pew and its pulpit, its sales of vegetables and grains for the masses of the departed, and its meetings at the Church doors.[11]

Furthermore, Mr. Esdras Minville, Director of the Ecole des Hautes Etudes Commerciales de Montreal, reports that Mr. Bourassa contends the French Canadian owes to his priest nothing less than his *survivance.*[12]

Again, in 1929, Msgr. Perrier, now Vicar General of Montreal, reviewed the role that the parish has played in maintaining the spiritual life of the French population, in saving their national life, and in preparing them to shoulder the responsibilities of social and political life. He then adds how Msgr. Landrieux, Bishop of Dijon, after a visit in Canada, was impressed by the function and structure of the French Canadian parish.

Moreover, Msgr. Perrier claims that a parochial bulletin is necessary to multiply divine teaching and to penetrate into the hostile quarters of the Province.[13] Father Cloutier, in the Semaine Sociale of 1935, declared that each parish should have activities animated with supernatural motives and charity. As such, we find today, a Conference of Saint-Vincent de Paul, a Sacred-Heart League, scouts and jocists, an association for women and young

---

[11] *Le Devoir,* Montréal, July 4, 1910, cited in Adélard Dugré, *La Paroisse au Canada-français* (Montréal: Ecole Sociale Populaire, 1929), p. 6: ". . . le peuple canadien ne conservera sa foi, sa langue et son caractère ethnique que si la vraie paroisse canadienne demeure, avec son curé familial et paternel, son église au clocher d'argent et son banc d'oeuvre, son école et son couvent, sa salle de paroisse, sa place d'église et sa tribune, ses ventes de légumes et de grains pour les 'messes des âmes' et ses réunions aux portes des églises."

[12] Esdras Minville et al., *L'Agriculture* (Montréal: Editions Fides), p. 295.

[13] S. s. du Canada, Chicoutimi, 1929, pp. 223-232.

girls, a workshop, and a Committee for maternal assistance in nearly all important French Canadian parishes.[14] Lest, however, the influence exerted by the parish in French Canada remain circumscribed in limited space and thus foster the already existing individualistic tendencies of the French Canadians, beneficial enterprises and interparochial meetings are recommended to stimulate Christian activities to react against pernicious teachings and fight the "license of the street."[15]

Much more conspicuous has been the role of the parish in the rural life of French Canada. Father Lamarche, O.P., at the 1928 meeting of the Semaine Sociale, called the parish a real farmer's information center. Without the parish, he maintains, there would be no means of communication between the agriculturists and the agronomes. The rural pastor is expected to provide for the advancement of the spiritual life of his parishioners, as well as to foster a love for farming, and to organize sane recreation. Thus, to react against the monotony of certain services in some country Churches, Father Lamarche asks that agricultural religious feasts be organized. There is a Breton proverb which says, "Whoever quits the farm turns to the left." Father Lamarche believes in that proverb and does not think it is lost time for a pastor to preach fidelity to the soil. His suggestions for healthy recreation for the country folk range from skating, conferences, plays, to musical recitals. Strangely enough, when Msgr. J. H. Cousineau, then Rector of Saint-Esutache, proposed in 1928, a rink for skaters of both sexes, criticisms poured in from people "too civilized to bother with reasonable things." The priest, however, maintained that this sport was more hygienic, more wholesome, and less dangerous than the tavern or other promiscuous meeting places.[16]

It is clear, then, that the Church, in Canada, has always encouraged the agricultural work of the pioneer. At the present time, it preaches a return to the land as "one of the best means to assure the economic life and the general prosperity of the country. Of the French Canadian woman, the Church demands that she keep her husband and her boys on the farm, that she

---

[14] S. s. du Canada, Joliette, 1935, pp. 238-239.
[15] S. s. du Canada, Chicoutimi, 1929, p. 239.
[16] S. s. du Canada, Saint-Hyacinthe, 1928, pp. 295-305.

make life agreeable for them, that she ennoble their life through her moral influence, her virtues, and finally that she bear a large number of children who will love the soil and adopt their father's trade. The farmer must take a certain pride in his work. Thus, we find Father Philippe Perrier quoting Frederic of Prussia: "If I could find a man who could produce two stalks of corn instead of one, I would prefer him to all political geniuses."[17]

No less important in the thought of the Semaine Sociale is the social role of the various religious orders in French Canada. They are aware that the proper aim of a religious order is to attain perfection in spiritual life by means of prayer and sacrifice. The main preoccupation of a religious is the interest of his soul. A consecrated soul is thus a living demonstration of the Gospel, a champion of its dogma and moral, a hero of the Cross by example silently preaching its austere fruitfulness. Were the religious orders to accomplish nothing more than to recall to the mind of the people the beauty and the necessity of poverty, flee from the innumerable dangers of an easy life, denounce outrightly egotism under its various forms, in short, widen the path of salvation by the power of example, they still would be looked upon as the greatest benefactors of society.[18]

But, the Semaine Sociale notes again that in a concrete manner the religious orders accomplish more than the personal sanctification of their members. If one examines the work of the religious, he finds them examining the history of the past, scrutinizing the mysteries of Holy Scripture, restoring the rites and splendor of the Roman liturgy. In a word, they continue as true sons of Saint Benedict, Saint Bernard, Saint Dominic, and Saint Ignatius of Loyola enriching the intellectual world with works of great value.[19]

Again, as the Semaine Sociale demonstrates, religious orders have played a considerable role for centuries: founded hospitals, organized parishes, opened schools, orphans' homes and boarding schools, conducted colleges, seminaries, and universities, taken charge of reform schools and prisons. Little wonder that today religious orders of women, such as the Hospitallers, the Grey Nuns,

---

[17] S. s. du Canada, Rimouski, 1933, pp. 257-264.

[18] S. s. du Canada, Sherbrooke, 1924, pp. 63-67.

[19] *Ibid.*, p. 69.

and the Sisters of Providence, have been put in charge of most of the hospitals built by French Canadian states and cities. The mental hospital, Saint-Michel Archange, formerly known under the name "Asile temporaire de Beauport" of Quebec is now under the care of the Sisters of Charity. It is a University hospital open to medical students. The imposing building of seven stories, ten in the central tower, harbors 1,600 patients out of a total of 3,500 distributed in the other pavilions.[20] The Clinique Roy-Rousseau, contiguous to the Saint Michel-Archange Hospital, was opened in 1926 under the direction of Doctor Albert Brousseau of Paris. This was the first neuro-psychiatric center in the Province of Quebec. The hospital has room for two hundred patients, is affiliated to Laval University, and administered by the Sisters of Charity of Quebec who own the clinic.

The Sisters of Providence have the direction of a similar institution in Montreal known as "Hôpital Saint-Jean de Dieu." In these two hospitals, as well as in all the others, the sisters are not preoccupied with the problems of unemployment, vacations, and worldly amusements. These distractions are outside the domain of lives entirely devoted to charity, abnegation, and the welfare of unfortunates.

Christian people cannot help noticing the devotion and sacrifices of these religious. As a consequence, they have been shown unlimited confidence and veneration. Even institutions most difficult to direct have been confided to their care. Thus, the Women's Prison of Quebec, now known as Our Lady of Mercy, has been under the direction of the Good Shepherd Sisters since 1931; similarly the Quebec Reform School for girls has been under the direction of the same sisters since 1944. In Montreal, the Sisters of the Good Shepherd also have charge of a reform school, Lorette at the Val-des-Rapids. The boys are sent to Mont Saint-Antoine under the care of the Brothers of Charity.[21]

Early in the century, Mother Gérin-Lajoie had realized that prevention is a better policy than cure. With this in view, she conceived the idea of founding a community devoted exclusively

---

[20] Richard Lessard, "Les Hôpitaux universitaires," *Laval Médical,* IX (September, 1944), pp. 486-489.

[21] Interview with Judge Arthur Laramée, July 19, 1944.

to a social apostolate. The Institut de Notre-Dame du Bon-Conseil of Montreal was consequently founded in 1923. It aims, in general, to bring new aids to the social work of women and in the midst of the French Canadian parishes to constitute religious associations, auxiliaries of Catholic action. Its specific aim is to provide for women and young girls that supplementary formation which is needed to infuse new strength into the Christian life of the family, in the professional milieu, and in Catholic social service. To carry out this program, various activities have been undertaken. The Ecole d'Education Familiale et Sociale gives a practical and realistic preparation for family life. The *Cercles d'Etudes* serve the function of the average post-graduate schools in the intellectual field. The *Patronage* and *Foyer* are centers of social formation where for a nominal weekly fee, young girls, who are at a distance from their homes, may find adequate social surroundings. In some parishes, a visiting Sister is assigned to go to the different homes, make records, and return them to the pastor. Indeed, social service with its various economic, religious, psychological, and medical activities, is the life-work of this group of trained Sisters. Mother Gérin-Lajoie herself spent some time at the New York School of Social Work to learn the techniques of social service.[22]

Another form of contemporary social work met with in French Canada, one recommended by the Popes and by the disciples of the Semaine Sociale, is that of the Third Order of Saint-Francis. Leo XIII, in his encyclical *Auspicato* states that it is one of the most certain means of combatting socialism, because it helps the rich to become benevolent and charitable and disposes the poor to face conscientious toil and courageously accept his lot.[23]

There are, moreover, religious communities in French Canada whose principal work consists in providing for the material needs of the poor. Some are all-embracing; they provide instruction, needs, quarters, food and clothing. Such a community is that of the Brothers of Saint-Vincent de Paul, who become "poor with the poor." Their zeal does not end with immediate relief of distress. They follow up their youthful protégés. After having taught them a trade and found a position for them, they oc-

[22] Interview with Mother Gérin-Lajoie, July 11, 1944.

[23] S. s. du Canada, Sherbrooke, 1924, p. 71.

casionally convene them for a summary report on their activities. In this way, a great number of children have become useful citizens of society instead of disturbers of the existing social order.[24]

To turn to old-age pensions—some thinkers of the Semaine Sociale disapprove of this form of public assistance and other such governmental aids, on the ground that they burden and complicate public administration. They are liable to become the toy of covetous politicians. Besides, philanthropy is inferior to Christian charity. Man, by nature, "needs to love and to manifest his love; the gift made with love and joy calls for love."[25] Such is the charity of Christ and of His followers who strive to alleviate human miseries.

This charity of Christ finds expression in the work of the sisters who are in charge of Foundling Homes. The Grey Nuns have such an institution in Montreal harboring some six hundred, and the Good Shepherd Sisters have one in Quebec which hospitalizes about eight hundred. Father V. Germain, Director of the Adoption Service at the Crêche de Saint-Vincent de Paul in Quebec, adequately summarizes the work of this institution. He claims that it offers four distinctive services: religious, social, domestic, and relief to the poor. For the abandoned newly-born, it provides the sacrament of baptism; for the fallen-away, every opportunity for conversion; for those in danger of social evils, excellent means of perseverance. It also takes care of those indigents who are a burden to society, and seek foster homes for unfortunate children. The Crêche is a substitute for the home. The sympathetic reception given by the Sisters to all who seek refuge within its walls has won notable conversions and the number of recidivists is very small as compared with that of permanent rehabilitations. And in this, the Sisters seek but the glory and love of the Good Shepherd of Souls.[26] The Order of the Servants of the Immaculate Heart of Mary, known as Good Shepherd Sisters, which was founded to help the unmarried mother, has progressed

---

[24] S. s. du Canada, Chicoutimi, 1929, p. 167.

[25] *Ibid.*, pp. 168-169.

[26] V. Germain, *Les Chroniques de la Crêche* (Québec: Victorin Germain, 1943), p. 1.

and broadened its field of work to include the protection of young girls and children.

There remains to consider the value of religious orders in French Canada from an economic point of view. Judge C. E. Dorion, a pioneer of the Semaine Sociale, in a course given in 1929 tells of an American arriving in Quebec, who upon seeing the Grey Nuns' Convent exclaimed: "Would it not be better if all those convents were factories?" That question, Judge Dorion goes on to say, gives proof of such misinterpretation and prejudice, that one stands aghast and finds himself unable to conjure up the only possible fact: man lives not on bread alone and has need of infinitely more than what can be produced in factories. He can only wonder why the visitor does not question the existence of clubs, theaters, dancing halls, and other places of amusement. Mr. Saint-Pierre, the learned Professor of Social Science at the University of Montreal, ably answered the above question in a pamphlet entitled: *What Are All Those Nuns Good For?* Making use of statistical data and accurate calculations, he shows how the religious orders particularly the Grey Nuns and the Sisters of the Good Shepherd, are reducing governmental expenses by accepting for a moderate fee to care for its poor and sick.[27]

The Semaine Sociale is well aware that the religious orders truly occupy an important place in three fields considered today as public service: education, the care of the sick, and help given to the poor. Unlike so many other countries, French Canada did not come under the influence of a Voltaire or a Renan in its educational system; instruction has remained religious and has escaped the anti-clerical prejudices of the last century. Parallel with the increase in population, there has been an increase in schools and professors. If the priests, brothers, religious men and women, who live moderate lives, were to be replaced by an army of lay-professors, the cost to the State would be enormous. In 1923, we find a verification of this fact. In France, 21,000,000 francs were paid to lay-teachers for the instruction of 10,000 pupils, while the Catholic missionaries received only 7,100,000 francs for 500,000 pupils. For the figures representing the savings brought about by the orders engaged in the public service of the poor and sick, Judge

[27] S. s. du Canada, Chicoutimi, 1929, p. 161.

Dorion refers us to the above mentioned work. It is a veritable budget of Christian bounty.[28]

Nor is that all that can be said about the economic value of religious orders. The Trappists, for instance, were given by the State the direction of an Agricultural Institute. This gesture ratifies what Mr. Emile Condoyer answered to the question, "Of what use are these institutions?" In his work, *La Maison du grand silence,* that is, the Trappists' house, he writes,

> Has not a group of Trappists the same title to recognition as an agricultural project? Is it nothing to clear a region, to give it prosperity, to pay its tax without cheating, to sell its wheat without theft? Regardless of religious garb, it remains the most perfect corporation of agricultural workers. I believe that it serves society.[29]

Now, it is a known fact that to some people, the garb does matter. Those who allow their love of wealth to rule all their actions, do not care to meet on the street indications of such love of poverty. The religious garb, with its wide plaits, veil, and medieval lines, its sandals and cowl, stands in sharp contrast to the scant clothing of the average modern. To the worldling, the religious habit represents stability; it bespeaks the superiority of the religious life unencumbered as it is by style and novelty.[30]

A survey of the social thought of the French Canadian Church would be incomplete without a consideration of the Lord's day and what it implies in the Catholic Province of Quebec. To every French Canadian worthy of the name, Sunday is the day set aside by the Catholic Church to pay homage and respect to God. As early as 1922, the principles and advantages of Sunday rest were discussed by Father Trudeau, O.P. His concern with the matter is

---

[28] *Ibid.,* pp. 163-169.

[29] *Ibid.,* p. 169 cited in *Le Droit,* July, 1929: "Une communauté de Trappistes, . . . n'a-t-elle pas le même mérite qu'une exploitation agricole? N'est-ce rien que défricher une région, y faire naître la prospérité, payer ses impôts sans tricher, vendre son blé sans voler? Qu'importe le froc, elle reste la plus parfaite des corporations des travailleurs de la terre, je pense qu'elle sert une société."

[30] S. s. du Canada, Chicoutimi, 1929, p. 184.

explained by the fact that French Canada is outwardly Catholic; besides, the Sunday question is partly an economic and social problem with which public opinion has to cope.

Without a doubt, the weekly Sunday pause has its benefits. Man needs rest to satisfy his craving for worship. By his very nature he is attracted to higher things. It was Alfred de Musset who said, "Malgré nous, vers les cieux, il faut lever les yeux." And it was Jehovah Himself who gave His decalogue to Moses on Mount Sinai, of which the third commandment reads: "Remember that thou keep holy the Sabbath Day. . . ."[31]

Evidently, then, the moral advantages of the Sabbath injunction redound to the benefit of the individual, the family, and society. One does not attend religious services without experiencing some sort of salutary change. Neither worker nor aristocrat can taste the joys of family life or even establish his authority and influence on solid principles if Sunday rest is not guaranteed him. Society, too, benefits by this decree. Inequality in ordinary life is a fact, equality before God is another fact, and the latter appears especially in temples of worship. The average faithful, lost in the press of universal Church, may not know who his neighbor is, but the two at the moment are equal, because both bow their heads to the same Master. There are also physical advantages of the Sunday repose. Man wears himself out with use and his organs thus impaired cannot be replaced. Consequently, he needs rest to repair such losses as are incurred by the workings of nerve and muscle. Statistical data show that production increases as the number of workers increases due to longer life and a greater capacity for work.[32] And this capacity is strengthened by an exact observance of the third commandment. This leads up to the study of the course given in 1922 by Msgr. Eugène Lapointe on *Sunday Work in Our Industry.* He can scarcely reconcile himself to imagine the Catholic Province of Quebec with its masses of Catholic workers bent under the humiliating yoke of Sunday toil, a monster imported from the United States with the pulp and paper industry. He further reports how, back in 1914, one could see of a Sunday

---

[31] S. s. du Canada, Ottawa, 1922, p. 118.

[32] *Ibid.,* pp. 124-130.

morning the population of Donnacona, Grand'Mère, Shawinigan, Tugue, and Jonquière separate into two groups: the one, well-dressed, directed its steps towards the Church; the other, in overalls, going with bowed head and shameful countenance towards the mills. What is more significant is that Msgr. Labrecque, Bishop of Chicoutimi, had already condemned this inhumanity in a pastoral letter dated December 15, 1912. Price Brothers Company gave it no heed. The Jonquière and Kenogami factories, however, under pressure of the Catholic workers, granted a concession: Sunday work was stopped for the full twenty-four hours. Shortly afterwards, Msgr. Lapointe points out, a small number of non-Catholic members of the International demanded and obtained the closing of the mills from 7:00 a. m. Sunday until 7:00 a. m. Monday. At this point, all that could be done was to demand protection from the government. Upon investigation, the mills were forced to close. This they refused to do. The government then appealed to the tribunals, and five companies: Price Brothers, Laurentide, Wayagamac, Belgo, Donnacona, were fined. None the less, Sunday work persisted; in fact, it still persists in places even though there are two laws, federal and provincial, forbidding it. Here Msgr. Lapointe asks whether the French Canadians are still masters at home or whether, thanks to the almighty dollar, their laws are not dead letters![33]

It was precisely at that time that, under the impetus of the President of the Semaine Sociale, a campaign, known as the *Ligue du Dimanche*—then the talk of the Country—was launched. Its immediate aim was to bring about the observance of the law relating to the Sabbath rest. By 1925, forty thousand persons had rallied to the movement. The following pledges prove that they were in earnest. They promised:

> Not to work on Sunday, for monetary gain or material advantages whatsoever;
> Not to suffer anyone to work on Sunday under their auspices or for them;
> Not to frequent and not to allow persons in their homes to attend theaters on Sunday;

[33] *Ibid.*, pp. 133-140.

> To combat the plague of Sunday work by all the means at their disposal.[34]

Moreover, about five hundred of the total 1,200 municipal councils in the Province of Quebec approved the activities of the League and asked that justice be dealt the workers. Requests, signed by nearly fifty thousand persons, were sent to the General Procurator. The latter was asked to intervene in the combat and to demand respect for Sundays by forcing employers to close their factories on that day. Thus, as early as 1925, upon the request of the Honorable Prime Minister, the paper mill of Kenogami closed on Sunday.[35]

In connection with these endeavors, there was also passed a law prohibiting in the Province of Quebec Sunday movies for gain. In addition, the League sponsors an annual Semaine du Dimanche. So far, Mr. Esdras Minville claims that there has been a slight progress in the keeping of Sabbath rest.

Another initiative, connected with the Church, which is discussed in the Semaine Sociale of Canada, is the closed layman's retreat. Its founder is none other than the distinguished President of the Semaine Sociale, Father Archambault. Started in 1909, the 'closed retreat' has become the consolation of French Canadian leaders and the great hope of Canadian men of action. His Excellency Msgr. Bruneault, Bishop of Nicolet, believes that it is one of the most efficient means of forming men of good will.[36] In this school of salutary discipline, the soul is purified and sanctified; it is taught what ardor, labor, and effort the Christian apostle must bring to his contacts with his brothers in Christ.

After having participated in these holy exercises, the Jocists, Jecists, and Jacists, for instance, understood the meaning of their motto: "Proud, pure, joyous, conquering"; the members of the

---

[34] S. s. du Canada, Trois-Rivières, 1925, p. 315: "Ne pas travailler le dimanche, dans un but de gain ou avantage matériel quelconque; Ne pas permettre qu'on travaille ainsi le dimanche sous leurs ordres ou pour elles; Ne pas fréquenter et ne pas permettre aux gens de leur maison de fréquenter les théâtres le dimanche; Combattre le fléau du travail du dimanche par tous les moyens à leur disposition."

[35] *Ibid.*

[36] S. s. du Canada, Sherbrooke, 1925, pp. 71-72.

Saint Vincent de Paul Society have been transformed into sublime beggars,[37] and even the travelling salesman becomes a fervent apostle. As Mr. Felix Desrochers says, the last-mentioned fact is nothing less than miraculous. Formerly, he asserts, these proverbial travelling salesmen had made use of their tongue without the gift of tongues. They had more liking for "spirits" than for spirituality. Their attraction had centered more about hotels than at altars. Men of methodical action, rather than men of Catholic action, they had exerted a pernicious influence on their surroundings rather than a religious one. But in 1914, as a result of a closed retreat, these same commercial travellers became apostles. One of their number convened them and at the suggestion of the late Father Louis Lalande, S.J.; fourteen of the newly-converted founded the *Cercle catholique des Voyageurs de Commerce* which was the nucleus of the *Association Catholique de Voyageurs de Commerce* of Canada, and became in 1938 the *Association professionnelle catholique des Voyageurs de Commerce*. Its aim was to organize the dispersed forces of the profession and direct them towards a religious and intensively social apostolate. To attain this objective the members had to become true Catholics, living a truly divine life and capable of transmitting this life to others. This was a direct application of the principles of Catholic Action in the true sense of the term, even before Pius XI had given his directives to the Church at large.[38]

The Saint Vincent de Paul Society is another organization fostered by the Church. The Semaine Sociale has proclaimed its accomplishments in several of its conferences. To the 1924 meeting, C. J. Magnan explained the aims, influence, method of organization, qualifications of members, and the unity of action of the conferences of the Society. Its principal aim, the speaker declared, is the sanctification of its members by the practice of works of mercy. It is an association of both prayer and charity deriving its force from the supernatural spirit which animates it. This society is noted for the simplicity of its organization. Basically, there is the Conference: this consists of a group of some thirty to

[37] Lorenzo Gauthier, *Pour un ordre social chrétien* (Montréal: Edition de l'Ecole Sociale Populaire, 1941-42), pp. 149-153.

[38] S. s. du Canada, Québec, 1941, pp. 188-189.

fifty practicing Catholics, who meet weekly and discuss their visits made to the various needy families in the vicinity. Men possessed of a deep faith, a sincere desire for personal sanctification, and a great love of the poor, abounding in humility, abnegation, zeal, and generosity, are the true confrères of a Conference of Saint Vincent de Paul.

In Canada, there were two hundred and fifty active conferences in 1924, of which one hundred and seventy were in the Province of Quebec, besides twenty particular Councils, twelve Central Councils and a Superior Council, located in the city of Quebec. The six thousand active members visited and helped annually four thousand families. The receipts and expenses reached a total of $300,000 during these years. Quebec, Lévis, Montreal, Trois-Rivières, Joliette, Ottawa, Toronto, London, Hamilton, Halifax, Vancouver have active Councils. There are also isolated Conferences in many small villages throughout the Canadian provinces. Moreover, during crises the Society acts as an intermediate agent between capital and labor, between the laborer and the employer.[39]

Thus far, the attempt was made to show how distinctly the Semaine Sociale of Canada represents the continuous influence of the Church on French Canadian social thought. There remains to point out the reason for this persistent influence. Compared with other countries, the religious situation in the Province of Quebec is enviable. The relations of Church and State are amicable and the Church receives from civil authority a singular respect. The Church is free to hold religious demonstrations, processions, and congresses.[40] In the words of Father Villeneuve, now Cardinal, at the 1927 assembly in Quebec, one may admire, but without too great enthusiasm, the condition of the Church in Canada at large, for the Church is separated from the State, when one considers its relation to the Federal Government at Ottawa. The same is true for all the provinces that have a Protestant majority. Besides, there does not exist, strictly speaking, a real union of State and Church even in the Province of Quebec. Modern liberalism and

[39] S. s. du Canada, Ottawa, 1922, pp. 310-323.

[40] André Siegfried, *Le Canada, puissance international* (Paris: Librairie Armand Colin, 1937), p. 183.

French liberality have inspired Canadians to show great tolerance towards foreign sects. Still, in matters pertaining to school organization, constitution of parishes, and freedom of religious institutions, one finds ordinarily a laudable spirit of understanding and a respectful alliance between the two authorities. Those who preside over the public destinies of French Canada have generally contributed to maintain these relations by their sincere faith and their great attachment to the Church. It is this situation that has awakened the admiration of foreigners who have observed the relations of Church and State in French Canada. It has, moreover, induced the French population to look hopefully to their religion for the social security of their public institutions.[41]

In fact, religious freedom for French Canada has come to mean freedom in the government of the Church by the bishops, freedom to appeal to Rome, freedom of worship, freedom of Catholic action, the Catholic press, Catholic organizations, and Catholic education. In short, the Church is not subordinated to the State, so long as it does not disturb public peace.[42]

Briefly then, to the French Canadian the Church is a great civilizing force. By instruction and supernatural aids, it helps sanctify its members. It regulates the conditions and formalities of marriage, and condemns evil practices.

For anyone there is adequate concrete evidence of the work of the Church: parochial social activities assist the needy and the various religious orders contribute aids to all levels of the social scale. The moral, social, and economic value of these orders may no longer be questioned, especially when one has examined Professor Saint-Pierre's careful study *What Are All Those Nuns Good For?* There is insistence on the observance of the Lord's day and French Canada has significant laws relative to the keeping of the Sabbath. The work of the laity taking the form of retreats and organizations is especially noteworthy. The relations of Church and State are nothing short of amicable; the Church is looked upon by civil authority with singular respect, and the State is helped in its legislative function by the diffusion of a social doctrine derived from the teaching of our social Popes.

---

[41] S. s. du Canada, Québec, 1927, pp. 316-318.
[42] S. s. du Canada, Saint-Jean, 1942, p. 61.

CHAPTER V

THE SEMAINE SOCIALE AND THE FAMILY

French Canadian social thought has stressed the fact that the family, together with the Church, private property, and agriculture, can save society from ruin. The present discussion will be concerned with the definition, constituent elements and aim of the family. Then follows a study of the rights and obligations of parents and children, the various needs of the family, and the factors responsible for its disorganization. Finally, possible remedies will be suggested, followed by a description of the French Canadian family as it existed before the infiltration of American fads and fashions.

In 1923, the Commission of the Semaine Sociale devoted an entire week to the study of the family, not so much because they discerned marked domestic disorganization but mainly because they were seeking constructive measures. Then, as now, the members aimed to show that, since no institution can be lasting if not based on immutable Christian doctrine, it is first necessary to recognize and spread this doctrine. Its promulgation alone can move the will of man to action. It is ideas that rule the world.

The affirmations of Leo XIII relative to the family are categorical. He declares the family to be the cradle of civil society. Again, in his words, domestic society has a logical and real priority over civil society.[1] These are age-old truths to which the Semaine Sociale adheres conscientiously and endeavors to spread by every means possible.

To the four main natural elements constituting family life even among the primitives, namely, a more or less stable union of mates, relatively or absolutely exclusive sex claim, common residence and common economic life, and long-range child rearing,[2] Msgr. Gag-

[1] S. s. du Canada, Montréal, 1923, p. 14.

[2] John M. Cooper, Temporal Sequence and Marginal Peoples (Washington, D. C.: The Catholic University Press, 1941), p. 44.

non, now Rector of Laval University, adds formal elements constituting the French Canadian family specifically.

Under such headings as: essential characteristics, fundamental principles, and important laws affecting the formation of the family and governing its economy, he qualifies two of the above natural elements. In the first place, following Leo XIII's teaching, he emphasized the Catholic doctrine of the sanctity, unity, and indissolubility of marriage and reminded the married of their mutual obligations: conjugal fidelity, cohabitation, mutual love and assistance. In connection with cohabitation, Msgr. Gagnon deplored the introduction of American styles and customs into the French Canadian Christian conception of the nuptial chamber and warns against the abuses of certain public resorts—abuses that often lead to serious disorders.

The French Canadian thesis on the family as determined by natural and revealed doctrine may then be stated as follows: the family is a natural, a hierarchical, and an autonomous society. It is natural and necessary for various reasons, namely, to propagate the species, to educate children, to build society. The family is a hierarchical society in that the members forming it although fundamentally equal, are not equal in regard to status, rights, etc.; each has distinct, natural and divine rights. The parents have the right to command their children.[3] This authority, given by God, should be exercised with kindness heightened by a sense of dignity. But C. J. Magnan adds that because of original sin, kindness and dignity do not suffice; firmness becomes necessary or else authority crumbles. Justice and impartiality, too, should be joined to firmness for the least injustice is revolting to children. Finally, charity and piety coordinate and vivify every exercise of this authority.[4] Again, in the words of Msgr. Gagnon, the family is an autonomous society, that is, independent of the State. It owes this autonomy to its priority of existence. Leo XIII repeatedly affirms this fact in his encyclicals:

> . . . we have the family; the "society" of a man's own household; a society limited indeed in numbers, but a

[3] S. s. du Canada, Montréal, 1923, pp. 21-31.

[4] *Ibid.*, pp. 225-229.

> true "society," anterior to every kind of State or nation, with rights and duties of its own, totally independent of the commonwealth.[5]

The family is autonomous, especially so in connection with the education of its children. The role of the State is rather one of encouragement, assistance, and protection. It has always been the policy of the Semaine Sociale to combat undue interference of the State in the life of the family and in the education of children.[6]

On the other hand, the children are expected to cooperate with the parents. The Civil Code of Quebec states that "the child at all ages must honor and respect his father and mother."[7] At the 1925 meeting of the Semaine Sociale, Father Archambault deplored the decadence of authority in families where the children no longer obey their parents. They are masters at home; caprice alone rules their conduct, and parents fail to intervene, precisely when they are duty bound to do so. There follows a whole series of abdications, and as a consequence of such behavior, the world is visited with a generation of weaklings.[8] Ferdinand Roy holds similar views when he declares that in olden times children were *generally* disciplined, insubordination was the exception; but, today, the process is reversed: discipline is rare; parents no longer command, children no longer obey.[9] And yet, authority is as necessary today as it was formerly. The words of Bossuet apply here: "Where each one may do what he wants, no one does what he wants; where there is no master, everyone is master; where everyone is master, everyone is a slave."[10] Antonio Perrault realizes that to command today requires much tact, clear-sightedness, justice, and charity. Parents cannot prevent young boys or girls from questioning commands received, nor even from examining the personality issuing the order. That is why to maintain sentiments of love and respect, the parents must command with wisdom, and give proof

[5] *On the Condition of Labor* (New York: The Paulist Press, 1939), p. 8.

[6] S. s. du Canada, Montréal, 1923, p. 38.

[7] *Ibid.*, p. 239.

[8] S. s. du Canada, Québec, 1927, p. 28.

[9] *Ibid.*, p. 54.

[10] Jacques Bossuet, *Politique tirée de l'Ecriture sainte,* liv. I art. 3, cited by Antonio Perrault, S. s. du Canada, Québec, 1927, p. 404.

that they are possessed with a sense of the dignity of life. The power of the parents must be derived from a love which shall attract children to what is good, and help them progress intellectually and morally. Authority demands the gift of one's self. Obedience must not be a soulless submission. It must be submission to a beloved superior from whom one seeks protection.[11]

As early as 1921, Mr. Antonio Perrault stated that family education should be imbued with Christian ideas, oriented towards social and eternal life.[12] In 1923, Fadette (Mrs. Henriette Saint-Jacques) demanded that early family education include a sense of patriotism. It is her belief that a child of six is capable of being a "petit Canadien-français" who knows why he is a Canadian, and wherein he is French.[13] The following year, Mrs. Louis F. Codère, sensed this social responsibility, and while speaking about the *foyer* pleaded for order in the home; she brought out the importance of teaching children the art of disposing furniture in a harmonious fashion; of teaching them economy in the organization of general and particular expenses, the whole endeavor being animated by a deep religious sense.[14]

At the 1927 meeting of the Semaine Sociale, Father Maheux specified that family education should be physical, intellectual, moral and religious.[15] Again at the opening session of the 1935 assembly, Bishop Papineau reminded his audience that Christian parents have the obligation to educate their children and pointed out how it can best be accomplished.[16] The family, in the words of Father Gosselin, Professor at Laval University, is the first school of formation. It is first in the order of nature and of time. It takes the child at the very dawn of his existence, orients, represses or stimulates the initial activities of his intelligence and will. The home influence is usually lasting.[17] Judge Dorion believes that one's character preserves amidst the vicissitudes of life the early form received in the home. It is rare, he adds, that

[11] *Ibid.*, pp. 405-406.

[12] S. s. du Canada, Québec, 1921, p. 407.

[13] S. s. du Canada, Montréal, 1923, p. 296.

[14] S. s. du Canada, Sherbrooke, 1924, pp. 139-148.

[15] S. s. du Canada, Québec, 1927, p. 116.

[16] S. s. du Canada, Joliette, 1935, p. 17.

[17] S. s. du Canada, Nicolet, 1940, p. 106.

a complete deformation of the moral being is produced, that the nostalgia for good does not appear sooner or later to one who has known its charm during his early life.[18]

Now, the Semaine Sociale realizes that to accomplish this difficult formative and educational task, the French Canadian family has certain definite economic needs. As Pope Pius XI pointed out:

> These goods should be sufficient to supply all needs and proper conveniences, and to uplift men to that higher level of prosperity and culture which, provided it be used with prudence, is not only no hindrance but is of singular help to virtue.[19]

In the first Semaine Sociale of 1920, Mr. Edouard Montpetit directed attention to the fact that the American government had spent forty million dollars to build workers' homes in eleven cities. The example, he continued, is worth imitating especially in the overpopulated Canadian cities.[20]

Every family needs a home. Dr. J. A. Baudouin, in 1923, pointed out that many sociologists and moralists have always been concerned with the housing problem. Making use of special studies that were made and general statistical data, he showed that filthy housing quarters constitute one of the most important causes of illness and death. He advocated a "casier sanitaire" which would give accurate current knowledge about the sanitary conditions of all the houses in a municipality. It is the best means of permanent information that the authorities possess concerning housing conditions. For example, in 1915 Lachine had 257 dark rooms; five years later under sanitary provincial regulations, the number had been reduced to ninety-one. Again, to bring about an improvement in possible future buildings and to foster hygienic conditions among the people at large, Dr. Baudouin recommended that the control of construction be in the hands of municipalities; that a program of rational regulations relative to slums be enforced; that courses in hygiene as an essential condition to success be con-

[18] S. s. du Canada, Trois-Rivières, 1925, p. 122.

[19] *On the Reconstruction of the Social Order* (New York: The America Press, 1938, p. 22.

[20] S. s. du Canada, Montréal, 1920, p. 92.

ducted to influence public opinion; and that a manual of hygiene be placed in every home.[21]

The following year, at the Semaine Sociale session in Sherbrooke, Mr. Arthur St. Pierre, Professor of Sociology at the University of Montreal, in a course entitled, *The Little Urban Property,* gave an elaborate study of the workingmen's living quarters. Citing statistical data on what had been done in the line of slum clearance in Europe and in the United States, he concluded that much remains to be accomplished in his own Province and urged that the Federal plan of housing be adopted by the Provincial Government to provide suitable homes for workingmen and to do away with the "depressing, demoralizing, and homicidal atmosphere of the crowded flat."[22]

Nor did the Semaine Sociale proposals on housing improvement end there. In 1940, at the Nicolet meeting, Father Archambault deplored the persistence of slums in the large cities of French Canada.

> Large families crowd into quarters without air, space, or light; and so become prey to physical and moral tuberculosis. And we wonder that birth rates are lower under such conditions! But to turn to lodging quarters is like passing from Charybdis to Scylla. Modern constructors have nothing to offer to the large family but small crowded quarters where a couple of children may live: mere pigeonholes![23]

At the same session of the Semaine Sociale, Father Richard of the Ecole Sociale Populaire, in a conference on *Housing and the Family,* proved very effectively that the housing problem is a serious one in French Canada, particularly so in Montreal where

---

[21] S. s. du Canada, Montréal, 1923, pp. 102-122.

[22] *Ibid.,* pp. 176-213.

[23] S. s. du Canada, Nicolet, 1940, p. 19: "Des familles nombreuses s'entassent dans des logis sans air, sans espace, sans lumière: proie offerte à la tuberculose physique et morale. Comment s'étonner que la natalité baisse en de telles conditions? Mais voici les quartiers neufs. Nous tombons de Charybde en Scylla. Là où il faudrait de vastes habitations familiales, les constructeurs modernes n'ont à vous offrir que d'étroits logements où se casent à grand'peine un couple et un enfant: des pigeonniers!"

there is such an excessive concentration of industry. He referred his audience to the 1934 study made in Montreal by the Montreal Board of Trade and the City Improvement League, which brought out the seriousness of its housing shortage following upon the depression of 1929. Although there is no statistical evidence on the housing situation in the other cities of the Province, Father Richard goes on to say, there exists, nonetheless a more or less crucial problem of housing, particularly in Quebec,[24] Trois-Rivieres, and Hull—important enough to affect the physical, intellectual, moral, and national life of the French Canadians.

Although a Federal law was passed in 1938 to help fight slums, its application was impossible because social-minded, disinterested, and competent leaders were lacking and public opinion did not favor the measure. Truly, Father Richard feels that the time is ripe for the élite, already conscious of their social responsibilities, to face the issue and safeguard human and Christian values by launching a crusade for better homes.[25]

According to Msgr. Plamondon, speaker at the Semaine Sociale of 1923, the aids given the family are never too numerous. They are listed under services of reparation and preservation: they include the *Pouponnière* or the *Crêche,* already discussed in the preceding chapter; the *Garderie* or Infant Schools where children are kept during the day to help the sick mother or the mother of a large family. It may be noted here that the speaker considered the Infant School the resort to remedy an abnormal situation. A somewhat less ideal service to the family is the orphan home or the boarding school, because this institution is intended as a substitute for parents. The benefits derived from such institutions must not lead one to overlook their drawbacks. Children in boarding schools do not live a normal life but one that is apt to impart false notions of what life really is. On the other hand, there are problem children who may well attribute their salvation and even

---

[24] Since that time, a collective study on the housing conditions of Québec under the title *Le Logement à Québec* has been made by the students of the School of Social Service at Laval University under the direction of Father Gonzalve Poulin, O.F.M., Director of the School of Social Service, Mr. Roger Marier, Assistant-Director and Mr. Jean C. Falardeau, Director of the Department of Social Research.

[25] S. s. du Canada, Nicolet, 1940, pp. 145-155.

their social positions to the virtues imposed upon them during their stay in a boarding school. Other adjuncts to the family include such instruments of formation as help complete family education: the school, the workshop, the *Maison de Famille,* associations, study clubs, and *patronages.*[26]

The Semaine Sociale does not overlook social insurance in its various forms as an aid to the family: insurance against sickness, accidents, maternity risks, old age, unemployment. All of these are diverse applications of the same principle: cooperation against risks. In Canada, there are two legislative provisions pertaining to social insurance: old-age pensions and the Provincial laws relating to industrial accidents. Quebec adopted her old-age pension law in 1936. Compulsory insurance against sickness exists in Canada only for those illnesses said to be industrial, those resulting from industrial accidents; the Province of Quebec, in 1931, accepted this principle and made compulsory the contribution of indemnities for certain sicknesses.

In 1938, Paul H. Guimont, Professor of Political Economy at the School of Social Science in Quebec, advocated corporative social insurance, that is, insurance through mixed and industrial funds, placed under the control of public administration. These funds should receive the contributions of the insured, the employer, and the State. Participation in this cooperative scheme would be compulsory.[27] Judging from the present development in the field of social security, we would expect further attention to be given the subject in the future.

Unemployment insurance exists today as a service of the Federal government. The employees, however, contribute a fraction of their salaries each week. For that contribution, they are given stamps equal to the money deposited.[28]

Family allowances are another need of which the Semaine Sociale is fully conscious. In the proceedings of the Semaine Sociale of 1927, Father Cloutier speaks of their introduction in Grenoble as early as 1916, of their popularity in France in 1925, and he

---

[26] S. s. du Canada, Montréal, 1923, pp. 204-213.

[27] S. s. du Canada, Sherbrooke, 1938, pp. 250-257.

[28] Interview with Mr. M. Caron, August 22, 1944 at the University of Montréal.

advocates them in French Canada to alleviate the lot of the workingmen and to render social relations more cordial between employers and employees.[29] The following year, we find Father Georges Bilodeau contending that it is more important to see to the needs of large families than to provide for old-age pensions. Furthermore he calls attention to the solution proposed by Father Léon Lebel, S.J., a pioneer advocate of the Family Allowance Program in French Canada, to settle the problem of the large family. He further deplores the emigration of so many French Canadians—a movement which represents tremendous losses in human capital; each individual was evaluated for that period at $3,000. This figure multiplied by the 200,000 Canadians who left the Province of Quebec within the past few years adds up to a fabulous amount.[30] Again, at the Semaine Sociale of 1929, Father Arthur Robert refers to Father Léon Lebel's pamphlet published two years previously in which the problem of family allowances is discussed in an enlightening fashion and bolstered with objective data.[31]

In 1938, at the Sherbrooke meeting, Father Lebel himself expounds what he calls the "véritable solution" to the problem of the large family. The remedy would consist of organizing the economic regime of the country in such a way that the revenues of the heads of families would be proportional to the number of their dependents. These revenues would come from two sources: wages to which the principle "For equal work, equal wage" would apply, and family allowances for which the principle, "Give to every one according to his needs" would hold. Father Lebel refuses to consider family allocations as wages or as alms. They are rather the remuneration for the eminent services rendered to society and to employers. They are not a utopia since they are already realized and even generalized in Belgium, France, Italy, New Zealand, Spain, and Holland.[32] Australia also has its law of Family Allocation since 1926.[33]

---

[29] S. s. du Canada, Québec, 1927, p. 237.

[30] S. s. du Canada, Saint-Hyacinthe, 1928, pp. 101-102.

[31] S. s. du Canada, Chicoutimi, 1929, p. 132.

[32] S. s. du Canada, Sherbrooke, 1938, pp. 115-117.

[33] Interview with Father Léon Lebel, S.J., July 21, 1944, at the Collège de L'Immaculée Conception.

Due to low wages and to the large number of children in the French Canadian family, these allowances are a necessity in the Province of Quebec.[34] It must be remembered, however, that family allowances alone are unable to solve the family problem. The definition as given by Father Bouvier, S.J., is not all inclusive: "family allowances are a compensation conceded by society, in view of the common good, to those fathers, who, through economic conditions are unable to gain a revenue sufficient to support a large family."[35]

The recent law providing for family allowances as enacted by the Canadian Federal Government realizes for many a great hope. By some it is regarded as an attack against provincial rights in connection with education, civil rights, the social domain, and fiscal power. For example, Article 3 of the new law provides a decreasing rate of compensation for the fifth and further children. So then, a family of four children under six years of age would regularly receive twenty dollars a month. If these children are the eighth, ninth, tenth, and eleventh of the family, the allowance will be eight dollars instead of twenty. In short, the law punishes the families which accept the children that God gives them; it fines the parents who provide the first and principal wealth of the country: human capital. No other country in the world has adopted a legislation with an "échelle décroissante." And so, the well-informed French Canadians hope that this law will be amended before July, 1945, at which date it should go into effect.[36]

Let us now pass from what the Semaine Sociale considers the needs of the family to some of the more complex problems of family life. Heading the list of factors working towards a breakdown of families in general is divorce. As early as 1920, we find Mr. Henri Bourassa, with his genuine French Canadian effusion, upbraiding the French Canadians for their indifference towards matters affecting the moral status of the whole of Canada. He

[34] Léon Lebel, *Family Allowances as a Means of Preventing Emigration* (Montréal, 1929), pp. 25-28.

[35] Emile Bouvier, "Un Projet d'allocations familiales," *Relations,* August, 1944, p. 202.

[36] Bouvier, "Les Allocations familiales à Ottawa," *Relations,* September, 1944, pp. 240-241.

tells about a French Canadian Senator, a devout Catholic, who asked without creating the slightest wonder, "Why deprive the Protestants of Quebec of the advantages of this legislation (relative to divorce) if they desire it?" Mr. Bourassa sees in divorce a social plague.[37] In the words of Father Villeneuve, present Cardinal, divorce crushes the social cells of the family one by one. How then can it be expected to "survive"?[38] At the 1923 meeting, Father Henri Martin admitted that divorce in the Province of Quebec is not the social plague that it is in many countries of Europe or in the United States, though he remarked with equal justice that efforts are made each year by certain deputies in the Parliament of Ottawa to render the issuance of divorce bills easier for Canada at large.[39] Mr. Léon-Mercier Gouin, present Senator, brands divorce as anti-Christian, anti-social and anti-juridical.[40] The Catholic population of French Canada is still too imbued with living faith to relegate the holy state of marriage to the rank of a free union, is Father Plamondon's belief. Nevertheless, divorce is on the verge of uprooting the "tree of society."[41] This is also the opinion of Mr. C. E. Bruchési, prominent lawyer of Montreal, who calls attention to an act of the Federal Parliament whereby the marriage of two Catholics residing in the Province of Quebec may be annulled and the parties relieved of their mutual obligations.[42] For that reason, Judge Dorion calls divorce the abolition of marriage.[43] No less emphatic is Mr. Joseph Barnard when he declares that of all Canadian laws the one that legalizes divorce is the most disastrous in its consequences.[44] Mr. Adelard Provencher claims that divorce is the executioner of children,[45] while Leo Pelland sees in divorce an out-and-out violation of divine law, a dreadful scourge of families and an attack on public morality.[46]

---

[37] S. s. du Canada, Montréal, 1920, p. 170.
[38] S. s. du Canada, Montréal, 1923, p. 52.
[39] *Ibid.*, p. 149.
[40] *Ibid.*, p. 183.
[41] *Ibid.*, pp. 190-191.
[42] *Ibid.*, p. 237.
[43] S. s. du Canada, Chicoutimi, 1929, p. 175.
[44] S. s. du Canada, Trois-Rivières, 1925, p. 81.
[45] S. s. du Canada, Nicolet, 1941, p. 70.
[46] S. s. du Canada, Ottawa, 1931, p. 224.

In the early forties, reports on the issuance of divorce bills in Canada appear more frequently than ever before. Father M. C. Forest, O.P., for example, tells of one instance where thirty divorce bills were presented and adopted at the Federal Parliament in less than twelve minutes.

Even though on one occasion, the Honorable Mackenzie King, Prime Minister of Canada, expressed the wish of establishing a divorce court in the Province of Quebec (with the exception of tiny Prince Edward Island, the only province of Canada without one), the suggestion was overlooked by the French Canadians who still cling to the ideal of the indissolubility of marriage. The French Canadian Bishops are strong in their insistence that the day when divorce will become legal, French Canada will undergo the sad experience of other countries and witness the slow but sure ruin of the family.[47] Quebec, then, has neither divorce law nor divorce court. For those provinces without divorce courts a divorce may be obtained only by a private Act of the Parliament of Canada. From 1918-1940, sixty-two divorce bills were thus granted for Quebec out of a total of 2,369 for the whole of Canada.[48]

Over and above the aforesaid problem of family organization occasioned by divorce, some members of the Semaine Sociale maintain that feminism in its liberal form is destructive of family responsibilities. As early as 1921, Miss Marie J. Gérin-Lajoie, future Foundress of the *Soeurs du Bon Conseil,* spoke of a Christian feminism, favorable to the development of a woman's personality, and directed towards awakening women to their providential mission and social role.[49] Again, in 1932, she describes as a 'liberal' feminism that which advocates the right to divorce, birth-control, an individualistic plan of life, and license in all its forms, and then opposes to it a Christian feminism which aims to obtain for women the right to work and the normal development of their faculties.[50]

---

[47] M. Ceslas Forest, "Encore le divorce," *L'Ordre Nouveau,* August 5 and 20, 1940, p. 1.

[48] *The Canada Year Book* (Ottawa: James A. MacKinnon, 1942), p. 130.

[49] S. s. du Canada, Québec, 1921, p. 287.

[50] S. s. du Canada, Montréal, 1932, p. 194.

It is against this "liberal feminism" that so many followers of the Semaine Sociale protest. In 1923, Msgr. Gagnon explained feminism as a theory which demands the same rights for women as for men. This feminism which swerves woman from her true path—her vocation of mother, educator and mistress of the household—should be condemned in proportion as it alienates woman from her role in the home.[51] Father Villeneuve called "radical feminism" that which ignores the authentic nature of woman, her physiology, her morals, her sublime vocation in the family and in society. He goes on to say that this view is absurd, subversive of society, and disrupts the family. Still this feminism is the fashion, in both social and political circles, in sports and industry, in studies and professions. There is another feminism, he added, one that will not make of woman a man, but rather the perfect homebuilder. That feminism will save society because it will save the family.[52] In this connection, it is Msgr. Courchesne's belief that a society in which the monastic form of life flourishes is well protected against this aggressive feminism which kills family life.[53] False feminism which tends to bring woman into the street and mix her in the turmoil of sordid politics has its source in pride and snobbery, in the desire for independence, change and adventure.[54] It is at this form of feminism that the disciples of the Semaine Sociale look askance, well aware of the pernicious effects it is bound to have on the French Canadian family.

Characteristic of the present decade is another menace to family life: woman labor outside the home. At the 1923 meeting of the Semaine Sociale, Msgr. Gagnon deplored the fact that women are obliged to leave their home and subject themselves to the hardships of toil destined for man. It is an evil, he added, that should be attacked as soon as possible, not only because it takes women away from their natural domain, the home, but because it increases unemployment among men, and thus causes them to put off marriage till they are in a position to support a family.[55]

---

[51] S. s. du Canada, Montréal, 1923, pp. 35-36.
[52] *Ibid.*, p. 56.
[53] *Ibid.*, p. 255.
[54] S. s. du Canada, Joliette, 1935, p. 286.
[55] S. s. du Canada, Montréal, 1923, p. 36.

At the Montreal meeting of 1932, Sister Gérin-Lajoie presented some important statistical data concerning woman labor in French Canada: 490,000 women and young girls were then employed in the various fields of economic activity; about 18,000 in apiculture, more than 100,000 in factories, 20,000 in various other industries, 75,000 in commerce and finance, finally, 250,000 in diverse domestic occupations. Women were also employed in transportation, in fisheries and hunting, in mines and quarries, and even in construction. What is rather significant is that while the percentage of women employed in 1891 was less than 9 per cent, it had increased to more than 16 per cent in 1921. Sister Gérin-Lajoie realizes that such a condition is bound to lead to pernicious consequences and warns her country against these aberrations.[56] Father Lorenzo Gauthier, C.S.V., too, demands that this ill-omened abuse, which prompts married mothers to seek employment outside their home, disappear. Family wages, he feels, should be such that normal expenses and ordinary needs may be met without disrupting family life.[57]

More menacing than feminism to family solidarity is depopulation. At the meeting of 1920, Mr. Henri Bourassa alluded to the diffusion of contraceptive methods in Montreal and other cities of the Province of Quebec, as well as in countryside villages.[58] In 1923, Father Henri Martin, O.P., grouped the three agents of depopulation under mortality, decrease in birth rate, and emigration. It is the surplus of births each year that insures the normal growth of a people. In the Province of Quebec, Father Martin went on to say, birth rates were lower from 1910 to 1920 than they had been in the previous decade, showing a decrease from 393 to 347 for every 10,000 inhabitants.[59] During the economic depression of 1929 and thereafter, the birth rate showed an alarming drop, although there was a considerable rise again in 1941.[60]

The causes cited for this decrease in birth rates are many: intemperance, including overfeeding, the abuse of sports, alcohol,

---

[56] S. s. du Canada, Montréal, 1932, pp. 198-199.

[57] Lorenzo Gauthier, *Pour un ordre social chrétien,* p. 122.

[58] S. s. du Canada, Montréal, 1920, p. 171.

[59] S. s. du Canada, Montréal, 1923, pp. 143-146.

[60] S. s. du Canada, Québec, 1941, p. 50.

the taste for luxury, divorce, liberal feminism, the diffusion of neo-malthusian literature, late marriages, abortion, and voluntary sterility. Dr. Rochard adds dancing to this list of causes on the ground that it is responsible for many physical disorders, chief of which are nervous prostrations. But the great cause of this lowering of births is the diminution of faith, forgetfulness of the supernatural view of human life.[61] The only way to limit the family when there is a serious reason to do so, is by abstention, that is, continence.[62]

At the Nicolet meeting in 1940, Adelard Provencher, distinguished lawyer of Trois-Rivières mentioned the Ogino-Knaus method. He admitted that he is not a theologian, so cited Father J. Viollet:

> The fact that the husband and wife employ a natural means and not a fraudulent one to limit the number of their children may not be a sin in itself; it may become one, however, if they refuse the child through egoism and without a serious reason.
>
> Thus, the Ogino-Smulders method is not the ideal solution to the problems posited by the difficulties of conjugal life. It may be tolerated in a particular case, but the fact remains that the moral ideal will always be the simple and natural union of the parties, with attendant upon it, acceptance of the child; or as an alternative, continence, if for serious reasons, birth must be prevented.[63]

Another factor operative in family disorganization in the thinking of the Semaine Sociale is alcoholism. Its members devoted

---

[61] S. s. du Canada, Montréal, 1923, pp. 146-152.

[62] *Ibid.*, p. 312.

[63] J. Viollet, *La loi chrétienne du mariage* (Edition Mariage et Famille), pp. 18, 19, 21, cited in S. s. du Canada, Nicolet, 1940, p. 68: "Le fait que les époux emploient un moyen naturel et non frauduleux pour restreindre le nombre de leurs enfants peut n'être pas en soi un péché; encore qu'il puisse le devenir, si les époux refusent l'enfant par égoïsme et sans raison sérieuse.

"La méthode Ogino-Smulders n'est donc pas la solution idéale aux problèmes posés par les difficultés de la vie conjugale. Elle peut être la solution tolérée dans un cas particulier, mais il reste que l'idéal moral sera toujours l'union simple et naturelle des époux, avec acceptation des enfants possibles, ou la continence, si, pour des raisons graves, une naissance doit être évitée."

an entire social study week to a discussion of this problem from its various angles. They resorted to a subtitle: *Temperance, a Rule of Life,* and proved how temperance enters into savings, in the use of alcoholic beverages, in the just distribution of wealth, in the exercise of authority and political rights, and in national and international relations.

At the 1923 Semaine Sociale, Father Henri Martin gave Mr. Arsène Dumont's theory of alcoholism. The latter held that alcohol caused an increase in births while Dr. Legrain contended that it decreased human capital in quality and quantity. He based his assertion on the hereditary characteristics which are ascertained in alcoholics. Father Martin believes that the relation between tuberculosis and infant mortality on the one hand, and alcoholism on the other, are well established.[64]

Msgr. Perrier holds the same opinion and expresses it thus:

> How many families are in dire misery because the head is a victim of intemperance!
>
> Alcoholism completely disorganizes the family; and what is still worse, its dire consequences for the future are incalculable. . . .
>
> So many deficiencies await the wretched posterity of alcoholics: cretinism, epilepsy, tuberculosis, disordered appetite for strong liquors. Often the sin of the father is punished in the child to the third and fourth generation.[65]

The best treatment of alcoholism is found in the proceedings of the 1943 Semaine Sociale under the title *La Sobriété dans l'usage des boissons alcooliques.* Msgr. Perrier begins his conference by defining alcoholism as "the habit of drinking alcoholic

[64] S. s. du Canada, Montréal, 1923, pp. 147-148.

[65] S. s. du Canada, Salaberry-de-Valleyfield, 1943, p. 138: "Que de familles sont dans la misère noire, parce que le chef est une victime de l'intempérance!

"L'alcoolisme du père désorganise, complètement la famille; et ce qui est plus terrible encore, ses malheureuses conséquences ont une portée incalculable dans l'avenir. . . . Que de tares guettent cette malheureuse descendance de l'alcoolisme: crétinisme, épilepsie, tuberculose, appétit désordonné pour les liqueurs fortes. C'est ainsi que le péché du père est souvent puni dans les enfants jusqu'à la troisième et quatrième génération."

liquors frequently, even without intoxication—a habit which begets an almost invincible desire to drink and which weakens the organism because infecting it with a fatal poison."[66] He then refers to Dr. Joseph Gauvreau's warning against *bierisme,* probably a greater evil than alcoholism because more insidious and less apparent than the latter. Briefly he recalls the disastrous effects of alcoholism on the individual, the family, society, and the race.

Msgr. Perrier then distinguishes four phases in the history of French Canadian struggle against alcoholism. The first opposition came from the Church in the beginnings of the French colony and was intensified with the arrival of His Excellency Msgr. Laval, first Bishop of Quebec. The second phase took place during the middle half of the nineteenth century, when a crusade against intemperance was headed by Mr. Quertier and Mr. Mailloux. It was Mr. Quertier who hoisted the black cross and with his magnetic personality won over a large number to his society. The third phase came at the turn of the century. This time the Bishops took the lead denouncing alcoholism as a social plague of French Canada. Archbishop Bruchési and Archbishop Paul-Eugène Roy launched a crusade of temperance in their respective dioceses. The next and last phase of the fight against alcoholism started in 1939 when Cardinal Villeneuve, the Archbishops, and Bishops, published a collective letter on temperance. The reasons to continue the fight are many: excessive alcoholism constitutes an attack on the race and a national perversion; tuberculosis and insanity are frequent concomitants;[67] there is a close relation between toxemia and criminality; the illegal sale of alcohol leads to other crimes; alcoholism favors laziness and prevents the earning of an honest living.[68] In a word, it degrades the individual, ruins families, and weakens the nation.[69]

In accordance with the social thought of the Semaine Sociale, Msgr. Perrier offers suggestions to reduce the consumption of alcoholic liquors. The action of the government has been effective

---

[66] S. s. du Canada, Salaberry-de-Valleyfield, 1943, p. 136.
[67] *Ibid.*, pp. 137-149.
[68] S. s. du Canada, Chicoutimi, 1929, p. 305.
[69] S. s. du Canada, Salaberry-de-Valleyfield, 1943, p. 13.

in limiting the amount to be sold and in forbidding advertisements referring to alcoholic liquor.[70] Counter-propaganda, education, the abolition of taverns,[71] and individual action, are likewise indicated to combat alcoholism. He calls on the priest in the pulpit, the instructor in the classroom, the woman in the home, rigorous exclusion of all strong liquor, and finally everyone, by the force of example. Father Goyer, S.S.S., in a radio talk asked when the leader would appear, the learned sociologist, the true politician, who would be capable of formulating measures favorable to temperance. Be these measures preventive or repressive, they would serve to extend the efforts of the episcopacy, the clergy, the heads of families, educators, and finally the Lacordaire leagues which began as crusades to obstruct the ravages of alcoholism and to extirpate its disastrous consequences.[72]

In the opinion of the followers of the Semaine Sociale, another factor contributing to the disorganization of the family is the desertion of the farm. Life in the city is so much more pleasurable than in the country; its attractions are numerous and the passionate desire for novelty is inconquerable in modern youth. Consequently many French Canadians flock to urban centers. This desertion of the farm affects the very roots of life: housing of a large family constitutes an enormous problem in a city where landlords declare: "Limit your family, if you want lodging quarters." Father Gauthier claims that to find a decent home for a large family in an important city is an impossibility, and French Canadians are unanimous in the contention that nothing is more important to French Canada for its *survivance* than human capital.

The Semaine Sociale would consider its teaching incomplete if it did not offer immediate and appropriate remedies for these various evils alarmingly menacing the institution of the family. The remedies proposed are both spiritual and material. Father Martin, in agreement with Father Vuillermet, O.P., claims that

---

[70] *Ibid.*, p. 151: "La bière que buvait votre grandpère. . . . La bière est vraiment le breuvage du peuple. . . . La bière, pain de l'ouvrier."

[71] At the 1944 meeting in Ottawa, Father Desmarais, O.P., reported that there were 1,300 taverns in Montreal and only 206 in Toronto.

[72] S. s. du Canada, Salaberry-de-Valleyfield, 1943, pp. 150-155.

the only sure remedy for the disorganized family is to rechristianize it.[73] A rule of life that appreciates the value of time, health, and prayer supporting moral life, in the opinion of C. J. Magnan, provides contentment and guarantees happiness in family life.[74] Father Courchesne, present Bishop of Rimouski, shows how the religious practice of evangelical counsels is an efficient preventive to family disorganization.[75] Like Father Martin, Mr. Henri Bourassa, believes that the only means of salvation for the family is a lively faith and respect for the laws of sacrifice and love.[76]

Another powerful means against the perils menacing French Canadian family life is the faithful observance of Sunday duty. It is indeed, a favorable means of maintaining among the members of a family the cordial relations that secure for it permanency, dignity, and charm.[77] In addition, many followers of the Semaine Sociale advocate a sound education, particularly a diffusion of agricultural knowledge to keep the farmers and their sons attached to the soil. In agreement with Judge Laramée, of the Juvenile Court of Montreal, who considers the lack of parental education the greatest problem in French Canada,[78] Dr. Joseph Gauvreau recommends the reeducation of mothers,[79] while Mrs. Françoise Gaudet-Smet and Sister Gérin-Lajoie are in favor of immediate preparation for family life. Mrs. Gaudet-Smet tells of a preventive rather than curative custom in Japan, where instead of nursing the sick, doctors nurse the healthy. Each person pays for medical services as long as he remains in good health. As soon as he becomes ill, all payments cease. Similarly, it is by far preferable to prepare for happiness in the family rather than to make breaches that eventually will have to be repaired.[80] Sister Gérin-Lajoie also believes in giving woman a true family educa-

---

[73] S. s. du Canada, Montréal, 1923, p. 153.

[74] *Ibid.*, p. 229.

[75] *Ibid.*, p. 255.

[76] *Ibid.*, p. 287.

[77] S. s. du Canada, Trois-Rivières, 1925, pp. 308-309.

[78] Interview with Judge Laramée, July 19, 1944, at the Cours des Jeunes Délinquents.

[79] S. s. du Canada, Montréal, 1923, p. 172.

[80] S. s. du Canada, Nicolet, 1940, p. 88.

tion, particularly in the line of the domestic arts: cultivation of the soil, breeding of animals, food preserving, needle work, all of which enter into the so-called "secondary plan of life" recommended by the eminent psychologist Dr. Moore, to keep mentally fit. Indeed, no effort has been spared to prevent the deplorable exodus of mothers from the home. The Saint Vincent de Paul Society, Maternal Assistance, and *Goutte de Lait* have contributed their shares to the movement.[81] The latter is as necessary as the Maternal Assistance group. It is one of the best known means of instructing mothers on their duties of protecting their offspring from the dangers of artificial food. In fact, it was the high rate of infant mortality that gave rise to the institution of the *Goutte de Lait*. To conclude this list of remedies, we may say that the family can be helped by a better compensation for work, that is, higher wages, family allowances, provisions for keeping the mothers at home, and by a back-to-the-farm movement.

It seems to be the attitude of the representatives of the Semaine Sociale to resort to the past to bring out the dignity of the French Canadian rural family life. Thus, at the 1923 meeting, Father Lionel Groulx, prominent historian, cited Bishop Taché depicting the greatest wonder in French Canadian history.

> One of the greatest marvels of the Catholic Church in these last two centuries . . . is the French Canadian family. . . . It is a marvel which we admire more than the magnificent Gothic cathedrals of old France.[82]

The French Canadian rural family of centuries ago, constituted by the sacrament of marriage, registered very few illegitimate births. Only one out of a total of six hundred seventy-four children baptized prior to 1660, and only one more by 1690. As a result of a birth census made by Father Tanguay, it was ascertained that from a total of 165,195 births only 1,366 children

[81] S. s. du Canada, Montréal, 1932, pp. 205-210.

[82] S. s. du Canada, Montréal, 1923, p. 334: "Une des plus grandes merveilles de l'Eglise catholique en ces deux derniers siècles, . . . est la famille canadienne-française. . . . C'est une merveille que nous admirons plus que les cathédrales gothiques, pourtant si magnifiques de la vieille France."

were illegitimate, a proportion of 8.03 per 1,000 children. Strangely enough, the rule in all respectable French Canadian homes was, at one time, to reach a dozen children and even to go beyond the second dozen.[83] The 60,000 Canadians of 1760 have become today more than 4,000,000. This fecundity in human capital—valued at $7,000 each in the United States according to data given by Dr. Moore—has since been referred to as the "miracle canadien,"[84] to which French Canada owes its *survivance*.

Another characteristic of the old French Canadian rural family found particularly in the great "familles souches," is the authority exercised by the father of the family. Bishop Plessis used to say, "Utterance of my father, utterance of a king." The head of the old Canadian family was a sort of family priest when he blessed the first handful of wheat before placing it into the soil; or at table when he blessed bread before cutting it; or again when on the morning of New Year's Day he solemnly raised his hands over the head of his children to bless them like the patriarchs of old. In such a family, work was the universal profession. Every member helped according to his capacities. The father was not only a tiller of the soil; he was also mason, carpenter, black-smith, cobbler, saddler, and during the winter months, weaver and chair-mender. Bishop de Saint Valier, who had visited the country places of French Canada, asserted that:

> Each house is a well-disciplined community where morning and night prayers are said in common, the rosary is recited, particular examination of conscience made before meals, and where the fathers and mothers of families, in the absence of priests, see to the conduct of their servants.[85]

Still another characteristic of the French Canadian rural family is its admirable cohesion. This is fostered by the necessity of living

[83] *Ibid.*, pp. 336-340.

[84] S. s. du Canada, Sherbrooke, 1938, pp. 104-105.

[85] S. s. du Canada, Montréal, 1923, pp. 344-351: "Chaque maison est une petite communauté bien réglée où l'on fait la prière en commun le soir et le matin, où l'on récite le chapelet et où l'on a la pratique des examens particuliers avant les repas et où les pères et les mères de familles suppléent au défaut des prêtres, en ce qui regarde la conduite de leurs valets."

in intimate contact at least during the six months of the fall and winter seasons. The family gathered at the long dinner table, with twenty-five or twenty-six of the household participating in the noon-day mirth, was once a fine substitute for outside distractions.[86]

Significantly, Father Archambault reported in 1923, that French Canadian families perseveringly faithful to divine marriage laws are still numerous.[87] The world-wide reputation of the French Canadian family for its fecundity, its simple morals, and its Christian virtues, was pointed out by Judge Laramée at the 1941 meeting of the Semaine Sociale. But, deploring the decrease in birth rates and the consequent menace to morality, he added: "things change quickly."[88]

However, the French Canadian home is not constituted merely by "four walls" as Dickens has one of his characters say. It is much more than that. It is a reliquary which must remain free from the taints of anglicization and americanization; a sanctuary where children are trained for the race, for the country, for the Church, and for God.

The French Canadian rural family has preserved most of its essential characteristics while the French Canadian urban family has sporadically felt the impact of the forces working towards its disintegration, namely, divorce, feminism, depopulation, alcoholism, desertion of the farm, and women labor. So far the remedies proposed by the Semaine Sociale for the restoration of true family life in the form of aids, education, and domestic arts, are indications of the elite's endeavor to maintain the existence of the ideal French Canadian family of yore.

---

[86] *Ibid.*, p. 355.
[87] *Ibid.*, p. 15.
[88] S. s. du Canada, Québec, 1941, p. 143.

CHAPTER VI

The Semaine Sociale and the State

The Semaine Sociale looks upon the State as a very important, natural, social institution whose end should be the common good and whose duty is to strive to attain that end. In this chapter consideration of the State and of the city will involve a discussion of their meaning, rights and duties, characteristics, and functions. The various rights of citizens will then be indicated, together with the meaning of and justification for patriotism. Finally, democracy as a form of government will be considered with emphasis on the advantages and disadvantages of the democratic mode of state organization, and its reform.

From the founding of the "ambulatory institution," the disciples of the Semaine Sociale, mindful of the importance of the State as one of the institutions of divine origin capable of bringing salvation to French Canada, discussed its various aspects. At the first session of 1920, Msgr. Paquet considered the action of the State as one of the principal remedies for the social ills of the time; at the next two meetings questions of industrial State legislation, intervention and arbitration in conflicts between capital and labor were discussed. How the State should favor the stability and progress of the family was the subject of the fourth session, and justice the topic of the sixth session. Canon Desranleau, present Bishop of Sherbrooke, explained the rights and duties of the State in relation to property in the fifth and Father Georges Roy referred to the authority of the State in the seventh session. There followed in 1928 a discussion of the agricultural problem. The city came in for consideration in 1929 as an urban agglomeration, as a miniature State. In 1931, when the Semaine Sociale realized that State legislation enters into so many debated problems, a whole Social Study Week was devoted to the discussion of the State. Since then, the subject has appeared under one form or another at nearly every session.

At the 1931 meeting, Father Georges Simard defined the State as an organized political people. If the organization is elevated and perfected by principles of faith, the State becomes Christian. As such, the State has for its principal aim the common good.[1]

Previous to the foundation of the Semaine Sociale, various theories about the State had been current in Canada. There were economists, and particularly capitalists, who advocated the "laissez-faire" theory of the Liberal School. When the postulates of this theory had been demonstrated to be false, the socialists reacted and clamored for State intervention. In a middle position between the Liberal theory and the collective utopia stands the doctrine of the Catholic Church as expounded in *Rerum novarum.* Most French Canadians, particularly the audience of the Semaine Sociale, proclaim that the State has its responsibilities in the solution of various social and economic problems; in a word, the State has rights to guard and duties to perform and it may not be deterred from doing what is necessary for the common good.

One of the first to mention the duties of the State is Father Desranleau at the 1924 meeting in Sherbrooke. He declared that the State had the duty to protect, restrain, consolidate, and defend the right to own property and to limit, modify, and conciliate its use in accordance with the demands of the common good of society. Toward this end the State should determine by law the right to property, assure the exercise of this right, and solve the conflicts that may arise. Moreover, the State has the strict obligation to prevent fraudulent financial speculations.[2] Considering the duties of the State from an economic aspect, Father Nazaire Hamel, O.F.M., declared that the State has a double duty: to better the lot of the workingman and to protect him.[3] Father Edmour Hébert further insists that the State supervise industry to prevent abuses and elaborate a social legislation capable of settling equitably the relations of capital and labor.[4]

The State must respect the clergy and the possessions of the

---

[1] S. s. du Canada, Ottawa, 1931, p. 270.

[2] S. s. du Canada, Sherbrooke, 1924, pp. 97-101.

[3] S. s. du Canada, Québec, 1927, p. 169.

[4] S. s. du Canada, Ottawa, 1931, p. 141.

Church. Its legislation should be in harmony with the laws of the Church in matters primarily ecclesiastical. In addition, the State, in the thinking of French Canadians, should help the family but never dominate it.[5] It has the right, as Father Courchesne expressed at the 1925 meeting, to assure not only sound morality but also all types of human activities: production and distribution of wealth, agriculture, industry, commerce, hygiene, science, arts, literature, and journalism.[6]

That the State has the right to intervene in the economic order is truly the belief of the apostles of the Semaine Sociale. This intervention is necessary in the development of transportation routes, railroads, canals, subsidies to commerce and industry in the form of prizes, expositions, international conventions, and well-balanced custom tariffs.[7]

One of the State's main attributes is authority. Constant reference is made to this in the Semaine Sociale. To Father Archambault authority is the "mainstay of societies and the safeguard of individuals."[8] Father Georges Roy defines authority as a moral force to command, based on a certain superiority possessed by the chosen one with the correlative duty incumbent upon the subject to obey under pain of sin.[9] More simple is Judge Lemay's definition: authority is "established order."[10] The end of authority is the preservation of the community, that is, public order; it must also harmonize private interests and actions to the norm of the common good.

Relative to the source of authority, French Canadian thought seems to diverge slightly from the teachings of Suarez, Bellarmine and others. At the 1927 Semaine Sociale Msgr. Paquet refers to the encyclical *Diuturnum* of Leo XIII in which he shows that all human authority comes from God.[11] Similarly, he claimed, Pope Pius X in his letter to the *Sillon* proclaimed that transmis-

[5] S. s. du Canada, Trois-Rivières, 1925, pp. 61-62.
[6] *Ibid.*, p. 108.
[7] S. s. du Canada, Ottawa, 1931, p. 107.
[8] S. s. du Canada, Québec, 1927, p. 27.
[9] *Ibid.*, p. 143.
[10] *Ibid.*, p. 412.
[11] *Ibid.*, p. 38.

sion of authority is made directly from God to the subject of the authority and not indirectly through the people.[12] Still we find Mr. Jacques Cartier claiming that authority is given directly by God to the community.[13]

That authority is necessary is well recognized by the Semaine Sociale. Thus, Msgr. Rouleau reasons as follows: as the human body needs a soul for life, so the people need authority to constitute a society. The people are, as it were, the body of society while authority is its soul. When the soul departs from the body, dissolution and death result; if authority disappears from society, anarchy will undoubtedly follow.[14] Msgr. Chartrand is of the same opinion when he contends that a society without authority would be a "monstrosity,"—that is a body without a head. Authority is for society what the soul is for the animated being, a principle of force, unity, tendency, and preservation.[15] Because isolated families would be unable to defend their rights against attacks from the outside; because they could not provide the sum of material, intellectual, and moral goods necessary for temporal and eternal welfare, Father Lebel argues that the State has the authority and duty to legislate a domestic program adapted to the present needs of the French Canadian families.[16] Judicial authority is also necessary to maintain equilibrium between the liberty and the rights of individuals. Its sanctions are fines, confinement in prison with or without labor, corporal punishment, and execution.[17]

Though demonstrating that authority is a necessity, the Semaine Sociale also considers its possible abuses. A reference is made to this at the 1927 meeting by Father Mauger, O.P. The first type of abuse occurs when authority violates God's plan and promulgates laws opposed to the natural law. The second form of abuse occurs when laws sanctioned by authority are not for the common good. Father Mauger cites a significant example to this effect. Any legislation on marriage which overlooks the human and religious

[12] *Ibid.*, pp. 210-211.

[13] S. s. du Canada, Saint-Jean, 1942, p. 59.

[14] S. s. du Canada, Québec, 1927, p. 22.

[15] S. s. du Canada, Ottawa, 1931, p. 25.

[16] S. s. du Canada, Sherbrooke, 1938, p. 102.

[17] S. s. du Canada, Québec, 1927, pp. 276, 288.

values involved, or one that does not safeguard the natural and supernatural rights of citizens, constitutes an abuse of authority that is both unjust and dangerous, and should be considered void, since it is contrary to the common good and infringes upon the absolute rights of man.

The followers of the Semaine Sociale readily accept Saint Thomas' definition of law: "an ordinance of reason for the common good made and promulgated by whoever has charge of the community."[18] At the 1931 session of the Semaine Sociale, in his course on *Law,* Léon-Mercier Gouin speaks of laws as "rules of general conduct imposed and sanctioned by the Government."[19] Thus, in Canada, religious freedom exists; Canadian law assures protection to the existing religious sects. Moreover, the penal code is aimed at crimes against God, religion and morals; it punishes blasphemy, perjury, and violation of Sunday rest. The Canadian criminal law imposes capital punishment on murderers; it deals severely with those guilty of assault, rape, extortion, or theft.[20]

The Semaine Sociale agrees that the spheres of the military, ocean transportation, diplomacy and finance, lie within the domain of the State. It also concedes that the State supervise matters of hygiene and morals; that it have power to arouse, encourage, and even supplant, if needed, private initiative; and that it may demand qualifications for certain offices. Such a system makes for decentralization, for a distrust of false doctrine, and for a greater development of individual initiative.[21]

Like Saint Thomas and the Popes, especially Pius XI, the champions of the Semaine Sociale teach that the State, while maintaining peace, must assure man a sufficiency of material goods and thus facilitate a virtuous and enlightened life, in other words, it must preserve and multiply the spiritual and material advantages which constitute happiness in this world. Mention is thus made in the Semaine Sociale of social legislation, namely, the ensemble of those laws which are meant to insure citizens against dangers,

---

[18] *Ibid.,* pp. 186-194.

[19] S. s. du Canada, Ottawa, 1931, p. 56.

[20] S. s. du Canada, Trois-Rivières, 1925, p. 72.

[21] *Ibid.,* p. 378.

accidents, and the evils resulting from the modern economic order. This legislation would cover such things as acknowledgment of professional associations, fixed minimum salaries, respect for Sunday rest, hours of work, prohibition of night work when possible, protection of women and children in industry, the establishment of insurance funds against accidents, illness, old age, unemployment, and the setting up of tribunals of conciliation and arbitration to settle difficulties. In line with this social legislation, the State would favor such private enterprises as, housing projects, *jardins ouvriers,*[22] *caisses populaires,* mutual insurance plans, and cooperatives.[23]

It is significant to note that in Canada the sale of alcohol is under the control of the State. Mr. Eugène l'Heureux, prominent journalist, approves this measure and adds that the individual tavern should also be under State control.[24]

Somewhat out of the ordinary is Canada's legislation relative to bilingualism in the federal offices and services of the country. Some approve of this situation, others accept it as a timely measure to prevent "un plus grand mal." Mr. Saint-Pierre would have every French Canadian bilingual because he sees in this course a means to obtain better positions. Msgr. Perrier claims that it exists for the French element only. Truly enough, in Montreal, the French Canadian conductor on being asked which language he could speak, replied: "Here we speak both French and English." It is not always so with the English-speaking conductor. As an instance of true bilingualism, Father Elie J. Auclair, at the 1924

---

[22] The *Cité Jardin* is a recent innovation in French Canada. Sixteen houses, the first development of the total eventually to be called *La Cité-Jardin du IIIe Centenaire de Montréal,* 1642-1942, were completed in 1942. A second development of eighteen houses was finished in 1943. A third series of ninety-seven is nearing completion and a fourth of over one hundred is now in progress. This Garden City is situated on the beautiful Rosemont plateau. The apostles of this movement are Mr. Auguste Gosselin and Father Jean d'Auteuil Richard, S.J. For a description of this project see, Jean d'Auteuil Richard, "A Garden City in the Making," *Journal of the Royal Architectural Institute of Canada,* September, 1944, p. 155 ff. and Emile Gervais, "Deux cités," *Le Messager Canadien,* October, 1943, pp. 484-495.

[23] S. s. du Canada, Ottawa, 1931, pp. 141-142.

[24] *Ibid.,* p. 203.

meeting, tells of a group of Toronto citizens making a pilgrimage to Sherbrooke. An English-speaking student from the seminary greeted the pilgrims of Toronto in French, and a French-speaking student addressed them in English.[25] Bilingualism has its followers. Judge Trahan in the 1925 session at Trois-Rivières recalls his proclamation in Parliament and "à la face du pays" that "Canada is a bilingual country; that its Constitution must be respected regarding the two official languages."[26] On the other hand, we have Mr. Albert Rioux declaring that systematic bilingualism has been a failure in French Canada, almost a "national suicide."[27]

The rights of the State are limited in the thought of the Semaine Sociale, in relation to the family and the education of children. At several meetings these limitations were specifically indicated. In 1931, Bishop Forbes considered the State in its relations to God, the individual, the family, free association, and finally to the Church. Due to the fact that the State is a society of men essentially subject to God, it follows that the State, too, is subject to the Supreme Being. Consequently, it is subject to natural and divine rights. The power of the State, argues Bishop Forbes, is also limited by the rights and liberties of individuals. A third limitation is imposed by the rights of the family. The State is also restricted in the exercise of its rights in connection with private associations such as, humanitarian, scientific, industrial societies, financial companies, and workingmen's corporations. Finally, the Church with its rights and natural superiority is itself a limitation of civil authority.[28]

Similarly, at the same session of the Semaine Sociale, Father Dubois, S.J., sets down as the State's first limitation, the rights of parents; and as the second, the rights of the Church. Pontifical documents widen the field of social justice. This brings to the fore the virtues that should inspire any action of civil authority, namely, prudence, justice and charity. Prudence enables the State to pursue its end, the common good, by using the most appropriate

---

[25] S. s. du Canada, Sherbrooke, 1924, p. 361.

[26] S. s. du Canada, Trois-Rivières, 1925, p. 374.

[27] S. s. du Canada, Joliette, 1935, p. 79.

[28] S. s. du Canada, Ottawa, 1931, pp. 11-12.

means. In the use of these means, justice works for a firm and wise measure.[29]

The Semaine Sociale makes a precisely consistent allocation of functions among the Federal, Provincial, and Municipal governments of French Canada. Thus, the constitution of the State is very complicated because the country is administered on the principle of decentralization. This, however, is in accordance with the social philosophy of the Church which advocates two measures in a normal political order: one, the decentralization of powers and the second, the specialization of functions.[30]

In the course of the different sessions of the Semaine Sociale, we find repeated statements made on the role of the State in French Canada. At one time, the speakers will claim that State intervention is necessary to protect the interests of the weak and to assure respect for justice. At another time they want it to exert control over matters that deal with morals by suppressing whatever in public life might have evil effects on them. Again, they insist that the State collaborate with the farmer in solving his many difficult problems, without, however, sponsoring the "laissez-faire" policy, but helping rather to achieve the common good. Following this principle, Father Joseph Ferland, at the 1931 meeting, calls for a campaign to counteract the State's meddling in school matters, and to restrict it to helping the Church and parents rather than supplanting them. He deplores the conditions which lead to the needless introduction of secular instructors in schools directed by religious orders. The male lay students who complete their course in the normal schools under government control need teaching positions. The State cannot exact that the School Commission, answerable to the Municipality, hire them, so we find these same students directed to teaching positions in the girls' normal schools, conducted by religious orders. With the exception of Gaspé, a lay professor has been added to the staff of all the normal schools of the country. Father Ferland calls this a very abnormal situation.[31]

The Semaine Sociale devoted the entire 1929 course to the

---

[29] S. s. du Canada, Chicoutimi, 1929, p. 259.
[30] S. s. du Canada, Sherbrooke, 1938, p. 136.
[31] S. s. du Canada, Ottawa, 1931, p. 128.

study of the miniature State, that is, the city and municipality. In a restrictive sense the city is essentially a union of families, occupying the same territory and united in civil society. The French Canadian is very conscious of the distinction between city and country. Hence the disciples of the Semaine Sociale plan to study the city as one of the characteristics of the age: great human agglomerations, "tentacular centers" either by their geographical position or by their natural resources, and industries which attract workingmen in large numbers.[32]

The French Canadians distinguish two types of industrial cities: the free or "open" city where any one may come to live, establish an industry, and in which the industrialist is proprietor of his plants only and shares like all the other citizens in the municipal and educational expenses. Such cities are, among others, Quebec, Montreal, Trois-Rivières, Chicoutimi. Then there is the "closed" city, the "company town," where all property, mills, land, and houses belongs to a company, and in which no other industry may operate. This type of city is a modern institution. Father J. Bergeron calls it by the special name: "ville industrielle" because he feels he cannot call private property of one man a city, no matter how extensive it may be.[33]

Father Joseph Dufour makes a philosophical analysis of the city. The word "cité" to him has various meanings. In ecclesiastical parlance it is used to designate heaven or the Church; in popular speech it is used to refer to civil society or the State or even the "ville." Following Saint Augustine, who defines it as a multitude of men united by a social bond, he studies the city with that meaning in mind. Like the family, there are four elements constituting the city as a civil society: matter and form, intrinsic principles, efficient and final causes, and extrinsic principles. The material cause of the city is the multitude; the formal cause, authority; the efficient cause is the nature of man; and the final cause, the common good.[34] Father Archambault, citing Jacques Maritain, declares that in this world the city is ordained

[32] S. s. du Canada, Chicoutimi, 1929, p. 16.
[33] *Ibid.*, pp. 60-62.
[34] *Ibid.*, pp. 21-25.

to a temporal common good, which is not only of a material order but also and principally of a moral order.[35] In this connection J. E. A. McConville says "urbanism" is in theory the science of rational economic and methodological management of cities; in practice, the art of managing the resources of a city in such a way as to make them serve best the general interests of present and future generations.[36] Urbanism aims at alignment, orderliness and symmetry in city-planning, such that space, plenty of sunshine and air, wide and clean streets, are duly provided; in short, housing conditions, artistic buildings, appropriate quarters for various necessities and contingencies of urban life. This supposes that room must be found for parks and open squares. Outremont, a suburb of Montreal, may be cited as a fitting example of the application of these principles. Urbanism, then, is socially important. It is not merely a science and an art, it is an urgent necessity; for French Canadians, a national virtue. It no longer tolerates the development of a center by unscrupulous individuals who are more concerned about personal gain than about material and social improvement. At the 1933 meeting at Rimouski, Cardinal Villeneuve, differentiating between material and utilitarian "mental urbanism," condemned the latter which has attacked all modern civilization. Mental urbanism does not only endanger the temporal happiness of a population but also Catholicism itself.[37]

There is much migration from rural centers to urban centers. However, beauty and convenience are not the main attractions of cities. At the 1928 meeting, Mr. Alphonse Desilets listed as other lures: travelling facilities, invading tourism, the sensational press, the excitement of city life, the automobile, the airplane, all this "progress" tends to dissipate the imagination and desires of an ardent youth.[38] The supposed easy life of city-dwellers with its pseudo-advantages is a constant bait. Besides, industries need workers and in cities the official hygienic service is better developed. At the 1929 session of the Semaine Sociale, Dr. Joseph

[35] *Ibid.*, p. 17, cited from Jacques Maritain, *La Primauté du spirituel*, p. 25.
[36] *Ibid.*, p. 186.
[37] S. s. du Canada, Rimouski, 1933, p. 289.
[38] S. s. du Canada, Saint-Hyacinthe, 1928, p. 186.

Baudouin reported that as early as 1919 there existed a Federal Health Service and in 1887 a Provincial Health Service. These health services are given particularly in cities. The Provincial Health Service instituted health inspection, vital statistics, laboratories, sanitary measures, and care of venereal disease. In 1925, a similar service was established in municipalities having a population of 5,000.[39]

In the face of such obvious advantages of the cities, the Semaine Sociale does not overlook the dangers associated with urban populations. First of all, family life in cities is exposed to the menaces already mentioned in the previous chapter. The fetid emanations and the deleterious smoke of mills pollute the atmosphere which intoxicates where it should regenerate. Housing quarters, built to harbor as many people as possible, are often without air and light. There is a dangerous promiscuity about a city that is as depressing as conditions of work are uncongenial. At the 1929 session, Father A. Bissonnette, O.P., agreed that life in cities offers more comfort and luxury, but the tyranny of fashion is more overbearing, arduous labor creates more dissatisfaction, and poverty is more frequent. Intellectual life offers still greater complications; daily contacts with people of divergent views, the press, conferences and assemblies, and dangerous reading, are not without leaving their mark on the human personality.[40] The religious life of the community is not without feeling these baneful effects. Sunday observance is usually not the order of the day. Divorce is very prominent in cities. Some movies and theaters are dangerous, particularly so because they impart a false philosophy of life. The influence of newspapers, magazines and comics is not to be overlooked. Because dancing is no less a moral danger than filthy literature, "modern dances" are branded as indecent and forbidden in every city, diocese, and parish of French Canada.[41]

---

[39] S. s. du Canada, Chicoutimi, 1929, pp. 109-111.

[40] For scientific proof of the effects of reading on the adolescent, see the empirical study on *The Effects of Reading on Moral Conduct and Emotional Experience* made by Sister M. Corde Lorang, O.P., at the Catholic University.

[41] S. s. du Canada, Chicoutimi, 1929, pp. 84-97.

Like the State, the city has rights and duties which are peculiar to its nature. Father Joseph Dufour, in his remarkable course given in 1929, expounded these rights and duties in a scholarly manner. The city has the right to protect itself, to exact help from the State. It has the right of liberty; it may take all the necessary means to accomplish its duties. The city has also the moral right of being helped by other cities. It may not be harmed in its reputation. Finally it has the right to a "collective territory." The duties of the city may be summarized under three headings: duties toward God, toward others, and toward its own members. To observe the laws of God, to demand respect for His name, to render the worship that is due Him is the first and greatest of the duties of the city. To the State, the city owes obedience; to the other cities, justice and charity. The duty toward its own members is a double one: protection and assistance. The city must protect the life, property, health and liberty of its citizens. It must assist and stimulate private initiative, supplement it if it is insufficient, replace it if it is powerless, encourage it if it makes progress. That duty of assistance is threefold: it must help to attain physical, intellectual, and moral perfection.[42]

It was seen in a previous chapter how the parish played an important role in the Church. Very important is the role of the parish in the city. Msgr. Perrier reports Leo XIII as saying that to live humanely and to practice virtue, a minimum of security and even material resources are necessary. That is why the city must provide the needs of this life and the joys of a higher culture for an ever increasing number of people. Now, the French Canadian assumes an additional aim, that of establishing the reign of Christ on earth, and it can best be accomplished when we consider the parish to be a traditional and official institution, involving the intimate collaboration of priests and laymen. The constituent elements of the parish are its good Christian lay-members; they are its glory. A noted priest once said: "A people is worth what the men who compose it are worth." Msgr. Perrier further cites the revealing words of Pope Pius X. The latter asked of a group of cardinals what was most necessary today to save society. He re-

[42] *Ibid.*, pp. 26-31.

plied negatively to answers such as: build Catholic schools, multiply Churches, cultivate sacerdotal vocations, declaring that what was most necessary was to have in each parish a group of enlightened, resolute laymen, who would be true apostles.[43]

In the proceedings of the Semaine Sociale we find sporadic utterances on the rights of citizens in connection with the State. As early as 1924, Father Desranleau affirms that the right to life is "the father and king of all the other human rights." Outside of divine natural rights, all the other rights may be overlooked if they are an obstacle to this fundamental right.[44]

Another right upon which the Semaine Sociale looks with sympathy is the right to liberty. At the 1931 meeting, Father Eustache Gagnon, C.S.C., following Saint Thomas' teaching, defined natural liberty as "the ability to act or not to act, of being master of one's act"; and moral liberty as "the faculty to choose among the means which lead to a determined end." The power to do wrong no more enters into the essence of liberty than illness forms part of health.[45] Father Anselme Longpré spoke of liberty as the first and most important of rights. He asserted that no social reform is possible if one forgets the inalienable and sacred rights of man. On the other hand, he maintained that since man lives in society, restrictions on liberty may be imposed in view of the common good, but this right may never be sacrificed by a regimentation aiming at its annihilation.[46] At the Semaine Sociale of 1927, Mr. Antonio Perrault declared that human nature does not impose on societies any definite form of government. The people, because they are free beings, may designate the form which seems best adapted to circumstances, whether it be a monarchy, an aristocracy, or a democracy.[47]

The disciples of the Semaine Sociale considered the right of property important enough to devote an entire week to its study at its fifth session in 1924. Mr. Yves Tessier-Lavigne, Professor

---

[43] *Ibid.*, pp. 223-236.
[44] S. s. du Canada, Sherbrooke, 1924, p. 105.
[45] S. s. du Canada, Ottawa, 1931, pp. 98-99.
[46] S. s. du Canada, Saint-Hyacinthe, 1937, p. 70.
[47] S. s. du Canada, Québec, 1927, p. 391.

at the University of Montreal, claimed that the human person has a right to property because duty commands every one to attain his last end, and individual property helps in this free activity.[48] Father Longpré maintained a similar view. He declared that the right of property is natural, that is, resulting from the nature of man himself; it is necessary so that man may reach his destiny; consequently, it is innate in man who has for his author, the author of all nature, God.[49] Thus, from man's right to live and to protect his existence flows his right to property.

Following Leo XIII, Pope Pius XI formulated the right to a living wage and to the means of obtaining it, namely, the right to form unions. Pius XI demanded, and with him the Semaine Sociale, that wages correspond to the needs of the workingmen's family; that they be large enough to assure relative well-being and permit savings. Moreover, he wanted the salary to be such that mothers need not desert their homes to contribute to the subsistence of their charges. He even declared that it would be better for an industry to disappear than to offer workers an insufficient salary.[50] Following Leo XIII in his *Rerum novarum,* the Semaine Sociale recommends workingmen's associations because they afford opportune assistance to needy laborers.

Still another right of citizens upon which the Semaine Sociale insists is suffrage. At the Quebec meeting of 1927, Mr. Léo Pelland cited Father Vermeersch's definition of suffrage: "the legal and onerous faculty to designate the leaders of the people," and Father Lamarche in his interesting pamphlet on *Electoral Duty* added: "those who will have to take a part more or less important in the government of the country."[51] Mr. Pelland contended that suffrage is not a natural right, because for centuries it was not exercised. On the other hand, Father Gaudrault believes that the right of suffrage is nearer the nature of man than is generally conceded. He further explains that this natural right does not enjoin compulsory voting any more than the natural right of marriage

---

[48] S. s. du Canada, Sherbrooke, 1924, p. 48.
[49] S. s. du Canada, Saint-Hyacinthe, 1937, p. 67.
[50] S. s. du Canada, Montréal, 1932, pp. 242-243.
[51] S. s. du Canada, Québec, 1927, p. 200.

obliges everyone to marry; moreover, this right does not establish popular vote nor even universal suffrage: one man, one vote. Father Gaudrault does not call the right to vote an essential right, like the right to eat, to live or the right to reason; it is a secondary natural right, based on a natural need in view of the common good. The right of suffrage, that is, electoral duty, he goes on to say, is commanded for the common good and when this common good is menaced, abstention from voting may then be a serious sin.[52] Both Father Gaudrault and Mr. Pelland oppose universal suffrage; Mr. Pelland sees in it an application of the revolutionary doctrines of equality preached by Rousseau. Pius IX, himself a victim of the Italian Revolution, branded universal suffrage a "mensonge universel."[53]

More democratic, Mr. Georges Pelletier, Director of *Le Devoir,* citing at the 1942 meeting Father Lemonnyer's *Précis de Sociologie,* stated the principal functions of universal suffrage: it helps to formulate popular wills, to designate those who are to govern, it is also a means of control and defense and even serves as an outlet for the discontent of a people.[54] Popular suffrage is not without its abuses in the opinion of Mr. Pelletier. When the party is itself dishonest, the election is not the voice of the people. Party spirit may be dangerous and as such, cannot be a good judge of political values. In French Canada, as elsewhere, we find such abuses as purchase of votes, dishonest newspaper campaigns, election of incompetent officers, creation of *surcitoyens,* exaggerated expenses and favoritism.[55] To do away with electoral abuses, the Semaine Sociale, represented by Mr. Pelletier, recommends that French Canada acquire a democratic spirit and political liberty by means of proportional representation; that the teaching of civics, social duty, and patriotism, be inserted in the program of every school, that an honest press form an honest public opinion, that respect for the rights of minorities be developed.[56]

[52] S. s. du Canada, Ottawa, 1931, pp. 47-49.

[53] S. s. du Canada, Québec, 1927, pp. 212-213.

[54] S. s. du Canada, Saint-Jean, 1942, pp. 86-88.

[55] *Ibid.,* pp. 93-98.

[56] *Ibid.,* pp. 102-107.

Woman suffrage has adversaries in the Semaine Sociale. The first mention of woman suffrage was made in 1923 by Father Villeneuve. He called it a form of feminism and argued that the role of woman is essentially that of a mother; if the right to vote exposes her to become less of a mother, let suffrage perish. Woman suffrage runs foul of the legitimate instincts of the female sex.[57] Again, at the 1925 meeting of the Semaine Sociale, Mr. Joseph Barnard disapproved of the indiscriminate right of woman suffrage that the Federal government had inserted in its statutes after World War I. He justified the municipal law of the Province of Quebec which gives the right to vote only to widows and unmarried women owning property. He stated his position most emphatically:

> . . . when the father is in the home, for pity's sake spare the wives and the mothers; do not offer them, with the right of suffrage, less than what they have already, or at least are supposed to have: peace in the home and calm affection of their family![58]

Likewise, Mr. Pelland opposes woman suffrage because he feels that women should not participate in public disputes and political agitations.[59] Similarly, Mr. Ferdinand Roy labels it as feminism and adds that voting is a function which men perform badly enough by themselves, without making it worse by extending it to women. Then he quotes the obviously too bold statement of Arsene Houssaye: "Man would nearly always go straight ahead, if he did not meet a woman at each step. She is a charming travelling mate, but she does not know her way and prevents us from seeing ours."[60] On the other hand, Father Gaudrault is neither for nor against woman suffrage. In the Province of Quebec women voted

[57] S. s. du Canada, Montréal, 1923, pp. 56-57.

[58] S. s. du Canada, Trois-Rivières, 1925, pp. 84-85: ". . . quand l'homme est au foyer épargnez, de grâce, les épouses et les mères; ne leur proposez pas, avec votre droit de suffrage, moins que ce qu'elles ont déjà, et que ce qu'elles doivent surtout avoir: la paix du ménage et la calme affection de leur famille!"

[59] S. s. du Canada, Ottawa, 1931, p. 208.

[60] S. s. du Canada, Québec, 1927, p. 63.

for the first time in 1944. The French Canadians have an opinion different from other nations about the role of woman in society; they are in general opposed to her emancipation.[61]

The Semaine Sociale devoted several courses to the study of patriotism. The fatherland, in the words of Father Caron, O.M.I., is a divine-natural institution and they are reprobates who become its destroyers.[62] In practice, the fatherland of the French Canadian is actually the Province of Quebec and the French sections of the other provinces; everywhere else he is a foreigner;[63] but in mentality the French Canadian is naturally Canadian, essentially Canadian, and nothing but Canadian. If the Canadian sings "God Save the King" it is because he cannot do otherwise; his true national hymn, the only one that is a true expression of his patriotism is "O Canada, mon pays, mes amours." Laurier, at one time Prime Minister, expressed the opinion of his co-patriots in the following words: "I love France which gave us life, I love England which gave us liberty; but the first place in my heart is for Canada, my fatherland, my native land."[64]

Justifying this patriotism, Mr. Anatole Vanier, Director of the *Action nationale,* at the Nicolet meeting of 1940, cited the example of Christ Himself who, although He exalted the universal commandment of divine charity towards all men and all peoples, manifested a profound and special love for His townsmen. At one time He weeps over the future disasters of His beloved fatherland. Similarly, Pius XI in *Ubi arcano* favors moderate nationalism which he represents as the object of a particular vigilance on the part of patriotism. Pius XII in *Summi pontificatus* says that

---

[61] Interview with Father Pie-Marie Gaudrault, August 1, 1944.

[62] S. s. du Canada, Ottawa, 1931, p. 240.

[63] Gérard Filion, "Le Paysan et ses institutions sociales," *Agriculture,* ed. by Esdras Minville et al. (Montréal: Editions Fides, 1943), Chap. VII, p. 415.

[64] Georges Vattier, *Essai sur la mentalité canadienne-française* (Paris: Librairie Ancienne Honoré Champion, 1928), p. 344: "J'aime la France qui nous a donné la vie, j'aime l'Angleterre qui nous a donné la liberté; mais la première place dans mon coeur est pour le Canada, ma patrie, ma terre natale."

Christian doctrine does not prevent one from promoting the prosperity and the legitimate interests of one's fatherland.[65] Repeatedly, and in many places, the Semaine Sociale reminds hearers that the fatherland is a people with its institutions, its patriotism, and its religion; that the fatherland is the past with its memories, its heroes, and its triumphs.

It remains to consider a peculiar form of patriotism in French Canada, that is, the tenacity with which the French Canadian holds to his language. As early as 1921, Mr. Hogue reminded his audience that they have a language to defend, a language which is ignored by the Federal and Provincial powers, by associations, and public utility companies.[66] Judge Lemay in 1927 did more: he denounced the novelty of introducing a great number of English sign-boards amidst a population where an insignificant minority speaks English. "We are on the verge," he said, "of painting our Province in English. This afternoon I went through a village of Beauce where not a single person speaks English. Well, the three hotels of the locality displayed signs in English.[67] Canon Pellerin also believes that it is high time that French Canadians cease to give foreigners the impression of a "pays français au visage anglais." At present one finds in the Province of Quebec signs written in both French and English. In Ottawa, the reports and documents are printed in the two languages. Every one who has studied the Constitutional law of Canada is aware of these facts. President Roosevelt in 1943 acknowledged the bilingual character of Canada:

> My visit to the historical city of Quebec vividly reminds me that Canada is a nation founded on the union of two great nationalities. The harmony of their associa-

---

[65] S. s. du Canada, Nicolet, 1940, pp. 96-100.

[66] S. s. du Canada, Québec, 1921, pp. 350-351.

[67] S. s. du Canada, Québec, 1927, p. 414: "On est en train, . . . de peinturer notre province en anglais. Cette après-midi je suis passé dans un village de la Beauce où pas une seule personne ne parle anglais. Or les trois hôtels de la localité avaient leurs affiches en anglais."

> tion in equality may serve as an example to all of humanity.[68]

The Semaine Sociale consecrated its 1942 session to the study of democracy. At its first meeting Father Archambault commented on the various definitions of democracy. In the United States, the word democracy has become synonymous with respect for the human person, equality of rights, cultural and religious freedom. "A society where the dignity granted by God to the human person and where its immortal destiny are completely recognized" is Father LaFarge's definition.[69] In his broadcast of January 18, 1942, on the Catholic Hour, Msgr. Sheen declares that the "essence of democracy consists in the recognition of the value of the human person, seat of the inalienable rights conferred by God to man."[70] Again, at the 1942 session of the Semaine Sociale, Msgr. Forget elaborated Lincoln's definition of democracy as being a "government of the people, by the people, for the people." A government of the people, Msgr. Forget explained, is one of free men; consequently democracy must respect the liberties given to man by God Himself. Government for the people: democracy then must exercise its authority for the common good only or else degenerate into tyranny. Government by the people: democracy demands that citizens watch their representatives and hold them responsible for their actions.[71] According to Father Delos, O.P., Professor at Laval University, the characteristics of a democratic regime are in opposition to the totalitarian regime; these characteristics are the establishment of a reign of law, a constitution juridically formulated and instituted by the will of the people, a party government, a program of action, and a democratic spirit activating the people. Christopher Dawson writes that democratic equality is a tendency towards an "aristocracy for all."[72]

---

[68] S. s. du Canada, Salaberry-de-Valleyfield, 1943, p. 203: "Ma visite à la ville historique de Québec rappelle vivement à mon esprit que le Canada est une nation fondée sur l'union de deux grandes races. L'harmonie de leur association dans l'égalité peut servir d'exemple à l'humanité toute entière, en exemple partout dans le monde."

[69] S. s. du Canada, Saint-Jean, 1942, pp. 11-12.

[70] *Ibid.*, pp. 30-31.

[71] S. s. du Canada, Joliette, 1935, p. 155.

[72] S. s. du Canada, Saint-Jean, 1942, pp. 43-49.

It may be well to note here that the Semaine Sociale alludes to a real and Christian democracy, thereby giving the impression that certain democracies do not enter into their concept. For instance, Mr. Moïse Lebeau, Mayor of Saint-Jean, cites Leo XIII as declaring in 1901 that Christian democracy is Catholic popular action without a shadow of political interference.[73] In the opinion of Judge Amédée Monet, if Christian democracy wishes to continue to exist it must consider the common good of all in matters pertaining to education, help given to the sick, the lame, and the unfortunate. A Christian democracy must not only give people free air, but it must contribute greatly to assure the happiness of all.[74] Msgr. Forget refers to a "living democracy" as a movement of integration, a participation of all the organized forces: families, regions, professional and economic associations, to the progress of the whole society and development of public orders.[75] In the conference on *Democracy and Communism* Father Gustave Sauvé, O.M.I., Director of the School of Social Science at the University of Ottawa, speaks of a "real democracy"—a form of government with popular suffrage. The legislators, he adds, who are chosen by the people and invested with an authority coming from God, must safeguard the elements of society, namely, God, the individual and the family, and realize the common good through justice and charity.[76]

Democracy as it exists in French Canada needs reforms. There should be the repression of unjust monopoly; the development of cooperatives; the promoting of measures to ordain, discipline and render more efficient parliamentary proceedings; the imposition of more severe sanctions against electoral frauds; and finally, the establishments of professional corporative organizations.[77] These reforms may best be accomplished in the thinking of Mr. Montpetit by the social elite.

The Semaine Sociale admits that democracy as a form of government has both advantages and disadvantages. Mr. Jacques

[73] *Ibid.*, p. 23.
[74] *Ibid.*, p. 151.
[75] *Ibid.*, p. 215.
[76] *Ibid.*, p. 145.
[77] *Ibid.*, p. 204.

Cartier, prominent lawyer of Richelieu, lists the advantages as follows: democracy is in conformity with human nature; the community retains the exercise of authority given to it directly by God; democracy tends to the common good; and it safeguards the fundamental rights of individuals. The disadvantages of democracy fall under various points. It does not integrate the family as such in civil society. Oftentimes private interests are subordinated unnecessarily to common interests. Democracy has also manifested a tendency to increase bureaucracy. It permits a lack of initiative when a nation has to face serious economic and political crises.[78] Besides, modern democracy of the type born of the spirit of the French Revolution, as described by Father Furfey in his recent book,[79] may become an instrument of tyranny against the Church.[80]

It seems to be the tradition of the Semaine Sociale to be mainly concerned with the domestic problems of the State. Comparatively little is said on international relations. In 1944, however, some suggestions for international order were made. These will be indicated later.

By way of summary, it may be said that in French Canadian thought the State is a political organization established for the common good. French Canadians readily recognize, on the one hand, the responsibilities of the State in the solution of various social and economic problems, but on the other hand, abhor the unnecessary insurgence of the State in matters that can be settled by other social groups. The Semaine Sociale contends that State legislation should be harmonized with the laws of the Church. The State should help the family in the education of its children but without dominating it. Catholic social thought in French Canada proclaims that the State must assist but not interfere in matters outside its own "field of force." The Semaine Sociale recognizes the dangers and attractions of city-life. It insists that the city should be composed of families and homes where the virtues

---

[78] *Ibid.*, pp. 58-64.

[79] This type of exaggerated naturalism is well described in Paul H. Furfey, *The Mystery of Iniquity* (Milwaukee: The Bruce Publishing Company, 1944), pp. 152-167.

[80] S. s. du Canada, Saint-Jean, 1942, p. 64.

of the French Canadians may flourish, whence the vital forces of their nation may be drawn. That this may not remain a dream, every human person must be supplied with those means which are conducive to his final end. French Canadians sincerely love their fatherland, Canada. Quite obviously, they consider as their own the land which their forefathers explored and cultivated. They are attached to their language and to particular characteristics and traditions specifically French Canadian. Under the Canadian Federal Constitution and under French Canadian influence, Canada has remained a bilingual country and French Canadians cling to this right with patriotic emotion. It seems that the notion of democracy to the French Canadian designates any form of government which aims to solve the problem of the State by establishing a social order based on the rights and dignity which man possesses due to his reasonable nature and his spiritual individuality; any form of government which, in view of those rights and the common good, institutes a positive order of civil liberties and responsibilities.

CHAPTER VII

THE SEMAINE SOCIALE AND EDUCATION

The Semaine Sociale treated the subject of Education in 1935. This chapter attempts a brief survey of the history of education in French Canada, to be followed by a statement of its aims, agents and necessity. Then, the various types of educational institutions will be discussed, the educative value of youth movements indicated, and the influence of exterior agents such as the press, radio, and movies emphasized.

From 1760 to 1840, the English minority of *Bas-Canada*[1] practically controlled the destinies of Canada. It dominated in the executive as well as in the legislative council. Although, under the Constitution of 1791, the Catholic Canadians were a majority in the Quebec Legislative Assembly, the English minority were always opposed to educational legislation proposed by the French Canadians. The laws adopted by the Assembly were killed in the Council, and when these were referred to London, no answer was forthcoming. In 1800 the Protestant minority imposed upon the Catholic majority the so-called Royal Institution, a chain of schools, established to anglicize and proselytize the Canadians. The Catholic population received strict injunction from Bishop Hubert not to send their children to the neutral schools[2] of the Royal Institution. This Institution, having proved unsatisfactory, closed most of its schools in 1840.[3]

The *Acte d'Union* of 1840, imposed on Canadians and aimed at reducing their political influence, in the long run turned to the advantage of the French Canadians. Hippolyte Lafontaine, the political leader of *Bas-Canada,* favored and promoted the alliance with the sympathetic *Reformistes* of *Haut-Canada* under Sir

[1] In 1791 Canada was divided into two provinces known as *Haut-Canada* and *Bas-Canada.* The Province of Québec is in Bas-Canada.

[2] Neutral schools are schools where the Catholic religion is not taught.

[3] S. s. du Canada, Trois-Rivières, 1925, pp. 361-362.

Robert Baldwin. In 1846, Catholics dominated Parliament and obtained freedom of education for the regions bordering on the Saint Lawrence. At that time, each group, Catholic and Protestant, possessed and controlled its own schools. During the period of the Union, that is from 1840 to 1867, the Catholic majority treated the Protestant minority with justice and generosity.

Meanwhile, in 1859, the *Conseil de l'Instruction publique* was created. At first it consisted of both Catholics and Protestants, but soon the Catholics demanded that each sect decide on the choice of its respective text-books. In 1867, each Province had charge of its school organization together with the obligation to treat minorities with justice. Two years later, the *Conseil de l'Instruction publique* was divided into two committees, one Catholic, the other Protestant. The Council attends to program of studies, qualification of instructors and supervisors, choice of text-books, school regulations and normal schools.[4]

Although attempts have been made, by the *Bureau National d'Education* for instance, to seize the direction of education in order to place it into the hands of Parliament and take it away from the Provinces,[5] the law concerning public education in the Province of Quebec still respects the independence of local powers in the organization of instruction, guarantees the rights of the father of a family, safeguards those of the child, and bases all education on religious principles. While the Province of Quebec had had a compulsory school attendance law only since 1943, statistical data, collected by Dr. A. F. Argue and presented by Mr. Saint-Pierre for the nine provinces of Canada show Quebec ranking third on the list for school attendance, surpassed only by Ontario and British Columbia.[6]

The Province of Quebec is said to have given the Protestant minority a maximum of consideration, while the minorities in the other provinces are still awaiting justice.[7] For example, Mr. Raymond Denis, President of the *Association catholique franco-canadienne* of Saskatchewan, reported at the 1931 meeting of the

[4] *Ibid.*, pp. 363-366.

[5] S. s. du Canada, Montréal, 1923, p. 71.

[6] Arthur Saint-Pierre, "A Propos de supériorité," *L'Action Universitaire* (October, 1944), p. 52.

[7] S. s. du Canada, Trois-Rivières, 1925, p. 366.

Semaine Sociale, that in Manitoba the Catholics "solved" their educational problems in the same way that the Catholics did in the United States. They have to pay a double tax; the teaching of French language in their schools was suppressed and catechetical instruction relegated to half an hour after class. Worse still was the condition of the educational system in Saskatchewan. Here the State forbade religious to teach in their religious garb; the crucifix had to disappear, holidays could not coincide with holydays. Thus, schools had to be in session on All Saints' Day and Ascension Day. The French language was not to be taught during the first years of schooling.[8] Of course, since 1931 conditions have somewhat changed. In fact, Catholic schools supported by Federal funds are guaranteed by the Federal Constitution.

At the 1929 meeting of the Semaine Sociale, Canon Gaudreault asserted that the Catholic schools in French Canada have always been respected by the governing body and public men. This cooperation based on a cordial understanding between civil and religious authorities arouses the admiration and envy of other peoples. French Canadian children of the city, like their forefathers, speak the genuine French of France and often the correct English of Shakespeare; the rural inhabitants, in general, however, read and write French only. As elsewhere, the theologians and men of letters and science in French Canada are found not on the lower rung of the social ladder but among the upper classes of society. And it is in the French Canadian schools that this intelligentsia has been trained and given the principles which have preserved intact their moral formation. One likes to recall what LePlay wrote about French Canada, especially when he presented the French Canadians as a model nationality:

> Among the State-provinces of the British Confederation, the *Bas-Canada* is the one, which, by both its past and present organization of the family, of religion, of property, offers the best signs of a high destiny.[9]

---

[8] S. s. du Canada, Ottawa, 1931, pp. 308-310.

[9] S. s. du Canada, Chicoutimi, 1929, p. 69: "Parmi les Etats-provinces de la Confédération britannique, le Bas-Canada est celui qui, par son passé comme par l'organisation présente de la famille, de la religion et de la propriété, offre les meilleurs symptômes d'une haute destinée."

The Semaine Sociale made education its main interest in 1935. It was that year that Mr. Albert Rioux pointed out the triple aim of the French Canadian school:

> to develop the man in the child confided to its care, to render him more manly; "specify" these men according to their origin and their traditions, that is, make them Catholics and French Canadians; anchor them in their milieu and orientate them towards the trade or profession which they are called to exercise.[10]

To this, Mr. Rioux adds a triple reproach, namely,

> to have sacrificed too often education to instruction and thus fallen into the practice of much "stuffing the brain"; to have neglected the national education of children; to have uprooted them from the social milieu in which they were called to live.[11]

At the 1927 meeting in Quebec, Mr. C. J. Magnan, Supervisor of the schools of the Province of Quebec, had declared that education, in the widest acceptance of the word, aims at the integral and harmonious development of all the physical, intellectual and moral faculties given by God to man.[12] Again in 1935, the same Speaker stated that the program of studies in French Canada is favorable to this integral development. This program carries the expression of Christian sentiment; in fact, the first article is concerned with the teaching of religion. Then, besides the other current, secular subjects taught in all schools, there is inserted, beginning with the third year of the primary school and moving up to the eleventh year, a methodical program of domestic economy

[10] S. s. du Canada, Joliette, 1935, p. 76: "1. Développer l'homme dans les enfants qui lui sont confiés afin de les rendre plus hommes; 2. Spécifier ces hommes selon leur origines et leurs traditions, c'est-à-dire en faire des catholiques et des Français canadiens; 3. Les ancrer dans leur milieu et les orienter vers le métier ou la profession qu'ils sont appelés à exercer."

[11] *Ibid.*, p. 77: "1. D'avoir trop souvent sacrifié l'éducation à l'instruction et d'avoir érigé en système le bourrage de crâne; 2. D'avoir négligé l'éducation nationale des enfants; 3. De les avoir déracinés, du milieu social dans lequel ils étaient appelés à vivre."

[12] S. s. du Canada, Québec, 1927, p. 72.

to prepare young girls for their future duties as mistresses of homes.[13] The writer has seen at the Ecole Allion in Ville LaSalle a class of little girls of seven or eight, at work with knitting or needle work under the direction of a certain Sister Saint Marie-Monique. Without doubt, this procedure helps to develop a love for the "foyer domestique." The impetus given to domestic art in the primary schools and in the convents has been remarkable within the last twenty years. Mr. C. J. Magnan reported that in 1935 there were in the families of the Province of Quebec 80,500 spinning wheels and 52,000 looms in active service.[14]

The Canadian Semaine Sociale, and particularly its President, insist that the principal agents of education are the parents, then the Church and the State. The tradition of home education is long established, dating particularly from the period 1760 to 1840 when the French Canadians were without schools and the parents and the Church were the only teachers. Now the public organization of education in the Province of Quebec is based on liberty, but the rights of the family are recognized and respected. It is indeed the family which attends to the education of the child while he is still in the cradle; moral education begins when the parents resist the child's first caprice. Like Father Archambault and Father Louis Lalande, Bishop Papineau claimed that education begins at the birth of the child. Then the mind is like clay in the potter's hand receiving without resistance the forms one wishes to give it.[15] To show the incomparable power of the words or examples of parents on the soul of their children, Father Archambault related how the Magistrate Henri Rollet acquired his great spirit of charity and eminent social sense. The latter attributed these virtues to his mother who taught him to show his love of neighbor —his playmates—by playing the games they wished to play. When he asked: "When may I play what I wish?" he was answered: "When you are alone." And this lesson of self-forgetfulness was remembered until his dying day which occurred in 1935 at the age of seventy-three.[16] Thus the disciples of the Semaine Sociale

[13] S. s. du Canada, Joliette, 1935, p. 285.

[14] *Ibid.*, p. 286.

[15] *Ibid.*, p. 321.

[16] *Ibid.*, pp. 23-24.

know and teach that it is during the first years of life that the child forms habits which will help him to become later an ideal adolescent, an honest and steady youth, a mature man with a strong soul, tender heart, and well-balanced intelligence.[17] Children need their parents to live and learn to live properly on this earth and especially to attain their last end.

The Church, in the words of the late Father Louis Lalande, S.J., at the 1925 meeting of the Semaine Sociale, is a great educational power through the ministry of its priests, possessing as it does the right and the obligation to teach all ages and all ranks of society. Father Lalande proceeded to explain the three principal theaters for the exercise of its function of education: the catechism class, the pulpit, the confessional.[18]

The State, as still another agent of education, has the function to defend the educational rights of the family, to give assistance to confessional schools by providing for material needs and facilitating new projects for both Church and school. The State possesses also a repressive control on all schools in matters of hygiene and morals.[19]

The Semaine Sociale agrees that the education given in French Canada must be threefold: Christian, social and national. There are countless repetitions of the idea that religious education is by far the most important. Among the members of the Semaine Sociale, there is an evident opposition to any neutral schools or mixed schools where religious instruction is given apart from the regular schedule. They believe that all teaching, all the regulations of the school, the members of the staff, the program and books should be inspired by a Christian spirit, in such a way that religion may truly be the foundation and the crowning of all teaching. For example Mr. Henri Bourassa stated in 1920 that religious and moral education should form the basis of all teaching and should be the first subject listed on all programs. According to him, religion takes precedence over science. He also expressed concern about the overcrowding of programs with new subjects to the extent that the time allotted to religious instruction

---

[17] *Ibid.*, p. 266.

[18] S. s. du Canada, Trois-Rivières, 1925, pp. 399-400.

[19] S. s. du Canada, Ottawa, 1931, pp. 74-78.

has been shortened even in schools under the direction of religious orders. He further stated that drawing, geometry, chemistry, botany, grammatical analysis and so many other non-digested and undigested subjects are far less important in professional and social life than a sound formation of the will and character.[20] Judge Dorion in 1923 branded education without religion as a crime.[21] He warned the French Canadians to beware of their adversaries who try to unify their laws with the hope that some day, through the materialistic and intellectual infiltration of the Anglo-Saxon world, the French population will adopt or be forced to comply with laws and a mentality totally different from their own, in other words, to concede to neutral schools. He cited the instance of the French population of Louisiana which is almost submerged in the American mode of life.[22] At the 1925 meeting of the Semaine Sociale, the same speaker asserted that no human society was ever without religion. In fact, those societies have perished which after attaining great material prosperity gave up religion to revert to the worship of material goods. Judge Dorion deplored the fact that so many Catholics underestimate the importance of the teaching of religion. "We give too much attention to Holy Scripture and the catechism in our colleges," has been a common criticism of too many French Canadian Catholics.[23]

Although the French Canadians have been justly chided as being individualistic, still the Semaine Sociale emphasizes the importance of a "social" education. This appears throughout the conferences, but particularly at the Joliette meeting of 1935. Father Archambault at that time called social education the primordial work of the present time, the work upon which the future of Christian civilization depends. This social education will give individuals a true understanding of their duties toward their neighbors, of the practical value of collaboration, of the expediency of considering the common good before all else.[24] In the opinion of Msgr. Lebon, the school, as well as later occupa-

[20] S. s. du Canada, Montréal, 1920, p. 175.
[21] S. s. du Canada, Montréal, 1923, p. 79.
[22] *Ibid.,* p. 70.
[23] S. s. du Canada, Trois-Rivières, 1925, pp. 128-129.
[24] S. s. du Canada, Joliette, 1935, pp. 21-23.

tions, should contribute to this education in sociability by positing a true conception of life and by habituating youth to forgetfulness of self. The false hedonistic theory that pleasure, wealth, honor, luxury, and comfort constitute life should be denounced openly and the beauty of self-giving exalted.[25] At the same meeting Father Eustache Gagnon, C.S.C., emphasized the fact that social education is indispensable as a reaction against the egotism and individualism with which modern environment is over-saturated.[26] Again, Father Georges-Henri Lévesque, O.P., eminent sociologist of Laval University, denounces the social irresponsibility of French Canadians in their daily actions, in their business and political life. Still he cannot fully understand how anti-social manifestations persist in a century in which we find so many social vocations; one meets sociologists and new social institutions at every turn. But all this, he is convinced, is superficial. That social problems have never before been so assiduously discussed may be due to the fact that people did not "act soon enough yesterday . . . or are trying to elude the obligation of acting to-morrow." In his opinion, there are too many social organizations in French Canada; they harm one another and have become embarrassing to the good citizens whom they weary by taxing their leisure, devotedness, and wealth. It is evident, that notwithstanding their necessity, they are timely measures aimed at the conversion, transformation and orientation toward a better social life and a more determined and serious social education of the individualistic French Canadians.[27]

Without doubt, it is the obligation of the school, as well as of the family, to develop a sense of social responsibility in the child in order to combat that excessive individualism characteristic of the French population. Father Archambault affirms that the relations of man to man in French Canada lack the charity that should characterize the sons of the same Father.[28]

To cite but one possibility of the application of this social edu-

---

[25] *Ibid.,* p. 38.

[26] *Ibid.,* p. 132.

[27] *Ibid.,* pp. 309-310.

[28] Archambault, "Pour réaliser l'ordre nouveau," *L'Ordre Nouveau,* December 20, 1936, p. 1.

cation in French Canada, one may borrow Rene Guinette's idea of cooperation relative to academic circles. His thesis is that too many teaching orders remain indifferent to what the others are accomplishing, where they might instead fuse their ideals, techniques, and difficulties. To foster better relations he proposes the initiation of a congress of education for Quebec. Representatives from each order would convene and the resultant exchange of ideas would prove beneficial.[29]

The inclusion of "national" education in French Canada is in accordance with the thinking of the Semaine Sociale. Its Honorary President, Cardinal Villeneuve, declared in 1935 that "domestic, social, and *national* education form part of the integral education of Catholic youth."[30] Bishop Courchesne and Father Archambault hold similar views. A course given by Msgr. Lebon on the nature and aim of education at the 1935 assembly contains a comprehensive study of the various forms of education. For him, national education must be particularly French Canadian. He adds that students should be warned against that excessive nationalism which selects national interest as the supreme criterion of truth and goodness. The best tribute, he goes on to say, that one may give to his country is the preservation of its distinctive beauty, its family strength, the school, and professional, civil and political life.[31] Also in 1935, Mr. J. Donat Dufour, Professor at the Normal School of Sherbrooke, studied *civisme*. He defined it as teaching "the virtue of a good citizen, his zeal for public interest." After having quoted Mr. Montpetit's views concerning the expediency of the teaching of civics in the schools, he referred to practical methods. He recommended the publication of an elementary manual of social ethics in catechetical form. To foster a love of family, country, and region is another excellent means to teach *civisme*. Still another means advocated by Mr. Dufour is to organize the school like a true civil society, to offer pupils a concrete field for social action. The speaker reminded his audience of the insufficiency of civic education in French Canada.[32]

[29] René Guénette, "Un Nouvel aspect de la coopération," *L'Action Universitaire,* XI (October, 1944), pp. 18-22.

[30] S. s. du Canada, Nicolet, 1940, pp. 22-23.

[31] S. s. du Canada, Joliette, 1935, pp. 40-41.

[32] *Ibid.,* pp. 56-73.

At the Nicolet meeting of 1940, Father Paul-Emile Gosselin gave an enlightening course on *L'éducation nationale.* He defined civic education as that form of education which renders man apt to use the rights conferred upon him by his privilege of citizenship and accomplish the duties imposed by this privilege. That education which prepares youth to accomplish its obligations towards the nation and country is known as patriotic education. It can be best given if Catholicism is lived in its full intensity and amplitude. The study of history in the classroom will then resuscitate the national past with its timely lessons. Likewise the study of language will help build the foundation of an education truly national. Besides religion, language, and history, geography and the natural sciences will contribute their share. Even mathematical problems may be related to the life of the people. Patriotic songs will have their place in Canadian folklore. Various projects outside of the school program can also help to foster a national spirit: literary circles, leagues of good speech, habits of home purchase, patriotic societies, a juvenile grouping of the *Société Saint-Jean-Baptiste,* and finally, public demonstrations on national feast days.[33]

The press, that "handy refrigerator of the ideas of modern man," exercises a pernicious or a healthy influence on youth and informs citizens of many social and political problems. The radio, the "talking daily," whose action is even more sustained, more penetrating and more comprehensive than the news column, should, besides giving amusement, be an organ of instruction both intensive and extensive. The university, the "brain of the nation" as Cardinal Villeneuve called it, should help form sound public opinion. All these should contribute to "national" education the knowledge and expediency which will induce the French Canadians to practice social virtues of impartiality, love of public good, the will to collaborate for the common good, and to serve before being served.[34]

Education would be considered incomplete by the Semaine Sociale if it did not include agricultural training. From the very beginning the Semaine Sociale asserted the expediency of such

---

[33] S. s. du Canada, Nicolet, 1940, pp. 107-118.
[34] S. s. du Canada, Saint-Jean, 1942, pp. 210-212.

a vocational education. Mr. Georges Bouchard in 1924 cited a 1910 United States study showing that the income of farmers who had attended high school was found to be $304 more than that of the farmer who had attended only the district school; the difference indicates the need of rural schools particularly in French Canada.[35] Also in 1924 Father Favreau called to the attention of the French Canadians the wisdom of the Americans who organize their agricultural instruction on a university basis.[36]

At the 1928 meeting of the Semaine Sociale, after having defined ruralized education as the art of making one understand and love the farm, Msgr. Allard gives three ways of inculcating in children this love of the land: conversation about agriculture, rural-life literature, a resorting to the peculiar emulation that possession of and responsibility for certain goods will give children.[37] Mr. C. J. Magnan also believes that rural primary schools can foster farming vocations provided their programs be rural in content and the mentality and aspirations of the teaching body all tend towards one and the same goal, rural-mindedness.[38]

Another concern then of the French Canadians in general and the Semaine Sociale in particular is rural-life education. That is why we find in the Semaine Sociale descriptions of the accomplishments of schools established to re-ruralize French Canadians. In 1928, Mr. Henri Bois, Director of the School of Agriculture of Sainte Anne-de-la-Pocatière, described the three principal establishments for rural education: Macdonald College at Sainte-Anne-de-Bellevue; the School of Agriculture of Sainte-Anne-de-la-Pocatière, and the Institute of Agriculture at Oka.[39] Worthy of

---

[35] S. s. du Canada, Sherbrooke, 1924, pp. 264-265.

[36] *Ibid.*, p. 280.

[37] S. s. du Canada, Saint-Hyacinthe, 1928, p. 107.

[38] *Ibid.*, p. 125.

[39] *Ibid.*, pp. 143-144: Macdonald College, an Anglo-Protestant institution, founded in 1907 and affiliated to McGill University, is a private institution comprising a Department of Agriculture, a Normal School, and a Domestic Art School. The School of Agriculture offers two principal courses. After the four year course a Bachelor of Agricultural Science degree is given. Thenceforth if any Bachelor wishes to continue his studies he must register in the Graduate School. The two-year course is that of the Intermediate Schools. The college farm is used for extensive experimentation. The

mention also in this connection is the Ecole de Médicine vétérinaire of the Province of Quebec.[40]

In 1933, Msgr. Allard, Chaplain of the Ecole d'Agriculture of Sainte Martine, gave an enlightening course on *L'enseignement agricole moyen.* Citing the Intermediate School of Agriculture at Rimouski established in 1926, as a model for the bulk of the French Canadian population, he then described the second such school, Ecole Sainte Martine, founded in 1932, in the Province of Quebec. Attendance at the courses is of six months duration from the latter part of October until the end of April, for during that period, the farmers can do without the help of their sons. It is the hope of Msgr. Allard that this intermediate rural teaching will help increase the number of rural elite and develop a rural civilization which will have the opportunity of realizing legitimate ambitions.[41]

It is significant to note also that in 1935 a summer session of six weeks for rural teachers was inaugurated in Rimouski at the request of Bishop Courchesne and with the financial help of the Minister of Agriculture and the Provincial Secretarial Office. The courses include: general agriculture, rural and domestic economy, pedagogy and domestic hygiene.[42]

Besides rural education, the Semaine Sociale treats classical and higher education. Numerous are the classical colleges in the Province of Quebec but the French Canadians consider their

---

Institut agricole of Oka, founded in 1893, is a private institution under the direction of the Trappists fathers, and affiliated to the University of Montreal. Its program is similar to that of Macdonald College. Still another private institution intended to spread rural education in French Canada is the *Ecole supérieure d'agriculture* of Sainte-Anne-de-la-Pocatière founded in 1859. This private school, with its farm, forms the Department of Agriculture of Laval University. It follows the same program as the schools described above.

[40] Firmin Letourneau, "La Politique agricole," *Agriculture* (Montréal: Editions Fides, 1943), pp. 373-375: Since 1928, the *Ecole de Médecine vétérinaire* is under the direction of the Trappist Fathers of Oka. It is affiliated to the University of Montreal and has won recognition from the American Veterinary Medical Association. The course is of five years and leads to a doctorate.

[41] S. s. du Canada, Rimouski, 1933, pp. 174, 179.

[42] S. s. du Canada, Joliette, 1935, p. 87.

universities a notable accomplishment in the field of social education. As early as 1920, the Ecole des Sciences sociales, economiques, et politiques was established as a separate department at the University of Montreal by Mr. Edouard Montpetit with the approbation of Msgr. Gauthier, then Rector of the University. This Social Science School is typically French in origin. After three years in Paris, Mr. Montpetit with the collaboration of specialists was ready to launch his new undertaking.[43] Among the more distinguished chosen as professors at that time were: Janet, Levasseur, Albert Sorel, and Paul Leroy-Beaulieu. The subjects were grouped under sociology, economics, political science, and journalism.[44] In 1943, the Institut de Sociologie at the University of Montreal was founded as a center of scientific research. Its aim is to seek solutions for the social problems bearing on the milieu in which the University is called to exercise its intellectual activity. Mr. Arthur Saint-Pierre, Professor of the Social Science School, is director of this research center. Perhaps because of the conservatism of Quebec, only in 1932 did Laval University found a School of Social Sciences, and this was annexed to the Department of Philosophy. In 1938, this School became autonomous, under its present Director, the Reverend G. H. Lévesque, O.P. Cardinal Villeneuve has emphasized the necessity of universities and their social role:

> . . . We need universities, not to make of them laboratories of vain speculations, rich museums where one may store away on labeled shelves mummified systems. Our Catholic and French Canadian universities must lead our public thought, under pain of losing prestige. We look to them as our monitors: guides in the case of those who attend, and social guides for the ensemble of our people.[45]

---

[43] Interview with Mr. Edouard Montpetit at the University of Montreal, September 20, 1944.

[44] Edouard Montpetit, *Pour une doctrine* (Montréal: Librairie d'Action Canadienne-française, 1931), p. 240.

[45] S. s. du Canada, Saint-Jean, 1942, pp. 212-213: "Il nous faut des universités, non pour en faire des laboratoires de vaines spéculations, de riches musées où l'on puisse collectionner, en rayons à étiquettes, des systèmes momifiés. Nos universités catholiques et canadiennes-françaises doivent diri-

As has been previously noted, the Semaine Sociale abhors neutral schools. When the Government founded neutral technical and commercial schools, the French Canadians did not consider this initiative in harmony with Catholic principles. Father Joseph Ferland expressed this view at the 1931 meeting. He was aware, however, of the amelioration of the situation relative to the Ecole des Hautes Etudes Commerciales—a neutral school destined to give a solid professional education in commerce, finance and industry. Founded in 1907 by the Government, opened in 1910 and affiliated to the University of Montreal in 1915, its influence is on the whole beneficial. The neutral technical schools also, he noted, have improved somewhat. These schools, one in Montreal founded in 1907 and the other in Quebec in 1910, aim to prepare those destined to work in industries to reach commanding positions. In Quebec, a priest, designated by the Ordinary and attached to the school, gives lessons in religion to the students who wish to attend; Father Ferland claims that these courses should be compulsory.[46]

The Semaine Sociale lays great stress on the educational value of youth movements. In 1935, Father Oscar Bélanger, S.J., discussed at some length "scoutisme." The membership, numbering some 3,000,000, speaks favorably for the popularity of this institution; one finds scouts in both China and Japan; the Soviets bolshevized, Mussolini fascistized, and Hitler nazified them. In Canada, Father Bélanger tells us, Msgr. Gauthier was the first to bless *scoutisme* in his discourse in 1927. Bishop Cloutier and Bishop Comtois encouraged it emphatically, while Bishop Ross in 1927 declared it well adapted to the French Catholic culture of Canada. Specifically, it is truly a method of education which utilizes, encourages, develops, directs and elevates the natural desires of a boy thus enabling him to acquire habits of purity, loyalty and devotedness. Baden-Powell, its founder, designated five chief aims: formation of character, health, courtesy, service

---

ger notre pensée publique, sous peine d'être submergés. On attend d'elles des directives de vie, de vie personnelle pour ceux qui les fréquentent, de vie sociale pour l'ensemble de notre peuple."

[46] S. s. du Canada, Ottawa, 1931, p. 127, and *Almanach du peuple* (Montréal: Libraire Beauchemin, 1943), pp. 425, 435.

to one's neighbors, and the search for God.[47] The institution has its pledge, its principles, its laws;[48] it insists upon the three virtues, honesty, devotedness, purity, upon the proverbial daily good turn, and has worked out a marvelous organization to accomplish these aims. Naturally, in French Canada the scout movement has to be integrally and authentically Catholic. The little scout says, "Upon my honor, with the grace of God, I promise. . . ." A chaplain, who should be an intellectual and a psychologist, forms part of the troop; he is on occasions director of souls. The Scout-leader, too, must be possessed of a strong sense of spiritual values. The two should work towards the success of Catholic scoutism which at present is a form of Catholic Action in French Canada.[49]

Another institution of educational value alluded to in the first chapter is the *Association de la Jeunesse Canadienne-française* or briefly the A.C.J.C. As early as 1923, Father Plamondon, C.S.V. referred to the A.C.J.C. as a group comprising excellent young men intent on intellectual work and piety.[50] Canon LeBon feels that this work can best be accomplished by Study Clubs. A bachelor's degree is not all that is necessary in life, he goes on to say, but religious, moral, and social questions arise which can best be discussed and debated in Study Clubs.[51] Sister Gérin-Lajoie in 1935 sponsored the activity method in which each member has some responsibility in the organization. Thus members are expected to prepare individual treatment of problems, to exchange ideas and discuss the plans proposed. The subject matter of these discussions usually embraces religious and social questions. The Study Clubs are under the direction of a priest who corrects false opinions. The A.C.J.C. is responsible for numerous religious, national and social undertakings,[52] and for the maintenance of the traditional rights of French Canadians. An instance of this is the campaign it undertook to preserve the use of French in calling

---

[47] S. s. du Canada, Joliette, 1935, pp. 111-117.

[48] The pledge, the three principles, and law are given in the S. s. du Canada, Joliette, 1935, pp. 117-118.

[49] *Ibid.*, pp. 118-129.

[50] S. s. du Canada, Montréal, 1923, p. 215.

[51] S. s. du Canada, Québec, 1927, p. 104.

[52] S. s. du Canada, Joliette, 1935, pp. 166-184.

telephone numbers.[53] Moreover, the A.C.J.C., in the words of Judge Dorion, is a bulwark against falsehood, calumny and scandal. Its members form a moral militia and its works are widely known throughout Canada.[54] The A.C.J.C. had in 1935 four hundred and eighty-six study clubs in twenty-one dioceses.[55] In fact, Mr. Louis de G. Fortin, Professor of the Ecole d'Agriculture de Sainte-Anne, believes that the A.C.J.C. is the organism which is best prepared to undertake the rural reform movement.[56] At present, it publishes two periodicals: *Vivre* and *Le Semeur.*[57]

The *Jeunesse Ouvrière Canadienne* (J.O.C.), the *Jeunesse Agricole Canadienne* (J.A.C.), and the *Jeunesse Etudiante Canadienne* (J.E.C.) are classified among youth movements militating for social education in French Canada. The J.O.C. and the J.O.C.F., the young girls' section, founded in 1931 by Father Henri Roy, O.M.I., after extensive studies and much investigation on the condition of laboring youth in the slums of Montreal, are well suited to the needs of young Christian workers. The energetic Father Roy began this amazing work by talking to the leaders of "gangs" about their lives and soon had a number of converts, intent on their unfailing pattern: "See, Judge, Act." Father Roy, while in Belgium, was a student of Canon Cardijn, founder of the famous Jocist movement in that country.[58]

The journals of J.O.C. are four in number: *La Jeunesse ouvrière, Pour garder, Le Militant,* and *L'Aumonier jociste.* The services of the Jocists include: *Pré-Jocisme,* some ten summer camps, facilities for thrift, a Jocist calendar, publications such as *Faites ça . . . et vous vivrez, Pour aimer* and *Un problème et une solu-*

[53] Interview with Mr. Guy Vanier, July 5, 1944.

[54] S. s. du Canada, Joliette, 1935, p. 204.

[55] *Ibid.,* p. 165.

[56] S. s. du Canada, Rimouski, 1933, p. 117.

[57] S. s. du Canada, Joliette, 1935, p. 92.

[58] Leonard Austin, "Miracles in Manchester," *The Torch,* March, 1944, p. 16. The late Bishop Peterson of Manchester invited Father Roy to try his technique in his episcopal city. In four years the whole face of Manchester was changed, at least of the French-speaking population. Three times the Jocists held their meetings in the Provincial House of the Sisters of the Presentation of Mary in Hudson, New Hampshire, where they impressed the sisters with their piety.

tion. Besides issuing propaganda stamps, the J.O.C. of Montreal has a juridical service, the benefits of which are well recognized. Each of the ten Jocist federations has its medical center. That the movement has proved popular and effective is attested by the impressive marital ceremony of one hundred four couples at the 1939 Jocist Congress in Montreal.

Around the city of Joliette, the J.A.C. took its first roots. This was in 1933 with the approbation of Bishop Papineau. At first limited to the Diocese of Joliette, Jocist thought gradually spread throughout the Province. The diocese of Sherbrooke now has eleven Jocist cells of which two are of the J.A.C.F.; Bishop Gagnon officially authorized the J.A.C. in this diocese in 1935. The Secretarial Office of Sherbrooke also has a cell in the diocese of Saint-Jean of Quebec and one in West Canada. The diocese of Quebec and Rimouski are also organizing their rural youth.

The J.E.C., started in one of the French Canadian colleges, has since aroused the attention of many educators and of a large number of pupils. Its journal the *JEC* is widely read and appreciated. It has a monthly publication *Le Conquérant* for its directors and militants. In 1935 there were eight cells. Ottawa and Montreal have its feminine units known as the J.E.C.F. Among the services of the J.E.C. we note a Study Jecist Camp for militants, chaplains or future chaplains of various sections.

These youth movements whether Jocist, Jacist or Jecist, intensify their action on common elements such as: will to conquer, the apostolate of comrade to comrade, the use of concrete and realistic methods of investigation, and the concern of forming Christians imbued with a profound supernatural life. This type of social pedagogy, in the opinion of Father Donat Hénault, where the learned becomes educator is perfectly suited to the youth of French Canada,[59] and fullfills the wish of Pope Pius XI as expressed in *Quadragesimo anno:*

> In order to bring back to Christ these whole classes of men who have denied Him, we must gather and train from amongst their very ranks auxiliary soldiers of the Church, men who know well their mentality and their aspirations, and who with kindly fraternal charity

[59] S. s. du Canada, Joliette, 1935, pp. 105-108.

> will be able to win their hearts. Undoubtedly the first and immediate apostles of the workingman must themselves be workingmen, while the apostles of the craftsmen and merchants should themselves be of the same class.[60]

Besides studying the educational value of youth movements, the Semaine Sociale pass to a consideration of the influence of such agents as the press, the radio and the movie. "Her Majesty, the Press," as the famous journalist Stephane Lauzanne called it,[61] has always irresistibly influenced public opinion. The influence of the press on public opinion was recognized by Leo XIII.[62] Pope Pius X was willing to sell his pastoral cross and sacerdotal ornaments to save his journal. Benedict XV, when told by the Vicar General of Geneva of the urgent necessity of building a church replied: "No, no, do not build; first, you must assure and develop your paper, it is the most important activity."[63] Pius XI declares that the "work of the Catholic journal is indispensable and the most efficacious. It is a need of the time."[64] The press has been called the fourth power of the State, a power as cogent as the other three: the legislative, the executive and the judiciary.[65] At the 1930 meeting of the Semaine Sociale, Victor Barrette, editor of *Le Droit,* calls the press a formidable machinery, a "Fourth Estate" knowing neither boundaries nor customs. It is a "surpuissance" and today, he added, it is all-powerful in the service of lust. In years past, its glory was to stimulate political passions, today the pointing of false pleasures is its chief concern. The role of the newspaper is to educate; unfortunately it has turned into a school of scandal. Nor is the French Canadian press, the speaker continued, without defects.[66] As Mr. Omer Héroux had done, Father Gaudrault censures the party press when he advocates free press.[67]

---

[60] *Quadragesimo anno, op. cit.,* pp. 41-42.

[61] Alfred Labelle, "La Presse, puissance sociale," *L'Action Universitaire* October, 1944), p. 60.

[62] S. s. du Canada, Ottawa, 1931, p. 51.

[63] S. s. du Canada, Chicoutimi, 1929, p. 146.

[64] S. s. du Canada, Joliette, 1935, pp. 25-26.

[65] Labelle, *op. cit.,* p. 60.

[66] S. s. du Canada, Joliette, 1935, p. 216.

[67] S. s. du Canada, Ottawa, 1931, p. 52, and Chicoutimi, 1929, p. 211.

The radio is another influential agent of education. A newcomer to modern society, it has already invaded not only the city and the country, Victor Barrette declared, but even the street and the home. The radio has become today a musical press; tomorrow it will be a picture press. It is a school equally favorable to good and to evil, to beauty and ugliness, accessible to hearers of all age and condition. Mr. Barrette then described the typical radio program:

> With silvery voice, it [radio] announces the Semaine Sociale, and abruptly invites us to drink of the famous beer which . . . our great-grand-parents drank! With a golden voice it carries the talk of the Catholic Hour and with the same voice carries us off a few seconds later to a crowd of dancers "en nage" and of saxophones "en delire."[68]

There results from all this, the speaker claimed, a "defrenchifying" of the home that leaves behind an impression of animality, a frenzied search for noise, pleasure and money. The newspaper has one voice, the radio has thousands; the former distracts one the space of an hour, while the latter keeps one constantly in a world of dreams and songs, of prayers and pleasures. The radio becomes a newspaper, a concert hall, a pulpit; theaters all in one. It speaks all languages, and is understood by everyone. The press is of interest to adults only; the radio is open even to youngsters. To offset the pernicious influence of the radio, His Eminence Cardinal Villeneuve recommends crusades of all sorts to render the education derived from radio broadcasts artistic and moral; people must learn to choose programs that will preserve the Christian atmosphere of the home.[69]

The Semaine Sociale of 1929 referred to another exterior agent of education. Father Bissonnette, O.P., depicted realistically what

---

[68] S. s. du Canada, Joliette, 1935, pp. 218-219: "D'une voix d'argent, elle fait la réclame pour une Semaine sociale, et brusquement elle nous invite à boire cette fameuse bière que . . . ses arrière-grands-pères buvaient! D'une voix d'or elle porte le sermon de l'Heure catholique et de la même voix elle nous transporte, la seconde suivante, au milieu de danseurs en nage et de saxaphones en délire."

[69] *Ibid.*, pp. 219-220.

he calls the "cinéma de bas étage"—the vestibule of the houses of prostitution. He holds that this type of movie is on the borders of French Canada awaiting an opportunity to be installed. After mentioning the "cinéma de second ordre" for the lower rung of society, he describes the movie "à la mode" with its colossal ads. The evil of movies, the speaker explained, lies in the profound influences of those new ideas the falsity of which simple and honest souls do not surmise but which, nevertheless, attack the old traditional social French Canadian life.[70]

At the 1935 session of the Semaine Sociale, Mr. Barrette called the movie the "University of imbeciles," but admits with Cardinal Villeneuve and the Archbishop of Ottawa that it could become an intellectual, moral and religious activity in the hands of members of Catholic Action. The speaker then cited such dangers as: desertion of the home on the part of the mother; disobedience on the part of children; false notions of life for youth of all classes. Even the heads of families become humiliated when the average father is represented as a man without power and nobility. The evil movie, like an exploiter, is not a pedagogue and even less an educator. Mr. Barrette recommended that families be educated in their duties towards the press, the radio, and the movie. The good press is often not appreciated to its full extent. Again this or that broadcasting station would put an end to overdaring programs if a *Ligue de pères de familles* emphatically demanded it. The movies ought to be rigorously censored by professors and parents alike.[71]

In 1931, Mr. Leo Pelland approved of a law then in force which forbade children below sixteen years of age, accompanied or not, to attend movies, and which required a censor, appointed by the Province, to check on films, billboards, and ads in French Canadian dailies.[72]

Briefly, then, education in French Canada, while legally vested in the Province, is under the control of the Church through its representatives on the Catholic Committee of the *Conseil de l'Instruction publique*. Education proper begins in the home.

[70] S. s. du Canada, Chicoutimi, 1929, pp. 90-93.

[71] S. s. du Canada, Joliette, 1935, pp. 221-224.

[72] S. s. du Canada, Ottawa, 1931, p. 224.

French Canadians are convinced that it is precisely as educators that parents possess the force of authority, example and teaching. The task of education would be incomplete in French Canadian thought if it did not include in its system social, national, rural, classical and technical elements. All these should be taught in a strictly religious atmosphere, one that is favorable to the admiration, esteem and development of Christian virtues and especially of Christian piety. The priest's collaboration is an important factor in the development of such a system of Christian education. Because the natural propensity of man is satisfied by association, youth movements constitute remarkable and influential agents of social education and have become important in time and extensive in space. The French Canadians borrowed the scout movement from foreign sources but infused into it the supernatural element. Not content with indicating the pernicious influence which the press, radio and movie may exert, the Semaine Sociale has shown that these may be utilized as agents of social formation, as instruments of moral elevation, as armaments for waging the good fight.

CHAPTER VIII

THE SEMAINE SOCIALE AND THE ECONOMIC ORDER

Aware of the importance of the economic order, the Semaine Sociale has given ample time and space to the study of economic problems. In line with the teaching of this Catholic institution, this chapter will consider in turn the definition of economics, the meaning of capital, and the functions of the economic order. It will discuss labor conditions, possible solutions to labor problems, the rights and duties of employers and employees, the chief causes of present economic disorders, rural life in French Canadian traditions, and finally, the causes and remedies for farm desertion.

By the economic order the French Canadians in general and the Semaine Sociale in particular understand the essential establishment of equilibrium or balance between the goods of production and those of consumption. The Semaine Sociale represented by Father Adrien Malo, O.F.M. at the assembly of 1932 in Montreal, noted the distinction between economics and morality but does not exclude the latter from the former. The supposed opposition between business, ethics and Christian morals does not truly exist. Saint Thomas directly asks the question: "Is business illicit by the fact that it incites cupidity?" and answers: "No." Profit, the objective of exchange, although in itself constitutes nothing that is honest and necessary, still involves nothing bad or contrary to virtue." Thus, economics deals with wealth and its ability to satisfy the normal needs of humanity, and for that reason studies the different operations by which natural resources are adapted to these needs, attempting thereby to establish laws which would provide for the greatest temporal well-being.[1]

In the light of the above statements, the Semaine Sociale admits the expediency of capital, defining it as "every economic good, more or less considerable, destined by its nature to provide for new utilities."[2] Father Arthur Robert of Laval University, at

[1] S. s. du Canada, Montréal, 1932, pp. 290-291.

[2] *Ibid.*, p. 331.

the Ottawa assembly in 1922, cited various definitions: Karl Marx said "that only money or its equivalent acquired in a previous bargain is capital"; Block defined capital as "an accumulation of products destined for production"; Hervé Bazin, "a part of the produced wealth placed in reserve and dedicated to reproduction"; to Victor Brants it "comprises all the produced wealth destined by the proprietor to a new operation." Finally, to Adam Smith, it was "that part of the stock from which a gain may be derived." Father Robert then declared that capital is a means of production of great value; a form of savings, a precious instrument which contributes efficaciously to the betterment of societies.[3]

To prove the legitimacy of capital, Father Robert argues that the inequality of wealth is one of the conditions of social prosperity and is the fruit of the natural inequalities of which God is the author. Pius X condemns the opinion in the *Sillon* that "inequality of conditions is an injustice or at least a minor injustice."[4] According to Catholic doctrine, the legitimacy of capital is derived necessarily from the right to private property,[5] from the just price, the inequality of material conditions, and the social character of economic wealth.[6]

In the words of Pope Leo XIII, capital as something legitimate based on justice, has a triple role to perform. First in its relation to the social classes, it represents the elite, the privileged class, and as such must respect the human dignity of the laborer. Secondly, the capitalist must take into account the physical capacities of the worker and prevent injury to his health. Thirdly, it is the role of the capitalist to give sufficient wages to his workingmen. Again in the words of Father Robert, without capital art and science, progress and scientific discoveries would be impossible. On the other hand, capital can not accomplish its role without the cooperation of labor.[7] The speaker applies Saint Mark's statement: "What therefore God has joined together, let no man put asunder" to the relations of capital and labor.[8] Similarly Leo XIII:

---

[3] S. s. du Canada, Ottawa, 1922, p. 50.

[4] *Ibid.*, p. 54.

[5] *Ibid.*, p. 55.

[6] S. s. du Canada, Montréal, 1932, p. 333.

[7] S. s. du Canada, Ottawa, 1922, pp. 62-66.

[8] *Ibid.*, p. 47.

"there can be no capital without labor, and no labor without capital."[9]

Father Lamarche, O.P., expressed the thought of the Semaine Sociale when he noted the social benefits of capital to humanity in general, namely, the introduction of modern comforts on a large scale and the linking of the past to the present and of the present to the future. He goes on to say that to cry: "Death to capitalism!" is as nonsensical as to cry "Death to man!" Mr. André Rousseau sees in man's ability to acquire capital "one of the attributes which gives man his prominent place in the order of creation."[10] To prove that capitalism need not be abusive, the late Father Louis Lalande, S.J., in a conference given at the 1922 session of the Semaine Sociale, reviewed in detail Léon Harmel's life as a Catholic employer. He first notes the three loves that filled the life of this industrialist: love of family, love of workers and, as source and inspiration of the first two, love of God. As early as 1797, the Harmel family established their factory at Val-des-Bois. Preceded by two generations of model employers, Léon Harmel took over the administration of Val-des-Bois in 1854. He soon became known as its "Bon Père." Upon his death at the ripe age of eighty-seven, the Bishop of Nice commented on the main objectives of all the activities of this renown Catholic employer:

> The work of Léon Harmel . . . may be summarized in the name which has attached to his person: the good Father Harmel. It is not only his seventy odd children, grand-children, great-grand-children, thirty-five of whom are fighting on the battlefields, . . . who have given him this name, filling every word with the love, veneration, gratitude, filial pride of three and four generations, . . . but the one thousand two hundred workingmen of Val-des-Bois, of whom he had established a second vast family. . . . To have widened the intimate circle of the Christian family, extending it from the home to the factory, from the domestic to the social order, that is his glorious and fecund work.[11]

[9] *Ibid.*, p. 67.

[10] S. s. du Canada, Montréal, 1932, p. 338.

[11] S. s. du Canada, Ottawa, 1922, pp. 282-286: "L'oeuvre de Léon Harmel, . . . se résume dans le nom désormais inséparable du sien: le Bon Père Harmel. Ce ne sont pas seulement ses soixante-dix enfants et arrière-petits-

For the workingmen, Léon Harmel founded cooperatives, *caisses de chômage,* bureaus of high finance, and attended even to the details of their intimate life. For example, at one time, as he was doing his rounds of inspection he came to a laborer with a bandaged hand. After inquiry about the accident, employer and employee, like father and son, left the shop together to go see a doctor.[12] His benevolent activities are too numerous to enumerate here; suffice it to quote six lines of his will which stand out as a living lesson to the industrial and laboring world:

> In whatever position you may be, love the poor. Whether happy or unhappy, give yourself to your suffering brothers.
>
> May your heart never be poisoned by hatred or envy.
>
> Love my dear workers; they were my children; take over my paternity; continue to bring my children to God and to do them good.[13]

His last advice to his sons follows:

> Above all respect in the worker the dignity of the man and of the Christian. I always said that the social question is just as much a question of dignity as one of wages; and the more I live, the more events confirm this belief. . . . Notwithstanding many apparent miseries, it is in the popular soul that one finds reserves of social salvation, because labor, the austerity of life and suffer-

---

enfants (dont 35 combattent sur nos champs de bataille et dont plusieurs y sont tombés glorieusement) qui lui donne ce nom avec l'accent qu'y savent mettre l'amour, la vénération, la reconnaissance, la fierté filiale de ces trois, de ces quatre générations, . . . Ce nom de père lui avait été donné par les 1200 ouvriers du Val-des-bois, dont il avait su se faire une seconde et vaste famille. . . . Elargir le cercle intime de la famille chrétienne, l'etendre du foyer à l'usine, de l'ordre intime à l'ordre social, voilà son oeuvre glorieuse et féconde."

[12] *Ibid.,* p. 293.

[13] *Ibid.,* p. 295: "Dans quelque position que vous soyez, aimez les pauvres. Heureux ou malheureux, donnez-vous vous-même à vos frères souffrants.

"Que votre coeur ne soit jamais empoisonné par la haine ou l'envie.

"Aimez mes chers ouvriers; ils étaient mes enfants. Vous reprendrez ma paternité; vous continuerez à les porter vers Dieu et à leur faire du bien."

> ing of all kinds are the greatest force to elevate humanity towards God. . . .
>
> Teach your children that the Incarnate Word loved the workers such that he wished to belong socially to their class. It would be wounding Him to the heart to scorn those whom he loved more than the others.[14]

Bishop Decelles of Saint Hyacinthe, at the 1937 opening session of the Semaine Sociale in that city, lauded contemporary industrialists in the persons of the Casavant brothers, Samuel and Claver, world famous manufacturers of organs. They always paid high wages to their employees; helped them to build a home in the vicinity of their workshop, in a word, were eminently religious and charitable. It was a custom with Mr. Claver, whenever he returned from some night trip, to go to the Cathedral for the seven o'clock mass and his daily Communion. During the last year of his life he spent some $12,000 for the missions and for the poor of Saint-Hyacinthe. The Casavant brothers could easily have become millionaires, but Mr. Claver did not even possess an automobile. Samuel, too, was a devout Christian, very influential in movements for temperance and education. Claver was a true saint and an amiable saint. In short, Bishop Decelles concluded, these two industrialists were without realizing it living incarnations of the doctrine enunciated in the encyclicals of Leo XIII and of Pius XI on the labor question.[15]

Again at the meeting of Chicoutimi, Father Jean Bergeron cited eminent industrialists such as Wilson in South America, Ford in the United States, and Lacroix in the Province of Quebec, as employers who still "render to God what belongs to God, to so-

---

[14] *Ibid.*, pp. 295-296: "Avant tout, respectez dans l'ouvrier la dignité de l'homme et du chrétien. J'ai toujours dit que la question sociale est autant une question de dignité que ce salaires; et plus je vais, plus les événements me confirment dans cette pensée. . . . Malgré bien des misères apparentes, c'est encore dans l'âme populaire que se trouvent les réserves du salut social, parce que le travail, l'austérité de la vie, la souffrance sous toutes ses formes sont les plus grands ressorts qui élèvent l'humanité vers Dieu. . . .

"Apprenez à vos enfants que le Verbe incarné a tellement estimé les travailleurs qu'il a voulu être socialement de leur classe. Ce serait le blesser au coeur que de mépriser ceux qu'il a aimés plus que les autres."

[15] S. s. du Canada, Saint-Hyacinthe, 1937, p. 15.

ciety what belongs to society and to workingmen what belongs to workingmen."[16]

It was mentioned above that the economic order consists in the equivalence between the goods of production and those of consumption. Production, then, in the thinking of the Semaine Sociale, is a means, not an end in itself. It aims to afford consumers the satisfaction of normal needs.[17]

Pope Leo XIII summarizes the duties of workers in reference to production in his encyclical *Rerum novarum* and the Semaine Sociale conforms to this teaching:

> . . . Religion teaches the laboring man and the workman to carry out honestly and well all equitable agreement freely made, never to injure capital, nor to outrage the person of an employer; never to employ violence in representing his own cause, nor to engage in riot and disorder; and to have nothing to do with men of evil principles, who work upon the people with artful promises, and raise foolish hopes which usually end in disaster and in repentance when too late.[18]

If the process of production supposes the loyal and generous collaboration of workingmen, this collaboration in turn presupposes perfect loyalty and a sense of moral value in the employer.

Exchange, as the second function of the economic order, through the merchant plays an important role in modern industry. The function of the merchant is to bring the finished product to the consumer. As long as the merchant respects the laws of a just price[19] and of legitimate gains without committing any injustice, he may, through his professional ability, his foresightedness and prudence, his administrative powers, realize an honest fortune.[20]

The cycle of all economic activity finds its ultimate point in consumption, the third function of the economic order. The consumer then, in the words of Father Edmour Hébert, plays a role

[16] S. s. du Canada, Chicoutimi, 1929, p. 54.

[17] S. s. du Canada, Saint-Hyacinthe, 1928, pp. 37-39.

[18] *Rerum novarum, op. cit.,* p. 12.

[19] Father Gilles Marchand, O.M.I., gave a masterly course on *Bénéfices et juste prix* in 1925. Cf. S. s. du Canada, Trois-Rivières, 1925, pp. 167 ff.

[20] S. s. du Canada, Saint-Hyacinthe, 1928, pp. 42-43.

of grave consequences in the economic drama. The Church has grasped the import of the consumer's responsibilities in the economic order and for that reason recommends that he be moderate in the use of worldly material goods. In fact, it is the consumer who orientates production and determines the nature and the quality of products. If stores are filled with articles of luxury, comfort, show, fantasy, the situation is due to the excessive demands of the consumer, to his useless squandering, to his foolish spending. Thus, the relation of economics to morality is made manifest. It is the teaching of the Church, Father Hébert holds, that contributes to the maintenance and harmonious development of the economic order: the producer by intelligent methods of production; the merchant by honest sales; and the consumer by restraint and wise moderation.[21]

That production in particular and the economic order in general may not be hampered by working conditions, the various phases of the latter should be studied with a view to remedying certain situations. This the Semaine Sociale has done, proposing special reforms for the French Canadian population.

The observance of Sunday rest and the benefits derived therefrom have already been discussed. The hours of work enter also into consideration. Mr. Arthur Saint-Pierre was the first to study *La Journée de travail* and it is from this masterly course that one may gather conclusive information. He readily admitted that this question is one of the most complex and most controversial ever met with in social economy and reverts to *Rerum novarum* for the doctrine concerning hours of labor:

> Daily labor, . . . must be so regulated that it may not be protracted during longer hours than strength admits. How many and how long the intervals of rest should be, will depend upon the nature of the work, on circumstances of time and place, and on the health and strength of the workman.[22]

Mr. Saint-Pierre gave the history of daily labor.[23] In 1889, Com-

[21] *Ibid.*, pp. 45-46.

[22] *Rerum novarum, op. cit.*, p. 26.

[23] S. s. du Canada, Ottawa, 1922, pp. 86-111.

missioner Freed's report to the government alluded to ten hours as constituting a day's work; it also mentioned the fact that employees in cotton mills worked thirteen or fourteen hours, whereas those employed in the houses of fashion were victims of "veillées meurtrières" and clerks in stores started their day at 5:30 a. m. to end it at ten or eleven at night. In 1922 Provincial Laws were put into effect and limited a week's work to sixty hours, sometimes even to fifty-five hours. With the coming of the International Organization of Labor the eight-hour day was definitely approved, although, to be sure, this limitation has not as yet met with world-wide recognition.[24] The benefits to be derived from such a legislation are important enough to be enumerated: advantages of health; opportunities for a more intensive family life than would otherwise be possible; facilities provided for self-instruction, for social activities, for the achievement of one's role as a genuine citizen. Some advocates of the reduction of hours of work consider this limitation a remedy for the unemployment plague of depression years.[25] Msgr. Eugène Lapointe in 1922, while speaking of the pulp industry in Chicoutimi, declared that the laborers in this industry never work longer than eight hours a day.[26] Mr. Pierre Beaulé, President of the C.C.T.C. at the popular meeting of 1932 proposed as a solution to the unemployment problem a five-hour working day.[27]

Conditions of work are also the especial concern of the Semaine Sociale. Dr. Hector Palardy gave an enlightening course entitled *Le Travail industriel et son hygiène* at the 1922 meeting in Ottawa. He advocated a rotation of occupations to offset the evils consequent upon repeated muscular effort and drudgery,[28] and warned against harmful industries, such as those in which dangerous substances, explosives, corrosives, and solid, liquid or gaseous poisons are manipulated. He also recommended filtration of air, ventilation, moderate temperature, sufficient lighting, proper nourishment, cleanliness, hygienic clothing, the use of respiratory ap-

---

[24] *Ibid.*, pp. 96-100.
[25] *Ibid.*, p. 101.
[26] *Ibid.*, p. 145.
[27] S. s. du Canada, Montréal, 1932, p. 369.
[28] S. s. du Canada, Ottawa, 1922, p. 72.

paratus when necessary, and suitable measures against accidents. To all this Dr. Palardy added that the employer should help establish, preserve or reestablish the "moral health" of his employees.[29] Mr. Antonio Perrault held similar views concerning hazardous work. The employer, he said, should foresee the habitual and possible causes of accidents. He should avert them by particular supervision and special precautions.[30] Very early the Semaine Sociale realized that child labor is detrimental to children and society at large and voiced on several occasions its opinion on the subject. In 1920, Mr. Arthur Saint-Pierre reported that the census of 1911 indicated a little more than 35,000 children of both sexes under fourteen years of age working for wages.[31] Father Edmour Hébert recommended the preservation of childhood, "for just as rough weather destroys the buds in spring, so too, an early experience of life's hardships blights the young promise of a child's powers and makes any real education impossible."[32] Mr. Edouard Montpetit mentioned the necessity of legislative intervention to forbid the labor of children under sixteen.[33] Father Henri Gauthier, in turn, painted a graphic picture of the young working girl and of the grave moral and physical consequences resulting from this situation.[34] At the 1923 assembly of the Semaine Sociale, Mr. George Pelletier disapproved of child labor as a means of increasing the family budget.[35] That same year Mr. Saint-Pierre listed the pernicious consequences of such premature work: physical harm, intellectual and moral "flétrissement," obliteration of all prospects for economic and social advancement.[36]

The Semaine Sociale is also aware of the disasters connected with wide-spread woman labor. In 1920, Mr. Saint-Pierre reported an increase of woman labor from one hundred eleven per thousand

---

[29] *Ibid.*, pp. 77-85.
[30] *Ibid.*, p. 195.
[31] S. s. du Canada, Montréal, 1920, p. 28.
[32] *Rerum novarum, op. cit.*, p. 26.
[33] S. s. du Canada, Montréal, 1920, p. 92.
[34] *Ibid.*, pp. 125-126.
[35] S. s. du Canada, Montréal, 1923, pp. 94-95.
[36] *Ibid.*, p. 130.

in 1901 to one hundred forty-three in 1911.[37] That woman should not be identified with man from an intellectual, physical and social point of view was Father Hébert's belief.[38] In 1920, Mrs. Gérin-Lajoie stated that in French Canada "the married woman who works is still an exception."[39] Dr. Palardy brought out the fact that woman, created by God for her role of mother, possesses a notably different physiology than that of man and thus in the employment of woman due consideration should be paid to this difference.[40] Miss Marie-Claire Daveluy, at the 1922 assembly in Ottawa, in her study of *Les Conditions morales de l'usine,*[41] deplored the shame and the "misère immeritée" of the women compelled to work in factories. The exploitation of their physical weaknesses, their moral distress, another destitution, are only one step removed from the cruelties of the sweatshop system.[42] Consequently Georges Goyau exclaimed: "Why, alas, do we not succeed in earning all our bread in all the sweat of our brow?"[43] Mr. Pelletier was likewise aware of the disastrous results occasioned by woman labor: the home remains without guardianship, the children without supervision, the house becomes neglected, meals remain unprepared.[44] The disorganization and the dispersion of the family, in the opinion of Mr. Saint-Pierre, are often the first consequences of the present industrial system.[45]

From the numerous references made to just wages it may be inferred that the Semaine Sociale is greatly concerned about remuneration for labor. This should "be enough to support the wage-earner in reasonable and frugal comfort."[46] A just wage, in the words of Msgr. Wilfrid Lebon, is one that represents the value of labor. However, the labor of the married man has not

---

[37] S. s. du Canada, Montréal, 1920, p. 28.
[38] *Ibid.,* p. 84.
[39] *Ibid.,* p. 105.
[40] S. s. du Canada, Ottawa, 1922, pp. 73-74.
[41] *Ibid.,* pp. 267-281.
[42] *Ibid.,* p. 270.
[43] *Ibid.,* p. 272.
[44] S. s. du Canada, Montréal, 1923, p. 94.
[45] *Ibid.,* p. 129.
[46] *Rerum novarum, op. cit.,* p. 27.

only an individual but a family value.[47] Father Hébert also considered the wage question as vital because it affects those intimate relations indispensable to the preservation of social peace.[48] Mrs. Gérin-Lajoie deplored the insufficiency of women's wages in industries as well as in stores.[49] Very different is Mr. Hogue's opinion about wages:

> Our fathers, with thirty cents a day, reared a family of twenty-six children. Today, with a starvation wage we [French Canadians] can bring up twelve. In the United States, high wages go to the care of a litter of puppies.[50]

Mr. Saint-Pierre, on the other hand, sponsored high wages. If capitalism as constituted today does not kill poverty, then poverty will kill it. Eminent men of the United States have understood this situation, Mr. Saint-Pierre believed, and thus formed the "school of high wages."[51] He cited Ford saying, "If it is proper for a manager to endeavor to derive from his industry the highest possible dividends, it is equally proper that this industry pay the highest possible wages."[52]

Pope Pius XI in *Divini Redemptoris* taught that the worker must, by his family wages, be assured of the sustenance of his own life and that of his family; he must be able to acquire a reasonable amount of goods, provide for the future, become a proprietor, and attain a degree of well-being and culture that will favor the practice of virtue.[53]

Against the raw labor contract, the Semaine Sociale has an

---

[47] S. s. du Canada, Montréal, 1932, p. 170.

[48] S. s. du Canada, Montréal, 1920, p. 73.

[49] *Ibid.,* p. 108.

[50] S. s. du Canada, Québec, 1921, p. 351: "Nos pères avec trente sous par jour élevaient une famille de vingt-six enfants. De nos jours, avec un salaire de famine nous en élevons douze. Aus Etats-Unis, avec de gros salaires, on élève des petits chiens."

[51] S. s. du Canada, Montréal, 1932, pp. 147-151.

[52] S. s. du Canada, Montréal, 1923, p. 139: "S'il convient qu'un gérant s'efforce de faire rendre à son industrie les plus forts dividendes possibles, il convient également que cette industrie paie les plus forts salaires possibles."

[53] S. s. du Canada, Sherbrooke, 1938, p. 414.

opinion to offer. It agrees with Msgr. Pottier's definition that, "it is an onerous and bilateral contract by means of which the workman rents his labor for wages."[54] In 1922, the labor contract in the Province of Quebec, as formulated in the Civil Code, gave rise to severe criticism on the part of Mr. Edouard Montpetit. These were repeated by Mr. Léon-Mercier Gouin at the Ottawa meeting.[55] Fortunately, the 1934 Provincial Law known as the *Extension juridique du contrat de travail* gives civil authority the power to bind all employers of a given region and for a certain type of work to a labor contract which imposes a determined wage. Thus, this wage becomes the just wage, not only because it is in conformity with the decisions of both employers and employees, but also because it is the legal wage.[56]

At the Trois-Rivières Assembly of 1925, Father Emile Cloutier explained the conditions required to make a labor contract just. First, the labor contract must be signed; secondly, the parties must freely adhere to it and with equal independence; and lastly, they must fulfill the obligations which they have freely accepted.[57]

It is somewhat significant that the Semaine Sociale devoted only one study to the problem of unemployment. In the study, made in 1932, Mr. Gérard Tremblay, *sous-ministre* of labor, expatiated in the light of *Quadragesimo anno* on the causes and remedies of unemployment. With regard to the extent of unemployment, Mr. Tremblay stated that the unemployed had become the "man of the day, . . . the man of fashion." Even during normal and prosperous periods the number of unemployed is remarkable. Incidentally, the writer while in Montreal was impressed by the large number of men seated in Viger Park at all hours of the day. According to the report of the *Bureau Internationale du Travail,* Canada in 1932 had 500,000 unemployed. Mr. Tremblay then went on to explain that he would not attempt to give all the causes

---

[54] S. s. du Canada, Québec, 1921, p. 179.

[55] S. s. du Canada, Ottawa, 1922, pp. 239-247.

[56] J. R. Villeneuve, "Le sens social," *La Vie des communautés religieuses,* December 31, 1934, p. 15.

[57] S. s. du Canada, Trois-Rivières, 1925, p. 190.

of unemployment.[58] Among the most potent of the moral causes he included state greed for gain, rivalry for speedy profit, and unbridled speculation. In the social order the causes are: disorganized social institutions, individualism, overproduction, abuse of credit, monetary problems, commercial difficulties, low wages, machinism, rural exodus, woman labor and seasonal employment. As remedies he proposed public works, reduction of daily working hours, limitation of child and old age labor, a return to the farm, unemployment insurance, labor insurance and directed economy. Mr. Tremblay concluded his course by attempting to convince his auditors that above all light on current social problems must come "from Rome, the See of the Vicar of Jesus Christ, the great friend of workers and the Master of human society!"[59]

To better labor conditions the Semaine Sociale has solutions to propose through its representative, Mr. Arthur Saint-Pierre, who discussed at length *La triple participation ouvrière* in a course given at the Trois-Rivières meeting of 1925. This discussion dealt with the profit-sharing, management-sharing and partnership contract in the industry in which a workingman is employed. Profit-sharing, the speaker contended, offers a limited rate of interest only, but it fosters the stabilization of the personnel and helps create cordial relations between employer and employee. In Canada, thirteen experiments were made in profit-sharing before 1918, eight of which were abandoned. Profit-sharing was said to have been instituted to prevent an increase of wages.[60] To conclude, the speaker was not over-enthusiastic about this method of bettering labor conditions.

The second form of labor sharing, known as management-sharing, aims to establish collaboration between labor and capital in order to promote their common interests. Mr. Saint-Pierre declared that its world-wide adoption would amount to a revolution. It is a form of industrial democracy, wholly an employer's

---

[58] Mr. Tremblay tells of an expert German who found as many as two hundred thirty-five causes of unemployment. Cf. S. s. du Canada, Montréal 1932, p. 101.

[59] *Ibid.*, pp. 104-139.

[60] S. s. du Canada, Trois-Rivières, 1925, pp. 207-212.

initiative, originating in Berlin in 1879 under a German industrialist Heinrich Freese. In 1885, Léon Harmel established management-sharing in his factory at Val-des-bois. In Canada the movement has taken the form of enterprise councils.[61]

Partnership contract, the third form of labor sharing, may be individual or collective. It is individual when the workers hold, each in his own name, one or more shares in the firm which hires them. It is collective when the personnel of a company, joined in a cooperative society, collectively possess a more or less considerable part of the company's capital. Mr. Saint-Pierre questioned the prudence of a laborer who confides his savings in the same institution in which he is employed. Should the institution close its door, the laborer would be without both wages and savings.

The results thus far acquired by these three forms of labor sharing are considerable, especially in Europe, and open a path to a possible solution of the labor problem.[62]

The family allowance, discussed in the chapter on the family, constitutes another answer to the economic question relative to family wages. We find allusions to its expediency as early as 1922. Father Cloutier cited Mr. Joya of Grenoble initiating monthly allowances for fathers having children under thirteen and gave evidence in support of the new procedure.[63]

Still another solution to the economic problem proposed by the Semaine Sociale is state intervention. Canon Harbour summarized the important points on this question at the Saint-Jean meeting in 1942. The mission of the State, he said, is to protect private property and savings; to establish conditions of labor favorable to the moral and physical health of workingmen. These comprise: Sunday rest, limitation of hours of labor, prevention of child labor, protection of working women, just wages, and social insurance.[64] Leo XIII demanded state intervention in the name of the common good and particularly for the protection of the

---

[61] *Ibid.*, pp. 212-229.

[62] *Ibid.*, pp. 229-234.

[63] S. s. du Canada, Ottawa, 1922, p. 167.

[64] S. s. du Canada, Saint-Jean, 1942, pp. 190-191.

laboring class. He mentioned the following cases which interest the public as well as individuals:

> . . . that peace and good order should be maintained; that family life should be carried on in accordance with God's laws and those of nature; that Religion should be reverenced and obeyed; that a high standard of morality should prevail in public and private life; that the sanctity of justice should be respected, and that no one should injure another with impunity. . . .[65]

Mr. Alfred Charpentier recommended the enactment of State legislation for the Province of Quebec, that would extend professional organizations for employers as well as for employees, by legalizing such organization and compelling registration of all those interested in the industry.[66] Professional organizations as a solution to the economic problem will be discussed in a separate chapter.

The French Canadians and the followers of the Semaine Sociale recognize the significance of cooperatives in the solution of their economic problems. Thus in 1937 they devoted an entire week to their study. By cooperatism, they understand the doctrine of those who see in cooperation a means of remedying the ills occasioned by an individualistic and capitalistic regime. Father Archambault, at the opening session quoted Bishop Decelles' definition of economic cooperation: "every social organization which aims, if not to eliminate, at least to reduce the number and the profit of the intermediate agents either in the interest of the producers or in the interest of the consumers."[67] Father Lucien Beauregard says

---

[65] *Rerum novarum, op. cit.*, pp. 22-23, and S. s. du Canada, Montréal, 1932, p. 276.

[66] S. s. du Canada, Montréal, 1932, p. 365.

[67] S. s. du Canada, Saint-Hyacinthe, 1937, p. 26: "Toute organisation sociale qui vise, sinon à éliminer, du moins à réduire le nombre et le profit des intermédiaires, soit dans l'intérêt des producteurs, soit dans l'intérêt des consommateurs."

Le Conseil Supérieur de la Coopération for the Province of Quebec was established in 1939 largely through the efforts of Father G. H. Lévesque, O.P. The Council publishes an official bi-monthly periodical entitled *En-*

that

> cooperation in the economic order means the placing in common of organized efforts with a view to realizing through the activity of an association based on justice and charity, that sufficiency of material goods the use of which is indispensable to man for the practice of virtue.[68]

The cooperative principles aim at the diffusion of profits rather than their concentration in the hands of a restricted number of individuals.[69] In the words of Father Armand Malouin, a cooperative is a

> society of persons who in the production, processing, sale or purchase, consumption of merchandise . . . or the use of credit, do away with the services of the usual middlemen—the merchants, industrialists, or bankers—with the objective of keeping for themselves the profits which would ordinarily revert to the middlemen.[70]

At the 1940 meeting of Nicolet, Mr. Leopold Paquin referred to cooperation as "the art of associating with other individuals to help them as well as oneself," a situation from which the motto "un pour tous, tous pour chacum" is derived. But to take part in

---

semble! Moreover, the University of Ottawa offers correspondence courses on cooperation. Twice a month the student receives for study the publication of a course, some sixteen pages in length. There are also questions to be answered. Twelve such lessons are sent and studied before a final examination may be taken to obtain a diploma. These courses are under the direction of Father Gustave Sauvé, O.M.I.

[68] *Ibid.*, p. 36: "La coopération dans l'ordre économique signifie la mise en commun d'efforts organisés en vue de réaliser, par le jeu d'une association faite de justice et de charité, cette suffisance des biens matériels dont l'usage est indispensable à l'homme pour pratiquer la vertu."

[69] *Ibid.*, p. 51: For detailed principles and applications of cooperatives in all its forms see H. H. Hannam, *La Coopération* (Ontario: The United Farmers of Ontario, 1937); Gérard Filion, *Notions élémentaires de coopération* (Montréal: La Librairie de L'U.C.C., 1939-1940); *La Coopérative de consommation* (Québec: Le Conseil Supérieur de la Coopération); and *Cercle d'étude* (Sainte-Anne-de-la-Pocatière: Ecole Supérieure des Pêcheries).

[70] S. s. du Canada, Saint-Hyacinthe, 1937, pp. 115-116.

an organization which requires one to think of others as well as oneself demands an upright mind and a sense of Christian responsibility, a dread of natural egotism, a sense of social duty and the practice of charity.[71]

The Church encourages this form of organization because it is an efficacious means of alleviating the lot of the laborer and the farmer by an equitable distribution of public health. In fact, the Church looks to cooperation to uproot individualism and to substitute in its stead the Christian practice of justice and charity, in a word, to achieve that new social order conducive to peace in the reign of Christ.[72]

The advantages of cooperation in general are many: availability of credit, reduction of purchase prices in the commodities of consumption, a better economic yield in production, the suppression of useless intermediate agents, an increase in gain on the sale of classified products. When a cooperative functions through the sole initiative of its members without subsidies from the State, the cooperators are easily convinced that they can manage their business and are truly the moulders of their common prosperity. The particular advantages are the elimination of individual patronal enterprise, the provision for urgent needs in credit, and production to serve the interests of the consumers. Above all, cooperatives exist to serve the people, not to pile up high dividends on real or fictitious capital.[73]

Father Philibert Grondin, diocesan missioner of Quebec, enumerated the qualities required of a true cooperator: honesty, patience, perseverance, humility, generosity, faithfulness; punctuality, discipline and discretion;[74] and Esdras Minville listed: a sense of one's social duties, individual and collective responsibilities, initiative, and a spirit of discipline.[75]

The first theorizers on cooperation were Robert Owen, a rich English industrialist and philanthropist of world-wide reputation,

---

[71] S. s. du Canada, Nicolet, 1940, p. 44.

[72] *Ibid.*, p. 47.

[73] S. s. du Canada, Saint-Hyacinthe, 1937, pp. 47-48.

[74] *Ibid.*, p. 237.

[75] Esdras Minville, *La Force conquérante de la coopération* (Québec: Le Conseil Supérieur de la Coopération, 1943), p. 6.

William Thompson, an Irish gentleman, and Dr. King, physician in Brighton, England. The first practical initiators of the cooperative movement were modest laborers, the "Pioneers of Rochdale." Their cooperative store opened by twenty-eight laborers in 1844 on Toad Lane Street was the first successful consumer cooperative known to history.[76] In Canada, the cooperative movement is linked with the name of Alphonse Desjardins alluded to in the first chapter.

The domain of cooperatives in French Canada comprises the entire field of economic activities. Mr. Jean-Baptiste Cloutier, speaker at the 1937 meeting of the Semaine Sociale, studied the various forms of cooperation: producer, which are concerned with various activities of production; farm, which represent the farmers' efforts at cooperation; credit, which specialize in financial activities to serve the well-being of the members; consumer, which function for service in buying, not for gain; and housing, which provide homes on a cooperative basis.[77]

Cooperatives are the golden mean solution, the middle way between capitalism and socialism. In their conception as well as in their function, cooperatives prevent the abuses of capitalism and correct the deficiencies of statism. They foster initiative, accomplish "great things with little people, while statism makes little people with great things."[78]

An example of sound cooperation—the experiment of Antigonish—was discussed by Father Livain Chiasson, organizer of cooperatives in the diocese of Chatham. He attributed the success of this movement to adult education undertaken in 1930 by the Extension Department of St. Francis Xavier University of Antigonish. The movement aimed to enroll the common people in a study and solution of their problems. Following in the footsteps of Dr. Hugh MacPherson, the apostle of cooperation, Father Coady and Father J. Thompkins played a major role in its later

[76] Filion, *Notions élémentaires de coopération, op. cit.,* pp. 5-7; S. s. du Canada, Saint-Jean, 1942, p. 116 and Nicolet, 1940, p. 43.

[77] S. s. du Canada, Saint-Hyacinthe, 1937, pp. 53-60: For a good study of the types of cooperatives see *L'Inventaire du mouvement coopératif* (Québec: Conseil Supérieur de la Coopération, 1944).

[78] S. s. du Canada, Saint-Hyacinthe, 1937, p. 64.

development.[79] With their associates they were responsible for the remarkable changes which took place in the Maritime Provinces. From cooperative stores and credit unions to marketing cooperatives, the movement passed to the field of industry. Father Coady first organized the fishermen of the Maritime Provinces. As a result, the lobster industry made rapid progress. The cooperative movement of Antigonish is full of promise for the future, Father Chiasson believes. Practical and adapted to the needs of the people, it is sound from the philosophical, religious, social and economic points of view. So far, the results obtained prove its expediency and the speaker hoped that the movement will progress until it reaches its objective: the realization of the social and economic well-being of the people.[80]

But until cooperation becomes the accepted practice, the Semaine Sociale recognizes the need of studying the respective rights and duties of both employers and employees as they function in the present economic order. The employers, in the words of Mr. Joseph Evariste Prince, are bound by duties of justice and equity towards their employees. "It is shameful and inhuman," he said, "to treat men like chattel to make money by, or to look upon them merely as so much muscle or physical power."[81] Justice demands also that employers derive a legitimate profit from their industry; that they pay their employees a family wage; that they do not overtax the strength of their employees; that they do not expose them to moral dangers;[82] that they be interested in their spiritual and temporal welfare; look upon them as brothers; give them good example and edify them by Christian lives.[83] To face these responsibilities, Father Eugène Tremblay said two attitudes must be present in the employers: a Christian spirit and a sense of

[79] Maurice Colombain has written an enlightening pamphlet on cooperative education entitled *Faire des hommes nouveaux* (Québec: Le Conseil Supérieur de la Coopération, 1943).

[80] S. s. du Canada, Saint-Hyacinthe, 1937, pp. 79-90; Nicolet, 1940, p. 49; and Sherbrooke, 1938, pp. 122-123.

[81] *Rerum novarum, op. cit.*, p. 13, and S. s. du Canada, Montréal, 1920, p. 82.

[82] *Ibid.*, p. 158, and S. s. du Canada, Trois-Rivières, 1925, pp. 28-29, 198-199.

[83] S. s. du Canada, Ottawa, 1922, p. 236, and Sherbrooke, 1938, p. 182.

social duty.[84] Summarily, Father Edmour Hébert declared that employers may sin in two ways: by systematically withholding, to the detriment of the general interest, production and by refusing reasonable living conditions to workingmen.[85]

The employees also have rights and duties peculiarly their own. Their claims to respect, just wages, the right to unionize, collective contract, conciliation and arbitration, in the opinion of Father Edmond Lacroix, are just and legitimate.[86] The employees, on the other hand, must furnish real and effective labor, conform to a just discipline for the success of the industry, respect the property of the employer, and not revert to violence to obtain just wages.[87]

Resorting to violence is not in accordance with the thinking of the Semaine Sociale but the pros and cons of the strike question were discussed as early as 1920 by Father Villeneuve, the present Cardinal. After defining the strike as "the abrupt and general cessation of labor profitable to employers, concerted by a group of employees, with a view to influencing employers by coaction—to grant them more favorable conditions than the present ones," he discussed the nature, bad effects, advantages and legitimacy, remedies and preventives of strikes.[88] Father Louis-Nazaire Hamel, O.F.M., called the strike "willed and concerted unemployment,"[89] and Father Philippe Perrier, now Vicar General, "a violent solution to a conflict."[90] In the proceedings of the 1938 Semaine Sociale, Father Perrier contributed an enlightening course on the teaching of the Church regarding the closed shop, sit-down strike, and picketing.[91] Speaking of the closed shop, he referred to Msgr. Ryan's affirmation that the closed shop is a "legitimate measure."[92]

---

[84] S. s. du Canada, Sherbrooke, 1938, p. 190.

[85] S. s. du Canada, Saint-Hyacinthe, 1928, p. 40.

[86] S. s. du Canada, Ottawa, 1922, pp. 209-221.

[87] S. s. du Canada, Montréal, 1920, p. 158, and Trois-Rivières, 1925, pp. 196-197.

[88] S. s. du Canada, Montréal, 1920, pp. 95-104.

[89] S. s. du Canada, Québec, 1927, p. 177.

[90] S. s. du Canada, Sherbrooke, 1938, p. 222.

[91] *Ibid.*, pp. 209-231.

[92] *Ibid.*, p. 210.

Concerning strike-breakers, he quoted from Msgr. MacLean's *The Morality of the Strike,*[93] and opposed legislation against sit-down strikes by citing Dr. Francis Haas, now Bishop of Grand Rapids.[94]

The Semaine Sociale devoted an entire course to the employee's right to work. As early as 1921, Judge C. E. Dorion discussed its nature, necessity, dignity and end.[95] Work is the proper activity of man, the manifestation of his life, the exercise of his physical faculties and of his intelligence.[96] It is a true prayer which elevates the soul. By work man accomplishes God's will, which prescribes labor in this natural condition in order to reach supernatural life. Thus natural and supernatural life rather than exclude each other complement themselves and support each other.[97]

Savings is another topic studied by the Semaine Sociale. In 1924, Judge Lemay stated that "gold is a bad master but can become a good servant." There are two ways to amass a fortune, he goes on to say, work and savings. He considered systematic savings in the form of deposits in banks or in *caisses populaires*. The French Canadians will become a thrifty people if they succeed in teaching their children practices of thrift. Alphonse Desjardins had grasped the situation when he founded school banks or penny banks.[98] These, under the direction of instructors, allow children to collect and deposit the small sums that they would otherwise spend on sweets or trifles. Impelled by the wish to increase their little capital in the School Savings Bank, children become thrifty.[99]

Again, at the 1943 meeting of the Semaine Sociale, Mr. Médard Leduc, public notary, studied the subject of savings under the headings: definition, nature, necessity, advantages and means of saving. Mr. Leduc noted among the means of saving: the keeping of a family budget, insurances of all types, penny savings, bar-

[93] *Ibid.*, p. 225.
[94] *Ibid.*, p. 226.
[95] S. s. du Canada, Québec, 1921, pp. 19-35.
[96] *Ibid.*, p. 19.
[97] *Ibid.*, p. 32.
[98] S. s. du Canada, Sherbrooke, 1924, pp. 136-137.
[99] S. s. du Canada, Chicoutimi, 1929, p. 152.

gaining and large quantity purchasing, sickness and accident prevention, assurance of the wife's collaboration, thrifty education of children. He concluded that individual savings for French Canadians constitute their national wealth, a necessary factor for their *survivance*.[100] That same year Mr. Albert Rioux, former sub-minister of agriculture, treated of the enemies of savings, both interior and exterior. The former were discussed under the heading: capital sins. He noted the State as among the exterior enemies; other enemies of savings are speculators and promoters of enterprises, publicity agencies, installment-plan purchases, usurers and bank loans.[101]

From a consideration of the enemies of savings, the Semaine Sociale turns to a study of the causes of the present state of economic disorder. First and foremost, it notes the suppression of corporations, a point to be treated in the following chapter. The capitalists' abuse of wealth is another important cause of the existing disorder. Malthus at one time feared that the means of production would not be sufficient to feed the entire population. Contrarily, Mr. Hermas Bastien declared at the 1938 meeting of the Semaine Sociale that production is too rapid and too abundant for consumption. Millions of laborers are deprived of work. They starve while coffee is being destroyed and wheat burnt. Every week in Montreal, the speaker continued, unsold milk is colored with a chemical powder, and to compensate for its loss, wages are lowered.[102]

The results of this situation are what might be expected: a great inequality in the distribution of wealth and class struggle. Inequality and antagonism are the consequences of this economic dictatorship.[103] Profit has become its god,[104] and when industries are overcapitalized, prices decrease, production ceases and the opposition of classes becomes prevalent; struggle of rural versus urban classes, of Franco-Canadians versus Anglo-Canadians, of Catholics

---

[100] S. s. du Canada, Salaberry-de-Valleyfield, 1943, pp. 55-70.
[101] *Ibid.*, pp. 71-91.
[102] S. s. du Canada, Sherbrooke, 1938, pp. 40-41.
[103] *Ibid.*, p. 37.
[104] *Ibid.*, p. 42.

versus Protestants,[105] of the bourgeoisie versus the proletariat. Magistrate Lemay asserted that there will be no peace as long as these people do not agree and do not cease to look upon each other as enemies.[106] Like Mr. Saint-Pierre, Mr. J. E. Perrault held a different view:

> In Canada, a country where the social classes are not stratified by centuries of hereditary prejudices, a country where the democratic system, allowing everyone to rise in the social scale, recognizes but one nobility, that of uprightness of will-power and work, there should be no room for defiance, antipathy and rivalry among citizens of the same country.[107]

That concentration of riches in the hands of a few capitalists forms part of the economic system of Canada finds confirmation in the inquiries which reveal that there were in Canada in 1934 two hundred thirty-five financial magnates.[108] Moreover, a census made in 1931 of the Province of Quebec shows a working population of 1,025,709 from the age of ten on, of which 535,203 were men wage-earners. The number of employers was 92,662, of non-employed 96,331. Such a mass of wage-earners as compared with the small number of employers does not seem to indicate a sound situation.[109] What is more serious is that modern capitalism appears to exercise absolute power over money, ruling the spiritual and moral values of humanity.[110]

It is significant to note that as early as 1920 Mr. Antonio Perrault asked of the French Canadians if the reproach expressed at the Congress of Breslau by Windthorst applied to them:

---

[105] *Ibid.*, pp. 44-45.

[106] S. s. du Canada, Montréal, 1932, p. 383.

[107] *Ibid.*, p. 350: "Au Canada, pays ou les classes sociales ne sont point divisées par des siècles de préjugés héréditaires, pays ou le régime démocratique, permettant à chacun de monter, ne reconnait qu'une noblesse, celle de la droiture, de la volonté et du travail, il ne doit pas y avoir place, entre les citoyens de ce pays, pour la défiance, l'antipathie, les rivalités."

[108] S. s. du Canada, Québec, 1941, p. 46.

[109] S. s. du Canada, Sherbrooke, 1938, p. 49.

[110] S. s. du Canada, Saint-Hyacinthe, 1937, p. 91.

"Everybody talks about the social question. Then he turns to smoke a cigar or drink a glass of wine and does nothing to bring about its solution."[111]

Another cause of the present economic disorder frequently stressed by the Semaine Sociale is the exodus from the farm with its accompanying abnormal situation: the overcrowding of cities. French Canadians leave the country either because land is not available or farming methods on a paying basis are unknown, or the farmers themselves are indifferent to advancement or finally, because revenues are not sufficient to cope with the increase in expenses.[112] The opposition of the Semaine Sociale to this exodus from the farm finds expression in the study of 1928 on the economic problem considered especially from the agricultural point of view. In addition, repeated references to this subject may be found throughout the proceedings of the Semaine Sociale. Thus in 1924, Mr. Georges Bouchard treated *Le Domaine rural canadien* describing the typical rural unit as a little farm of two to five acres in width and thirty or more in length.[113] It was Virgil who had said, and with good reason, "Admire if you wish the large farm, but cultivate a small one."[114] In 1933, Mr. Albert Rioux differentiated between family farming and speculative farming. The former represents a type of exploitation the extent of which corresponds to what a normal family is able to cultivate. The latter aims at the financial yield of the enterprise.[115] Saint Thomas in *De regimine principum* showed his preference for agriculture when he stated that "A being is much nobler when he is in a position to be sufficient unto himself. It is a deficiency to need others. . . ."[116]

Besides the independence that the farm confers on those who exploit it, country life is characterized by permanence and stability. Rural domains in the words of Mr. Bouchard constitute the best

---

[111] S. s. du Canada, Montréal, 1920, pp. 183-184.

[112] S. s. du Canada, Saint-Hyacinthe, 1928, pp. 97-99.

[113] S. s. du Canada, Sherbrooke, 1924, p. 251.

[114] S. s. du Canada, Rimouski, 1933, p. 189.

[115] *Ibid.*, p. 303.

[116] S. s. du Canada, Montréal, 1932, p. 216.

rampart against communistic tendencies.[117] It is true that agriculturists do not comprise the most learned class but in general they are intelligent, moral, and laborious, without haughtiness, yet proud of the fact that they nourish the great human family.[118]

Not only do farmers help to sustain the population at large, but they assure to the French Canadian nationality its force and value in number.[119] A similar view was expressed by Father Archambault declaring that the French Canadian *survivance* is closely linked to the land.[120] Mr. Antonio Perrault held the same opinion:

> . . . For the survival of our race nothing will ever equal the millions of parishes where the peasant . . . is sheltered from the assimilation and destructive morals of city life.[121]

Father Lionel Groulx declares that the land is as great a producer of men as it is of life. Large cities, on the contrary, like "frightful cannibals"[122] are devourers of humanity.

The moral value of rural life is also recognized by the Semaine Sociale. According to Father Archambault the country is the guardian of the moral life of the French Canadians. Nature brings them close to God, unites them with their Creator who is everywhere especially in the secret power responsible for the germination of plants and the ripening of fruits, and finally in the beneficial alternation of seasons. While city life multiplies the snares where virtue founders, the country protects it and facilitates its exercise.[123] Mr. Bouchard called the country "the heart of Canada." By strengthening this heart, he added, we strengthen the whole social organism.[124]

---

[117] S. s. du Canada, Sherbrooke, 1924, p. 252.

[118] S. s. du Canada, Saint-Hyacinthe, 1928, p. 191.

[119] S. s. du Canada, Ottawa, 1931, p. 304.

[120] S. s. du Canada, Saint-Hyacinthe, 1928, p. 33.

[121] *Loc. cit.*, ". . . Pour la survivance de notre peuple, rien ne vaut, rien ne vaudra jamais des milliers de paroisses où la classe paysanne, . . . demeure à l'abri de l'assimiliation et des moeurs déformantes des villes."

[122] S. s. du Canada, Rimouski, 1933, p. 329.

[123] *Ibid.*, p. 20.

[124] *Ibid.*, p. 142.

The social, national and human value of agriculture surpasses its economic value in the opinion of Father Lorenzo Gauthier, C.S.V.[125] When economists proclaim agriculture to be the "power of nations, the reservoir of life and the basic industry of countries," they have in mind family farming and not speculative agriculture.[126] Canon Courchesne, future Bishop of Rimouski, in referring to Gérin-Lajoie, a pioneer in French Canadian sociology, remarked how the latter was concerned about the migration of rural populations to the cities. To him, the fact that popular virtue finds in rural life the safeguards of the cloister without the burden of its austerities, constitutes a guarantee of the social health of the people.[127]

Moreover, the Semaine Sociale recognizes the economic value of agriculture. Farming, in the opinion of Mr. Oscar Gatineau, is a necessity to the life of all the population and constitutes the only industry dating from the creation of the first man and lasting to the end of the world.[128] Statisticians and dietitians have set up family budgets for five persons living in the country. One of these, called the poverty budget, amounts to $900; a second, health and decency budget to $1,729; a third reached the sum of $2,400. Now, if one multiplies this amount by the number of families in a rural parish, the economic value of farms becomes evident.[120] Thus Bishop Langlois is eager that French Canadians remain a rural people. He claims that a nation develops in accordance with its abilities. Although French Canadians may vie for dominance in other fields, they will remain absolute masters in agriculture. In a word, French Canada needs a rural elite.[130]

That the hygienic value attached to the country is another benefit of rural life is evident from the data given by Mr. Clarence Hogue in 1928. The infant mortality rate in cities, he said, surpasses that of rural districts.[131] In the country, work in the fields

---

[125] *Ibid.*, p. 292.
[126] *Ibid.*, p. 312.
[127] S. s. du Canada, Trois-Rivières, 1925, p. 113.
[128] S. s. du Canada, Saint-Hyacinthe, 1928, p. 215.
[129] *Ibid.*, p. 241.
[130] *Ibid.*, p. 312.
[131] *Ibid.*, p. 249.

helps children to become robust, healthy and strong. Their physique is better developed by fresh air, hygienic housing, and sane food.[132]

On the other hand, the agricultural situation creates an awkward problem, in the opinion of Mr. Bouchard, because its paying basis in financial returns is not sufficient. The marketing of products is often difficult because of the lack of consideration on the part of producer for the exigencies of the consumer; because of a defective system for the distribution of products, the conditions imposed by the Fordney Bill rendering less advantageous the exporting of many products to the United States. The absence of bookkeeping on the farm is also a cause of financial losses. Like Mr. Charles Gagné, Father Georges Bilodeau believes that the present agricultural situation is due to defects in the exchange system.[133] Again, the rural home is no longer a center of production; rather it is a place where young girls are too often lonely. In many a country home an unused piano or "a frozen stove" has been substituted for the spinning-wheel, skein-winder and loom. The education given in rural schools is not sufficiently rural in nature; the soul of the instructor has not been ruralized.[134] In 1928, Mr. Wilfrid Guérin made a strong plea for an institution of superior instruction in agriculture which would conform to the religious and national traditions of French Canada. He likened this deplorable situation to "placing the cart before the horse."[135]

It is true that experimental farming in Canada is relatively new. Nevertheless, Mr. J. A. Sainte-Marie, in a masterly course given in 1933, traced the development made through the centuries. After citing the fact that the first agricultural school was founded by Bishop de Laval in Saint-Joachim in 1670 and closed in 1715, he went on to name twelve other schools which were subsequently established in the Province of Quebec.[136]

---

[132] S. s. du Canada, Montréal, 1932, p. 219.
[133] S. s. du Canada, Montréal, 1926, p. 132, and Rimouski, 1933, pp. 148-152.
[134] S. s. du Canada, Sherbrooke, 1924, pp. 260-261.
[135] S. s. du Canada, Saint-Hyacinthe, 1928, p. 16.
[136] S. s. du Canada, Rimouski, 1933, pp. 56-57.

Addressing the farmers in particular at the Rimouski meeting of 1933, Father Alphonse Belzile praised their accomplishments:

> Your billboard is your land with the gold of its wheat and the savor of its fruit.
>
> You give the example of a moderate life, of a great spirit of labor, of a sound morality; you give well-disciplined children with good health and sound judgment. You render society many more services, but the enumeration already made is long enough to convince you of the great nobility of your profession; . . .[137]

Father Groulx expressed a similar appreciation when he said:

> It [the land] furnishes us with our basic powers; the best of our human capital, the best also of our social institutions. It creates for us economic prestige and a still greater power, namely, intellectual, moral and political strength because it keeps our middle class sane and vigorous, . . .[138]

The Semaine Sociale and its Rector realize that remedies must be applied to the various causes alleged for the desertion of the farm: *désaffection* of the land, as Mr. Bouchard expressed it, pseudo-attractions of city life, economic reasons, lack of ruralized education. Thus in the proceedings of the Semaine Sociale one finds helpful suggestions for the solution of the agricultural problem considered from the professional, economic, social and political viewpoints.

---

[137] *Ibid.*, p. 241: "Votre enseigne est votre terre, avec l'or de ses blés et la saveur de ses fruits.

"Vous offrez l'exemple d'une vie modérée, d'un grand esprit de travail, d'une bonne moralité; vous offrez des enfants bien formés, pourvus d'une bonne santé et d'un jugement droit. Vous rendez à la société bien d'autres services encore, mais l'énumération que j'en ai faite est déjà assez longue pour vous convaincre de la haute noblesse de votre profession; . . ."

[138] *Ibid.*, p. 339: "Elle nous fournit les forces de base: le meilleur de notre capital humain, les meilleures également de nos institutions sociales. Elle nous crée de la puissance économique, mais aussi une puissance plus haute qui peut s'appeler: puissance intellectuelle, puissance morale, puissance politique, parce qu'elle nous garde, saine et vigoureuse, . . ."

In the line of professional or economic remedies, Mr. Esdras Minville recommended at the Sherbrooke meeting of 1938, that the newly established Bureau for Scientific Research be provided with the necessary means for the realization of its end: the study of scientific problems which are the clue to a multitude of economic problems. It is expedient, he noted, that French Canadians know what they possess, the extent and nature of their wealth and its distribution in their province.[139]

At the Rimouski assembly of 1933, Father Archambault stated explicitly that rural education should start in childhood, in the home and at school, and be continued by the press, conferences, study circles, rural days and agricultural congresses.[140] At the same meeting of the Semaine Sociale, like Mr. Guérin, Mr. Albert Rioux recommended the reading of the bulletins prepared by the ministers of the federal and provincial agricultural departments, and the agricultural journals published in French Canada.[141] Bishop Langlois believes that to spread, maintain and fortify the agricultural class a rural elite should be formed—one which by the power of word, by reading and writing, would stress the importance of the exploitation of the land,—and little by little spread the truths learned and the information gathered.[142] Mr. Gagné even suggests that farmers who lack helpers take under their charge two or three novice-cultivators to initiate them into the work of the farm.[143]

A knowledge of pedology, the science which studies the nature and kinds of soil, is also recommended for farmers. At the Rimouski assembly of 1933, Mr. Auguste Scott gave a timely course on the classification of soils[144] and showed the expediency and advantages of such a classification and the conditions for productivity, thus enabling the French Canadians to solve efficiently their present economic rural problems. That same year Mr. Louis de G.

---

[139] S. s. du Canada, Sherbrooke, 1938, pp. 177-178.
[140] S. s. du Canada, Rimouski, 1933, p. 24.
[141] *Ibid.*, p. 317.
[142] S. s. du Canada, Saint-Hyacinthe, 1928, pp. 311-314.
[143] S. s. du Canada, Rimouski, 1933, p. 210.
[144] *Ibid.*, pp. 61-77.

Fortin discussed the role of agronomes. He first described the *fol agronome* whose quips caused agriculture to be defined as the "art of spending money scientifically,"[145] and then proceeded to point out the duties of the efficient agronome and his role on the farm.

Again, the Semaine Sociale advocates that agriculture as a profession be inspired with that spirit of solidarity which is so necessary to improve the soil and sell its products, and in addition protect itself by means of professional organization and associations. At the 1933 assembly of Rimouski, Father Edouard Beaudoin declared that such an association had already been established in French Canada but that it is still in the embryonic stage. None the less, farmers who wish to survive should encourage its growth. The struggle for economic life is not an individual but a collective fight. He held that farmers should demand legislative protection and should organize to counteract the influence of labor unions.[146] The motto *Cruce et aratro!* (with cross and plough) was given to agricultural associations by Father A. Desmarais at the 1938 meeting of the Semaine Sociale.[147]

Such an association, *Union catholique des cultivateurs* has existed in the Province of Quebec since 1924. It is a Catholic union recognized by the Bishops of the three ecclesiastical provinces of Quebec, Montreal and Ottawa.[148] The Provincial Minister of Agriculture, the Honorable Adélard Godbout, once said that if this Catholic Union did not exist, it would have to be founded.[149] Numerous other references to the timeliness of such a union is found in the proceedings of the Semaine Sociale. Father Gauthier referred to the apostolic role that it plays among the rural population. It has awakened the spirit of fraternity and developed the idea of social justice. Detached from all political ambition, unobstructed by the influences of coteries, passionate lover of the soil, competent to its finger-tips, conscientious of its responsibilities, the Union remains in the opinion of the people

---

[145] *Ibid.*, p. 97.
[146] *Ibid.*, p. 51.
[147] S. s. du Canada, Saint-Hyacinthe, 1928, p. 291.
[148] S. s. du Canada, Rimouski, 1933, p. 261.
[149] *Ibid.*, p. 318.

the agent of solidarity, the apostle of the rural gospel, the support of the wavering and the loyal and disinterested collaborator of ecclesiastical and civil authority.[150]

Canon Allaire[151] and Father Belzile are proud of the results obtained by this Union: the establishment of five hundred study clubs and of a professional journal, the *Terre de chez nous,* the organization of courses in the home, a daily program on the radio, the formation of a professional mentality, the purchase and sale of agricultural products, the providing of means to obtain credit, the construction of bridges, the use of chemical manure and of lime, encouragement for the return to and maintenance of farms, favorable legislation, the collaboration of the clergy to keep the members strictly Catholic.[152]

For commercial transactions, the Semaine Sociale, in agreement with all alert farmers, recognizes the necessity of establishing co-operatives of all types. The impetus to this cooperative movement was given by Frederic Guillaume Raiffeisen, who founded the first German *Ländliche Genossenschaftskasse* in 1849, and by the French Canadian parliamentary journalist, Alphonse Desjardins, for Canada in 1900. The saving and credit cooperative, known as *Caisse populaire Desjardins* is based on the following moral principles: moderation in the use of the riches of this world; detachment on the part of those who contribute to this work; mutual, loyal and fraternal aid in the name of the divine law of charity.[153] Mr. Desjardins' first attempt at cooperation was branded as nonsensical by some of his detractors. To these he replied: "It is possible that I am insane, but mine is a mild form of insanity. I have dreamed of helping the poor, I thought that it was high time to establish something to which the common people might turn to find support. With your principles of economic liberalism, money enslaves the common people, while with my cooperative organization money is rendered more humane in its function, which is to

---

[150] *Ibid.,* p. 300.

[151] S. s. du Canada, Saint-Hyacinthe, 1928, pp. 194-199.

[152] S. s. du Canada, Rimouski, 1933, pp. 246-252.

[153] S. s. du Canada, Saint-Hyacinthe, 1937, p. 173.

serve the people."[154] And Mr. Desjardins, encouraged by his pastor and several priests of the College of Lévis, in the pursuit of his noble work, proceeded with courage and will-power to put his plan into effect. The first paragraph of the second article in the Constitution of the *Caisses populaires* reads as follows: "The Society aims to protect its members against misfortune, the results of unemployment, sickness and poverty, by teaching them the inestimable benefits of economy and foresightedness resulting from cooperation, . . ."[155] Truly from an economic point of view these popular banks are the best credit organizations on a parochial basis. The cost of administration is small and the administrators knowing most of the people avert risks and losses in loans granted.[156] In the words of Mr. Desjardins himself, this organization does not enrich anyone: it is based on a just social thought of union for life rather than struggle for life. The *Caisse populaire* is established for the poor and rich alike, provided they are honest, laborious and sober. In 1912 there were more than 56,000 such credit unions in Europe.[157] In June 1941, there were 1,116 in Canada of which 665 were in the Province of Quebec with a total membership of more than 200,000 of which 161,818 reside in the Province of Quebec. Loans amounted to more than 115 million dollars.[158] The rural credit unions at present number five hundred twenty with 120,154 members and assets amounting to $23,670,595.01.[159]

---

[154] *Ibid.*, pp. 248-249: "Avec vos principes de libéralisme économique, disait-il, l'argent asservit le peuple, tandis qu'avec mon organisation coopérative l'argent est rendu plus humain pour remplir son rôle, qui est de *servir* le peuple."

[155] S. s. du Canada, Rimouski, 1933, p. 160: "La Societé a pour but de protéger ses membres contre les revers de fortune, les résultats du chômage, la maladie et l'indigence, en leur enseignant les bienfaits inappréciables de l'économie et de la prévoyance par la coopération; . . ."

[156] S. s. du Canada, Saint-Hyacinthe, 1928, p. 222.

[157] Alphonse Desjardins, *La Caisse populaire* (Montréal: Ecole Sociale Populaire, 1912), pp. 31-32.

[158] Jean Bergeron, *L'Agriculture et l'Eglise* (Québec: Jean Bergeron, 1943), p. 128.

[159] *L'Inventaire du mouvement coopératif, op. cit.*, p. 52.

From Canada the movement spread to the United States. Upon the recommendation of an English expert, the President of the United States, invited Mr. Desjardins to expound the details of his masterly work. As a result today there exist more than 10,000 credit unions in the United States.[160] One example of the beneficial function of this credit organ is given in the proceedings of the Semaine Sociale of 1940 by Mayor Arthur Martin who related the establishment of a credit union in Southbridge as early as 1910. As a consequence there is no slum in this city which boasts many active industries; the workers live in comfort and freedom and the perversive ideas widely spread in other industrial centers do not affect this slumless city.[161]

Since the launching of the cooperative movement, various types of cooperatives spread with astounding results. To cite one example of a consumer cooperative: the *Société des producteurs de Sucre d'Erable* of Quebec. Just when the maple syrup industry was about to disappear in Quebec under pressure of much exploitation, the establishment of a cooperative enabled the members to control prices and to assure the sale of their produce.[162]

The social remedies to prevent the desertion of the farm are also discussed by the followers of the Semaine Sociale. Already alluded to were the mutual insurances advocated by Mr. A. R. Gagné at the Saint-Hyacinthe meeting of 1937, and special amusements for rural dwellers and the establishment of *Cercles de fermières*. In 1928, Mr. Guérin reported that the poet Désilets was General Director of two hundred *Cercles de fermières*. The influence exerted by the wives, sisters and fiancées of farmers by this post-graduate work is remarkable. The home has become attractive due to the teaching of domestic arts; more resources have been added to the family bank due to an awakened domestic industry; a clinging to traditions encouraged, due to the fight against Americanization. "I do not know of a home where one speaks of

---

[160] Bergeron, *op. cit.*, p. 128.

[161] S. s. du Canada, Nicolet, 1940, p. 157.

[162] S. s. du Canada, Rimouski, 1933, p. 168. For a summary of the procedure in a *coopérative agricole* see Léo Filion, *La Tenue des assemblées dans une coopérative agricole* (Québec: Le Conseil Supérieur de la Coopération).

leaving it when the mother of the family is interested in agriculture,"[163] concluded Mr. Désilets.

As political remedies for the prevention of migration from the farm, the Semaine Sociale mentions state intervention and colonization. State intervention as advocated by Mr. Eugène l'Heureux should take the form of teaching farmers the real value of money. Let the State again induce new agricultural projects, create a system of emulation, encouragement and edification, foster professional ambition, favor the establishment and development of cooperatives, magnify in all circumstances the social role of the farmer, reduce to a minimum various taxes, improve working conditions, facilitate first the control of local markets and then those abroad, and spread agricultural science by all imaginable means: schools of all sorts, special courses, journals, experimental or demonstrational farms.[164] In short, let the State foster such conditions as will permit agriculturists to overcome their difficulties as easily as the other members of civil society.

Colonization, another means for the prevention of the exodus from the farm, was studied at the 1928 assembly by Father Jean Bergeron and again at the 1933 meeting by Mr. Minville. Father Bergeron by colonization means "to people a foreign country with natives, or one's territory with its own people or foreigners whom one wishes to incorporate into the nation." Thus there is both an exterior and an interior or domestic colonization. Exterior colonization may be agricultural or mercantile. Domestic colonization is especially agricultural; when industrial, it is called exploitation. The practical end of domestic colonization is to increase population and the production of commodities of prime necessity.[165]

Father Bergeron defined a colonist thus:

> A colonist is a French Canadian Catholic, born of farmers, raised on a farm, who has not been softened by the easy life of the village, who has not tasted of the enchanting and depressing pleasures of modern cities,

[163] S. s. du Canada, Saint-Hyacinthe, 1928, p. 17.
[164] S. s. du Canada, Ottawa, 1931, p. 199.
[165] S. s. du Canada, Saint-Hyacinthe, 1928, pp. 227-228.

> especially American cities, but who was accustomed to work and to privations at an early age 'who bore the yoke since childhood' in the words of Holy Scripture.[166]

Such colonists have almost vanished in the course of thirty years under the corrosive action of what is called "modern progress." Among the obstacles to colonization the speaker mentioned: seizure of millions of lots by speculators and the indifference of the public.[167]

Father George Bilodeau, colonizer of the plains of Temiscouata in the thirties, refers to a "loi du retour à la terre" and wonders why it has been given a name that fits a doll's head like a beaver hat. This law permits the purchase of land belonging to the municipality or to individuals, provided the cost is not more than one hundred dollars. It is effective only in as much as it favors the occupation of abandoned lots. The Federal government established a system of return to the land by sending the unemployed to new lands following it up with assistance equivalent to six hundred dollars.[168]

Colonization in French Canada is not a permanent institution. There are fluctuations and variations.[169] Mr. Minville advocated a permanent, political, progressive, and conquering measure of colonization which would utilize all the cooperation necessitated to establish French Canadian young men on farms—a form of activity which would assure the preservation and increase in number and quality of their human powers.[170]

Faithful to its mission of informing public opinion on present social problems, the Canadian Semaine Sociale organized in April 1944 a *Congrès de colonisation.* The papers presented awakened social thinkers to the urgent need of preparing programs of colonization for the post-war period and founded another society called *Aide à la colonisation.* Approved by the French Canadian

---

[166] *Ibid.,* p. 253.

[167] *Ibid.,* pp. 258-259.

[168] S. s. du Canada, Montréal, 1932, pp. 228-230.

[169] Interview with Mr. Esdras Minville at the Ecole des Hautes Etudes Commerciales, July 5, 1944.

[170] S. s. du Canada, Rimouski, 1933, pp. 236-237.

clergy, this organization aims to influence public opinion and public authorities, while the Society of Colonization aims to help the French Canadians to establish themselves on new lands.[171] As Cardinal Villeneuve said in his pastoral letter of March 29, 1934, colonization is a national and apostolic work. That all who are interested in their religion and in their country should be interested in the movement and lend their cooperation is the general belief of French Canadians.

In summary, holding that financial activities form an integral part of the economic order and that the rights of employers as well as employees should be safeguarded by the State, the Semaine Sociale rejects that exaggerated capitalism which is responsible for so many economic disorders. It advocates rural life for the French Canadian population aware of its various benefits, thereby offering practical, economic, social and political remedies for bettering conditions on the land.

---

[171] *L'Aide à la colonisation* (Montréal: Ecole Sociale Populaire, October, 1944), pp. 1, 8.

CHAPTER IX

The Semaine Sociale and Professional Organization

Professional organizations, which so engross the attention of all thinking sociologists today, have been effectively studied by the Semaine Sociale. First, Catholic syndicates as bases for such organizations will be discussed. Then the various types of unions, employers' associations and corporative groups will be considered as part of the French Canadian pattern of economic and social life.

Because professional organizations form an integral part of the economic order in the social thought of French Canada, the Semaine Sociale devoted the courses of the 1936 session to the study of these organizations. Besides this, repeatedly references are made in the various reports on the proceedings of the Semaine Sociale. In fact, each year a typical "manifestation ouvrière" is included in the program.

Now, syndicate in French Canadian thought is not synonymous with labor unions, especially when these are conceived as cells of a future socialist order. Rather the term refers to a professional union, an association of persons of the same profession or of similar professions with a view to studying, defending, and promoting their mutual interests.[1] Mr. Gérard Picard calls the syndicate a school of democracy for workers, employers and society at large.[2] For Father Philippe Perrier, it is an institution that has the same rights as the city does in contemporary society.[3] In the words of Father Edmond Hébert, the Catholic syndicate is born of the will of the Church. By associating for the protection of their rights in confessional syndicates, Catholic workers are obeying the Pope and are following the direction of the Church.[4]

---

[1] S. s. du Canada, Nicolet, 1940, p. 163.
[2] S. s. du Canada, Saint-Jean, 1942, p. 152.
[3] S. s. du Canada, Sherbrooke, 1938, p. 209.
[4] S. s. du Canada, Ottawa, 1922, p. 180.

Father Hébert holds that the Catholic labor union is above all a "home of charity and a school of justice."[5]

As was previously said, although an attempt was made in 1901 to introduce Catholic syndicates in Quebec, they were definitely and regularly established only in 1907 in Chicoutimi by Msgr. Eugène Lapointe, then Vicar General of the diocese. In Trois-Rivières the labor movement began in 1912 under the impetus of Msgr. Cloutier who delivered a series of instructions in response to the Pope's demand.[6] As a result in January 1913 the *Corporation Ouvrière Catholique* was formed with two hundred workers. In Sherbrooke, the Catholic syndicates first received attention when Father Leonidas Adam, Mr. Arthur Boulé and Mr. Joseph Laliberté met in a little hall on King Street to discuss the teachings of *Rerum novarum*.[7]

Catholic labor unions aim to insure respect among the various classes of society, to secure material comfort, to help the development of moral life, win recognition for the rights of workers,[8] foster harmony between capital and labor, bring about economic progress and amelioration in working conditions, establish social peace[9] and preserve the Faith.[10]

The principles of Catholic syndicates may be summarized as follows: the necessity for a maintenance of the inequality among social classes, liberty of work, and patronal autonomy.[11] Hence the Church's motto for professional organizations: "union without violence."[12] Mr. Alfred Charpentier at the 1935 assembly of the Semaine Sociale showed how the Catholic syndicate is a school of social formation because it is first a school of Christian brotherhood.[13] Social doctrine as taught by Catholic syndicates holds to the idea of private property tempered by social justice. It abhors

[5] Edmour Hébert, *L'Organisation ouvrière* (Montréal: Ecole Sociale Populaire, 1919), p. 10.

[6] S. s. du Canada, Trois-Rivières, 1925, p. 392.

[7] S. s. du Canada, Sherbrooke, 1938, p. 400.

[8] S. s. du Canada, Ottawa, 1931, p. 306.

[9] S. s. du Canada, Québec, 1921, p. 359.

[10] *Ibid.*, p. 385.

[11] *Ibid.*, p. 130.

[12] *Ibid.*, p. 44.

[13] S. s. du Canada, Joliette, 1935, p. 307.

the struggle among the classes and aims to establish collaboration between employer and employee. It teaches respect for established authority and affirms that every crisis has its origin in man, that any reform must begin with a renovation of the moral order and that success is more definitely assured by charity than by law and war.[14]

To attain the necessary spiritual reform of morals, syndicates must be Catholic and national. Father Gauthier in 1942, in his talk on *Syndicalisme* as a School of Democracy, explained how Catholic syndicates derive their inspiration from the Gospel of Christ and the encyclicals of the Popes. To remain national, he added, they must oppose international unions and in all legitimacy and justice must conform to the mentality, fundamental interests and sound traditions of French Canada.[15] While Catholic and nationalistic in regard to labor unions, they have approved of the work of the I.L.O. as will be indicated later.

Moreover, French Canadian labor unions count among their members a chaplain whose function is to reach decisions stamped with justice and charity and to give wise and disinterested counsels, such as are based on the teaching of the Gospel. In the words of Mr. Pierre Beaulé, the chaplain in the French Canadian union is the friend, the brother, the father of a large syndical family. He is the guardian and energetic defender of the rights of the workers and the tireless apostle of Catholic syndicalism.[16]

In a course entitled *Les Services syndicaux,* Mr. Saint-Pierre, as early as 1921, explained the principal services rendered by the unions. The study sections attempt to cultivate the syndical and social sense of its members. Thus, the press, placement bureaus, unemployment banks, professional courses, the service of professional relations, syndical mutuals, and cooperatives constitute helpful means of reconstructing and bettering the conditions of the workingmen in French Canada.[17] In line with this are the numerous directive powers given to syndicates, as enumerated by Mr. Simon Lapointe at the same session.[18]

---

[14] S. s. du Canada, Saint-Hyacinthe, 1937, p. 335.

[15] S. s. du Canada, Saint-Jean, 1942, pp. 160-165.

[16] S. s. du Canada, Ottawa, 1931, p. 301.

[17] S. s. du Canada, Québec, 1921, pp. 146-162.

[18] For a complete list of these powers see *Ibid.,* pp. 213-215.

Among other services which syndicates perform, Father Bonhomme, O.M.I., mentioned that of establishing places of amusement and of convening the members at an annual congress with a view to developing their professional interests and cooperation towards promoting French Canadian labor legislation.[19] In 1940, Father Alphonse Allard discussed the role and place of Catholic syndicalism in the Church and recommended the establishment of secretarial offices, the conduction of syndical study weeks, study clubs, propaganda assemblies, laymen retreats to imbue members with a Catholic spirit of charity, justice and moderation, and to render them cognizant of the beneficial action of the Church in social matters.[20] French Canadian labor unions are considered instruments of social peace, ramparts of the Catholic faith and of the ethnic influence of French Canadians. Their role is to develop among the laboring class a desire for social betterment. No less important is their function of preparing for the exercise of corporative activity; the Christian syndicate constitutes a magnificent ground for the exercise of corporative principles, a true school for their application, an association from which the leaders learn to teach and command and the members to execute and collaborate.[21]

The achievements of Catholic unions are numerous and important. As early as 1922, Mr. Pierre Beaulé reported that the Catholic syndicates of Quebec succeeded in obtaining an increase in wages without recourse to strikes. He attributed this to the "faith which guides us is our power, the clergy which helps us is our success." The syndical organization will become more and more the hope of the fatherland and of the nation, the true "porte-bonheur" of Christian organized work.[22] In 1931, the same speaker called attention to legislative measures obtained by Catholic syndicates: recognition of syndicates as possessing civil personality; minimum-wage law for women in industries; the reform of the 1927-28 law relative to industrial accidents; the nomination of a

[19] S. s. du Canada, Chicoutimi, 1929, p. 148.
[20] S. s. du Canada, Nicolet, 1940, p. 170.
[21] S. s. du Canada, Trois-Rivières, 1936, p. 383.
[22] S. s. du Canada, Ottawa, 1922, p. 261.

commission to establish social insurance; and representation at the International Conference of Labor at Geneva.[23]

The following year Msgr. Lebon declared that Pope Pius XI alluded to social insurance in *Quadragesimo anno*. Cavalleva defines social insurance as a system of social aid whereby a premium is paid beforehand during a specified period so that the worker may receive what he needs. These insurances cover such items as: involuntary unemployment, accident, sickness, incapacity, old age, maternity, or death. Catholic social doctrine approves this principle of insurance because it is in line with that Christian spirit and sentiment of justice of which every one should be possessed. As early as 1891, Leo XIII recognized the need to complement wages. Pope Pius XI in *Casti connubii* referred to the State's obligation "to supply the insufficient resources of personal effort."[24]

Father Archambault and his colleagues of the Semaine Sociale further hold that, although Leo XIII and Pius XI do not use the words collective agreements, these are nevertheless manifestly recommended when the Popes affirm that questions of wages should be settled not by the State but by an understanding between employer and employee. The French Episcopate voiced these recommendations in 1934 and shortly afterwards Cardinal Villeneuve expressed similar views on the measure: ". . . industries should consider collective agreements, and legislators can achieve a work of great social importance by favoring them."[25] In his course at the 1938 assembly in Sherbrooke on *Les Conventions collectives de travail,* Mr. Gérard Picard, Secretary of the *Confédération des Travailleurs catholiques* of Canada, borrowed Mr. Jean-Marie Arnion's definition of collective agreements:

> An understanding by means of which one or many employers or an employers' association on the one hand,

[23] S. s. du Canada, Ottawa, 1931, p. 302.

[24] S. s. du Canada, Montréal, 1932, p. 174. An excellent study on *L'Aide des assurances sociales* was made by Mr. Paul-Henri Guimont, Professor of Political Economy at the Social Science School of Laval University. Cf. S. s. du Canada, Sherbrooke, 1938, pp. 232-259.

[25] S. s. du Canada, 1938, p. 32: ". . . les industries devraient considérer la convention collective et . . . les législateurs feront une oeuvre de haute portée sociale en la favorisant."

and a union or any other grouping of workers on the other, determine the general conditions of work which should be considered when individual contracts for the loan of services are made.[26]

The agreements thus reached are then published in the Canadian *Gazette* for two consecutive months after which time, if no objections are forthcoming, they become compulsory.[27] The collective agreement, developed in Great Britain during the nineteenth century, favors professional organization, and the law of April 1934, sometimes called *loi Arcand,* relative to its extension in the Province of Quebec, modified since, provides for *comités paritaires* and bureaus of examiners, whereby persons interested in the industry have regulatory power under the supervision of the State. There were in 1938 seventy-one collective agreements in activity in the Province of Quebec.[28]

As soon as neutral unions with socialist tendencies appeared in French Canada, they met with opposition from the Church, as the latter readily perceived the danger inherent in such movements. In 1921, Msgr. Lapointe, pioneer of the Catholic syndical movement, reported the existence, to counteract this situation, of two hundred Catholic unions with some 50,000 members.[29] The following year, Mr. Achille Morin reported fifteen syndicates and two central councils in Hull.[30] In 1924, Mr. Antoine Laliberté realized that, though recruiting was difficult enough in Sherbrooke, none the less women syndicates and weavers' unions at the *Manufacture Paton* got a good start.[31] Again, in 1938 Mr. Omer D. Paulhus

---

[26] *Ibid.,* p. 199: "Un accord par lequel un ou plusieurs patrons ou un syndicat patronal d'une part, et un syndicat ou tout autre groupement de salariés d'autre part, fixent les conditions générales du travail que devront respecter les contrats individuels de louage de services."

[27] Interview with Mr. Saint-Pierre at the University of Montreal, September 20, 1944.

[28] S. s. du Canada, Sherbrooke, 1938, p. 202. Mr. Alphonse Bégin of the *Conseil central des Syndicats* of Montreal, summarizes the social measures obtained by the Catholic unions. Cf. S. s. du Canada, Salaberry-de-Valleyfield, 1943, pp. 161-162.

[29] S. s. du Canada, Québec, 1921, p. 383.

[30] S. s. du Canada, Ottawa, 1922, p. 260.

[31] S. s. du Canada, Sherbrooke, 1924, p. 354.

could report a central council in Sherbrooke with twenty-eight affiliated unions representing some 5,000 members. This in turn contributed to the establishment and development of four syndicates in Granby and Farnham with 1,500 members.[32] In 1927, Mr. Pierre Beaulé stated that there were 75,000 members belonging to Catholic unions in the Province of Quebec,[33] which meant that only four per cent of the French Canadian workers belonged to Catholic syndicates.[34] In Joliette, the movement was slow in making its appearance. But in 1934, friends from Montreal came to explain Catholic syndicalism to the workers of this city. That night forty-five of them registered and by 1935 there were 500 members belonging to Catholic unions.[35] By 1940 there were fifty-three cities in French Canada which had been affected by the Catholic syndical movement.[36]

Numerous are the advantages derived from Catholic labor unions. As early as 1921, at the Quebec meeting, Msgr. Paquet reminded his hearers that Catholic French Canadian syndicalism favors the interests of the professions, reconciles the classes which egotism separates, stimulates the cult of social virtues,[37] ameliorates the lot of workingmen exploited by certain employers, reacts against the incoherent individualism created by the French Revolution,[38] fosters the practice of honesty, combats socialism, Bolshevism and other modern perversive ideas, helps in the defense of the French language, keeps money in French Canada.[39] Catholic syndicates have also the common advantage of referring conflicts between employers and employees to judicial tribunals or better still to arbitration or conciliation. Three types of such tribunals, namely, ordinary tribunals, local authorities, and special tribunals were reported in 1921 as already existing in Great Britain, Germany and other countries of Europe.[40]

---

[32] S. s. du Canada, Sherbrooke, 1938, p. 391.
[33] S. s. du Canada, Québec, 1927, p. 412.
[34] S. s. du Canada, Montréal, 1932, p. 190.
[35] S. s. du Canada, Joliette, 1935, p. 306.
[36] S. s. du Canada, Nicolet, 1940, p. 159.
[37] S. s. du Canada, Québec, 1921, p. 49.
[38] *Ibid.*, pp. 83, 88.
[39] *Ibid.*, pp. 350-351.
[40] *Ibid.*, pp. 222-223.

In the Province of Quebec where two million persons depend upon wages for their subsistence, the urgency of belonging to Catholic national syndicates seems evident. Father Archambault, at the Montreal meeting of 1932, added appreciable advantages for the soul of the worker to the material advantages of combatting unemployment, assuring a reasonable wage and increasing professional services. Catholic syndicalism teaches the true doctrine of the Church on the inequality of classes, the rights and duties concerning property, the obligation of collaboration between capital and labor. It helps the laborer become a righteous, honest, and religious-minded citizen. Moreover, it benefits employers and society at large by establishing peace between two social classes, by assuring order—the foundation of society.[41]

Mention was made at the first Semaine Sociale of some early supporters of the Catholic syndical movement. Father Fortin of Quebec devoted his time to propaganda, organization and instruction. Father Archambault helped by the inauguration of laymen retreats and Father Lelièvre, O.M.I., the Apostle of the Sacred Heart, spread the knowledge of spiritual values. Mr. Henri Bourassa made a valuable study of national syndicates which serves as ample proof of his talent and of his admirable solicitude for the needy.[42]

The colleagues of the Semaine Sociale consider farmers' unions necessary in French Canada. This implies cooperation in agriculture in the form of cooperatives referred to in the preceding chapter. That this cooperative movement was launched with such remarkable success, Mr. Georges-Henri Saint-Cyr, Vice-President of the *Union catholique des cultivateurs* believes is largely due to the *cercles agricoles* established as early as 1870. These clubs, when sufficiently numerous, were combined in what became the *Union agricole nationale*. Its principal objectives were:

1. To improve the material and spiritual conditions of the agricultural class;
2. To induce farmers to combine their efforts, look to their interests, advance their cause and protect themselves by every means possible;

[41] S. s. du Canada, Montréal, 1932, pp. 386-387.
[42] S. s. du Canada, Montréal, 1920, p. 163.

3. To favor amiable understanding and true brotherhood;
4. To diminish the number of lawsuits by endeavoring to submit difficulties to arbitrators chosen from the members of the Union;
5. To demand respect for and render effective all the laws and ordinances helpful to agriculture.[43]

Women's unions form another type of Catholic syndicate in French Canada. Miss Marie J. Gérin-Lajoie at the 1921 meeting gave an enlightening course on *Le Syndicalisme féminin*. She tells how Miss Auclair reported that as early as 1906 and 1907 there existed an association of Catholic women instructors in Montreal and one of store employees, office-workers, and telephone operators. Syndicates of women then spread to the most important cities of French Canada. Whereas men's unions are preoccupied with measures of a technical, economic, and political order, women's syndicates are concerned with excessive demands on the part of certain employers, with hygienic conditions, and adequate moral protection. Miss Lajoie listed the advantages which had already been derived by women syndicates as early as 1921:

1. Better wages;
2. Greater employment stability: discharge for trivial motives became less frequent than formerly;
3. More respect from men-workers in factories. Improved deportment on the part of young girls;
4. Cessation of night work and its ensuing abuses;
5. More reserve and less favoritism or flirting on the part of certain employers or foremen;
6. Information about vacant positions.[44]

[43] S. s. du Canada, Trois-Rivières, 1936, pp. 129-130: "1. Améliorer la condition matérielle et intellectuelle de la classe agricole; 2. Amener les cultivateurs à agir de concert pour surveiller leurs intérêts, avancer leur cause et se protéger par tous les moyens possibles; 3. Favoriser parmi eux la bonne entente et la véritable fraternité; 4. Diminuer le nombre des procès en faisant soumettre autant que possible les difficultés à des arbitres choisis parmi les membres de l'Union; 5. Travailler a faire respecter et mettre en vigueur toutes les lois et ordonnances utiles à l'agriculture."

[44] S. s. du Canada, Québec, 1921, pp. 283-300: "1. Amélioration des gages; 2. Plus de stabilité dans l'emploi, les renvois pour des motifs futiles étant plus rares; 3. Plus de respect de la part des hommes dans l'atelier. Une meilleure tenue générale de la part des jeunes filles; 4. Cessation à peu

The most elaborate discussion of labor organizations was made in 1936 by a pioneer of the Semaine Sociale, Mr. Alfred Charpentier. The syndical movement, in the Province of Quebec is limited to three groups: the American International represented by the *Congrès des Metiers et du Travail du Canada* founded in 1892 and affiliated since 1881 with the American Federation of Labor; the Neutral National typified by the *Congrès Canadien du Travail,* founded in 1927 to supplant the old Federation of Labor; and the Catholic National represented by the *Confédération des Travailleurs Catholiques du Canada,* the C.T.C.C., founded in 1921 and of which Mr. Charpentier is president. In 1936 the C.T.C.C. had 43,000 members, eighty local unions included about half of this number; the other half were in ninety-six affiliates divided among eight federations. There are, moreover, a few independent unions some of which are typical of revolutionary unions. The Industrial Workers of the World, Mr. Charpentier tells us, appeared in Canada in 1912, was banished in 1918 and reinstated the following year; it is strongest in West Canada and aims at the abolition of the proletariat by the establishment of corporative socialism. In 1919, the *One Big Union* took over a good number of the members of the I.W.W.; of soviet inspiration, it groups its members by industries and geographic units in order to favor general strikes. The Worker's Unity League, founded in 1930 by the International of Moscow is still another example of a revolutionary union: it has been considered dissolved since 1935. The speaker concluded by affirming that the Canadian workers finally realized the folly of belonging to an international union and as a consequence enrollment in the latter has diminished steadily during the past years.[45]

A similar view was maintained by Father L. Gauthier when he referred to the expediency of enrolling in a Catholic national syndicate. One reason for the existence of the C.T.C.C., he said, is the dislike on the part of Canadian workers of being dominated by American unions. The C.T.C.C. believes that to allow unionism

---

près complète du travail du soir et des abus qu'il entraine; 5. Plus de réserve et moins de favoritisme ou flirt de la part de certain patrons ou chefs de département; 6. Renseignements sur les places vacantes."

[45] S. s. du Canada, Trois-Rivières, 1936, pp. 140-158.

from a foreign country, one that has neither the laws, customs, mentality, nor problems of Canada, is a grave economic error, a national abdication and a political danger.[46]

The neutral unions, in the words of Father J. B. Desrosiers, S.S., constitute a danger through their separation of morality from business and their exclusion of the Church from syndical questions. In truth these unions lack idealism, intent as they are on material goods only.[47] At the 1940 session of the Semaine Sociale, Mr. René Hamel declared that the defeat of France, Belgium and Holland is partly due to the infiltration of class internationalism which caused the destruction of national solidarity. Besides, he added, the fundamental error of every international union is to ignore the moral and religious aspect of human activities.[48]

In this connection there remains to be discussed the politico-social organization the Cooperative Commonwealth Federation, or C.C.F., represented in the Canadian Parliament by some deputies and favored by a few Catholics. Although this organization refuses to be branded communistic, Father Archambault asserts that its character is clearly socialistic. Needless to say, this scheme is not advocated by the Semaine Sociale. In 1937, an outstanding French-Canadian Mr. Camille L'Heureux analysed the movement. Mr. J. S. Woodsworth is said to have asserted that its program rests on principles truly socialistic. The Federation originated in 1932 at Calgary, Alberta, and aims to establish a cooperative community in Canada with a view to substituting for the present capitalistic regime a social order that will eliminate exploitation and class domination by creating a national bureau of directed economy. The three general principles advocated by the C.C.F. are excellent: human character of economy, cooperation, and directed economy. The difference between the C.C.F. and the Catholic social doctrine lies in the application of these principles. The C.C.F., it was asserted by Camille L'Heureux, destroys individual freedom, private initiative and exaggerates the social role of the State.[49]

---

[46] S. s. du Canada, Saint-Jean, 1942, pp. 163-164.

[47] S. s. du Canada, Salaberry-de-Valleyfield, pp. 170-172.

[48] S. s. du Canada, Nicolet, 1940, p. 177.

[49] S. s. du Canada, Saint-Hyacinthe, 1937, pp. 27-28; 91-112.

The Semaine Sociale is concerned with a better project than the C.C.F. plan to solve the economic-social problem of French Canada. It advocates associations of employers and employees as foundation stones for corporative organizations. Employers' associations (associations patronales) are groupings of employers of the same industry for the protection and defense of their interests. The aims of such an organization are: the establishment and maintenance of quality among the members; the promotion of mutual understanding and cooperation among commercial employers; the protection of their interests and the defense of their legitimate rights; the establishment, on bases of justice, charity and equity, of their relations with their employees by means of collective agreement and by a permanent mixed committee; the provision for uniformity and security in the relations between these same commercial employers and the public to assure mutual confidence; the attempt to prevent misunderstandings among the personnel; the solution of problems arising out of economic commercial relations; the organization of economic activity according to Catholic social principles; and the establishment of an information center to influence legislation. The advantages were enunciated by Mr. Edouard Coulombe, president of the *Association patronale du Commerce* of Quebec. Among these were: a substitution of order for disorder in the profession, the securing of fair treatment and freedom from economic dictatorships, the organization of a service of information, the study of changes and of technical services and the development of a spirit of collaboration. Similarly, professional associations are advantageous to the employees.[50] Mr. Gérard Picard, Secretary General of the C.T.C.C. adds that these professional employers' unions are means to arrive at a corporative organization of society, which could then be adapted to modern life and oriented toward the common good.[51]

In 1937, Father Charles-Omer Garant, Professor at the Grand Séminaire of Quebec, reported on an association of employers in the construction trade and a labor union of the same industry. For two years a collective contract had been set up between these two groups and a few meetings held. The speaker attended these

---

[50] S. s. du Canada, Québec, 1941, pp. 231-234.

[51] S. s. du Canada, Saint-Jean, 1942, p. 153.

meetings as chaplain of the Association of Employers. At the close of the assembly he was told: "We should meet oftener; we understand ourselves better when we speak to one another."[52]

The following year, at the Sherbrooke meeting of the Semaine Sociale, Mr. Picard was able to inform his audience that in Quebec one could count four such associations deriving their inspiration from Christian principles: the *Syndicat patronal des Maîtres-Barbiers et Coiffeurs;* the *Association des Constructeurs* of Quebec; the *Syndicat patronal de l'Imprimerie;* and the *Association patronale du Commerce.*[53]

As early as 1921, Father Emile Cloutier cited the Canadian Manufacturers Association as an example of such organization, extending as it did all over Canada and numbering 4,200 members, 994 of whom were from the Province of Quebec located in eighty-five urban and rural centers. Today it represents eighty per cent of the capital and eighty-five per cent of the industrial workers. It holds an annual general congress as well as provincial and regional meetings. There are, moreover, Executive Bureaus and Permanent Committees to study the question of transportation, tariff, insurances, legislation, commerce, industrial relations, publicity and education. The speaker admitted the importance of such an association and recommended groups of a similar pattern to the French Canadians.[54]

This explains the insistence of the Semaine Sociale on the formation of a corporative system, like the foregoing in character, but more extensive in scope and achievement. As early as 1921, Father Desranleau, at present Bishop of Sherbrooke, described the corporative regime of the Seventeenth and Eighteenth centuries.[55] In 1936 Mr. Jean Bruchesi treated the initial attempts to establish a corporative organization in various countries of Europe, the United States and Brazil.[56] In a course given at that same session of the Semaine Sociale by Mr. Leo Pelland accepted by Mr. Duthoit's definition of a corporative system: "The institu-

[52] S. s. du Canada, Saint-Hyacinthe, 1937, pp. 271-272.

[53] S. s. du Canada, Sherbrooke, 1938, p. 203.

[54] S. s. du Canada, Québec, 1921, p. 172, and Trois-Rivières, 1936, pp. 110-112.

[55] S. s. du Canada, Québec, 1921, pp. 56-73.

[56] S. s. du Canada, Trois-Rivières, 1936, pp. 202-235.

tion of a public and official body, intermediate between private enterprise and the State, charged with the maintenance of the common good in a determined profession."[57] Again, a professional corporation is a legally constituted body, which groups all the members of the same profession under a single authority, having the power to act in view of the common good and to impose its decisions on those concerned.[58] An outstanding authority on the subject, Mr. Maximilien Caron says that "corporatism is a doctrine which proposes the reform of our social organization."[59] And Cardinal Villeneuve at a Youth Congress gave as a password "Du corporatisme à plein."[60] Father Desranleau in 1921 enumerated the characteristics of corporations which were prominent before 1789: esprit de corps, professional honor, domestic character and religious spirit.[61] A profession in the mind of Mr. Leo Pelland implies discipline and organization;[62] therefore a corporative authority which is both lasting and peculiar to corporation becomes part of the system. Its essential functions are: to regulate the relations between employers and employees and the conditions that pertain to productive enterprise.[63]

Corporatism as advocated by the Semaine Sociale is based on the following precorporative elements: employers' associations and labor unions. It aims to fit in with the constitution of Canada without claiming any direct participation in government. Specifically social in character, but economic in the course of time, it projects the realization of an ordained economy taking into account the intelligence, will-power and true liberty of man.[64]

---

[57] *Ibid.*, p. 50: ". . . l'institution d'un corps officiel et public, intermédiaire entre les entreprises particulières et d'Etât, charge de la gérance du bien commun au sein d'une profession déterminée."

[58] "La Corporation professionelle," *L'Ordre Nouveau*, Montréal, December 5, 1938, p. 1.

[59] Maximilien Caron, "Le Corporatisme au Canada" in *Vers un ordre nouveau par l'organisation corporative* (Montréal, Ecole Sociale Populaire, 1940), p. 20.

[60] S. s. du Canada, Nicolet, 1940, p. 197.

[61] S. s. du Canada, Québec, 1921, p. 67.

[62] S. s. du Canada, Trois-Rivières, 1936, pp. 42-43.

[63] *Ibid.*, p. 194.

[64] S. s. du Canada, Nicolet, 1940, p. 185.

As to the legitimacy of professional organization, Father Alphonse Deguire, S.J., affirmed that that is legitimate which is in conformity with the will of God. Now an association is in conformity with natural law, the expression of the divine Will. It is necessary, then, to allow man to attain his end and perfection in conformity with the aspirations of the nature given him by God.[65] The Bishops of the Province of Quebec have voiced their approval of corporatism in the following words:

> We believe that the day will appear—soon, we hope —when the Province of Quebec will give the world an example of a corporative organization inspired on the encyclicals, which, although changing nothing in our constitution and yet adapted to our spirit and traditions, will play a most beneficial economic and social role. This will surely be the new order based on justice and charity which all good citizens look for. We hope for its coming and bless wholeheartily the courageous apostles of this salutary restoration.[66]

The above is truly the expression of Pope Pius XI's thought when he wrote:

> Let those free associations which already flourish and produce salutary fruits make it the goal of their endeavors, in accordance with Christian social doctrine, to prepare the way and to do their part towards the realization of that ideal type of vocational groups which we have mentioned above.[67]

---

[65] S. s. du Canada, Trois-Rivières, 1936, p. 71.

[66] S. s. du Canada, Saint-Jean, 1942, pp. 18-19: "Nous croyons que le jour viendra—bientôt, Nous l'espérons—ou la province de Québec donnera au monde l'exemple d'une organisation corporative inspirée des encycliques, et qui, sans rien changer à notre constitution, s'adaptant à notre esprit et à nos traditions, jouera un rôle économique et social des plus bienfaisants. Ce sera vraiment l'ordre nouveau, basé sur la justice et la charité, qu'appellent tous les bons citoyens. Nous souhaitons son prochain avènement et nous bénissons de tout coeur les vaillants apôtres de cette restauration salutaire."

[67] *Quadragesimo anno, op. cit.*, p. 25.

The objectives which govern the corporative regime, taken from Mr. Firmin Bacconnier, were quoted at the 1936 opening session of the Semaine Sociale by Father Archambault. They are: the regulation of production, both as to quantity and quality and the determination of a just price.[68] In the words of Mr. Alcide Côté, the elementary principles of corporatism rest on the peaceful coming together of two organizations—labor unions and employers' associations—to discuss the interests of the profession, the procedures of employers and employees of the same trade, having common interests, and animated by the same Christian spirit. The proper functioning of corporatism will thus do away with violent conflicts restoring equilibrium to the rights of the contending parties.[69] Truly, syndicalism, supplemented by corporatism carries within itself the hope of national economic discipline.

Again, this form of corporatism, as recommended by Mr. Maximilien Caron, bears no resemblance to Italian statism, although its integration into the democratic pattern of French Canada is advocated. It goes to the root of present social evils, namely liberalism and its credo, unregulated competition.[70] Mr. Minville's belief is that if a corporative institution is to be established on definite bases, it must not be imposed by law or by force; it must arise from the free will of the people interested and their awareness of the present social conditions and must be the result of a profound and general conviction of its necessity.[71]

In this regime, the State plays the role of regulator and supreme arbiter. "It guides, watches, urges, curbs" says *Quadragesimo anno*. Under its control and with its help, corporative groups act as associates. Father Archambault holds that such a corporative organization, if animated by a true Christian spirit, would transform the social life of French Canada. It would give a new structure to associations capable of offsetting the dangers of totalitarianism and of preserving democracy from perversive idealogies.[72]

Being non-political, the corporative organization does not par-

---

[68] S. s. du Canada, Trois-Rivières, 1936, p. 24.
[69] S. s. du Canada, Saint-Jean, 1942, pp. 156-157.
[70] S. s. du Canada, Nicolet, 1940, pp. 185-186.
[71] S. s. du Canada, Trois-Rivières, 1936, p. 245.
[72] S. s. du Canada, Salaberry-de-Valleyfield, 1943, p. 15.

ticipate directly in State government; only through an intercorporative council it may play the role of adviser in political meetings.[73] Mr. Maximilien Caron is of the opinion that the powers exercised by the corporation would have to be regulatory, disciplinary, arbitral and administrative, and that the corporative institution should be established on a provincial plan.[74] Several professors of the Semaine Sociale have shown the necessity of such a corporative organization in French Canada. Father J. B. Desrosiers applied to professional what may be said of a domestic organization. Corporatism is possible; moreover, it is necessary in all countries, and, no matter what the form of government may be, a country will be prosperous to the degree of prominence given to corporative organization. A country without such an institution is in need of serious reforms. Corporatism is necessary, he added, to safeguard the common good, and to restrain the liberty of individuals.[75] Father Alphonse Roux, Principal of the Normal School of Drummondville, stated that the corporative institution is the means of furnishing the social body with those elements it lacks to give its equilibrium and vigor.[76]

Back in 1921, Father Desranleau noted the benefits derived from the Guilds of the Middle Ages: assurance of peace and justice, friendly relations, community of interests, equitable distribution of profits, well-being, comfort and education. To be sure, medieval corporations had—as all human institutions have—disadvantages. He indicated three: inability to enter into a trade without the consent of the Council of Juries, never-ending lawsuits, too minute and narrow regulation of professional activity which hindered initiative and the spirit of invention.[77]

---

[73] *La Corporation professionnelle, op. cit.*, p. 1; S. s. du Canada, Nicolet, 1940, pp. 187, 192; Trois-Rivières, 1936, pp. 183-188; Saint-Hyacinthe, 1937, pp. 224-225.

[74] S. s. du Canada, Saint-Jean, 1942, p. 134: The term *corporation* as used in French Canada and incidentally in this dissertation is defined as follows: a body legally constituted, which groups all the members of the same profession under a single authority, having power to act in view of the common good and to impose its decisions on all those concerned.

[75] S. s. du Canada, Trois-Rivières, 1936, pp. 170-173.

[76] S. s. du Canada, Québec, 1941, p. 56.

[77] S. s. du Canada, Québec, 1921, pp. 68-70.

Mr. Antonio Perrault realized also that when vocational groups forget the objective for which they were established, the members, less and less imbued with Christian ideas, endeavor first and always to satisfy their personal egoism to the detriment of their competitors. At that point according to the eminent sociologist, Father Antoine, the corporation is a body without a soul, a body where an oligarchy reigns, the leaders monopolizing the charges to their profit and changing regulations to exploit the members.[78]

The role of the State relative to corporations was reviewed in Mr. Caron's course on *L'Organisation corporative*. The State should help corporations, supervise their activities so that they may not harm society but promote the common welfare. To know their needs and the results of their work is beneficial to the State in order to elaborate its legislation. The State will first intervene to grant a juridical personality to corporations and a corporative charter—a general law of corporations. Such legislation is required, moreover, to confer legal authority upon them to invest them with the various powers previously mentioned, for the State alone disposes of the "monopoly of coercion."[79]

Another authority on this question, Mr. Léon-Mercier Gouin, argued that since the State is already concerned with the general administration of a country, its postal system, customs, railroads and exterior defense, it has no time to supervise production, temper unbridled competition, pacify the relations between employers and employees and provide for the needs of the poor and unfortunate.[80]

There is sporadic mention in the proceedings of the Semaine Sociale of the possible types of corporations in French Canada. Father Emile Cloutier applies the corporative principle to the domain of industry. This industrial corporation would then comprise the capitalists, directors, managers, expert technicians, office clerks and laborers. Each of these categories would have its separate union; all the unions would be linked and contact between them maintained by mixed commissions; finally, the delegates

[78] S. s. du Canada, Québec, 1927, p. 389.

[79] S. s. du Canada, Sherbrooke, 1938, p. 316.

[80] Léon-Mercier Gouin, "La Solution corporative," *"Vers un ordre nouveau par l'organisation corporative* (Montréal: Ecole Sociale Populaire, 1940), p. 11.

representing the various unions would compose the superior corporative council. This council would be the directive organ of the profession; make regulations and supervise their applications; prevent the recurrence of difficulties and conflicts; and negotiate with other corporations and with public officials.[81]

At the 1942 meeting, Mr. Caron distinguished four types of professions suitable to a corporative regime, namely: agriculture, commerce, industry, and public services. Each type gives rise to one federation. Consequently four corporative federations would group all the individuals who take part in the economic and social development of the Province.[82]

Existing corporations in the Province of Quebec include those of the Bar, the medical profession, Chamber of Notaries. Other professions are similarly organized: pilots, dentists, architects and farriers. To take the Bar as an example of such an association: a lawyer must have a license from the Bar to practice his profession; he must observe the regulations of the Bar which determine the conditions under which he may enjoy the advantages and privileges of his profession. These same regulations may even forbid acts judged derogatory to the laws of the profession.[83] Thus, the corporation exercises a coercive power. It punishes violators by censure, reprimand, suspension and even definite expulsion.[84]

To summarize, the role played by professional organizations is primarily social and economic. Economically the corporation is concerned about the regulation of production and exchange, the determination of prices, the adaptation of products and services to the need of customers; socially, it conciliates the rights of employers and employees, organizes social services, professional teaching, placement, and insurances. With other corporations it collaborates to promote the common good. Thus it abolishes the struggle of classes, remedies the evils of individualism and inculcates in citizens a sense of collectivity whereby the common good is promoted.

---

[81] S. s. du Canada, Montréal, 1932, p. 260.

[82] S. s. du Canada, Saint-Jean, 1942, pp. 138-139.

[83] S. s. du Canada, Québec, 1941, pp. 230-231.

[84] S. s. du Canada, Sherbrooke, 1938, p. 314.

CHAPTER X

Semaine Sociale and Perversive Ideologies

In keeping with the Church's policy, the Semaine Sociale has always condemned the various forms of perversive ideologies: socialism, communism, individualism, liberalism, and racism. Frequent references to these destructive theories may be found in the reports of the "ambulatory University."

At the very first session of the Semaine Sociale two courses treated of socialism: one, *Un faux remède, le socialisme* given by Father Lucien Pineault, the other, *Les Conséquences funestes du socialisme* delivered by Mr. André Fauteux. Early in his course, Father Pineault formulated a definition of socialism:

> a system of those who teach that all productive goods must become the property of civil society, not by force and violence, as the anarchists and Bolshevists want it, but by political means, such as elections and laws and that, independently of all natural moral and religious right.[1]

At the 1924 meeting Father Henri Simard declared that socialism is above all a philosophical theory of the constitution of society preoccupied solely with the pleasure and happiness of this life. The speaker affirmed that socialism is opposed to the Catholic Church and its supernatural doctrine and is bent upon combatting it with all its might.[2]

---

[1] S. s. du Canada, Montréal, 1920, p. 40: ". . . le système de ceux qui enseignent que tous les biens productifs doivent devenir la propriété de la société civile, non par la force et la violence, comme le veulent les anarchistes et les bolchévistes, mais par les moyens politiques, tels que les élections et les lois et cela indépendamment de tout droit naturel, moral et religieux."

[2] S. s. du Canada, Sherbrooke, 1924, p. 49.

One of the pernicious errors of socialism is the denial of the right to property; for the benefit of the proletariat, all are despoiled of their property which is taken over by the State. To realize their supposedly benevolent project, moreover, socialists arouse the masses and enkindle hatred. Again socialism, denying the spiritual and sublime end of man, holds that human society is constituted only for man's temporal well-being.[3] As such it is concerned mainly with material goods and their distribution, with physical hygiene, with rest and labor and other matters of this nature. The socialistic endeavor to alleviate the poor man's lot is most laudable, to be sure. But the method socialists advocate is seriously at fault, especially as to its fundamental philosophy and in their demands as to the character of change in government and in the constitution of society concerning the right to individual property.[4]

At the 1931 meeting, Father Edmour Hébert reported on the collectivistic doctrine reviewed at the Congress of Gotha in 1875, where it was asserted that the means of production are exclusively collective property and belong to society; individuals have merely the use of them; agricultural and industrial production is social, that is, it can be exercised only in the name of the State; the socialistic State is to determine the prices of commodities and products; after deductions have been made on the general costs, the individual will receive his wages. It is he who should benefit of the dividends which heretofore had gone to the capitalists.[5]

In 1924, Father Simard referred to several tactics employed to spread socialism: instruction of the masses in the exaggerated knowledge of the evils suffered and in the irresistible power their numbers possess; the paying of socialistic missionaries who convene popular assemblies and lead discussions on the questionable merits of the system. In the *Montreal Gazette* of April, 1924, the same speaker reported that there was ample evidence that the spread of socialism in Canada has been in direct proportion to the energy expended by its "missionaries." In a news item whose

---

[3] S. s. du Canada, Montréal, 1932, p. 235, 241.

[4] S. s. du Canada, Sherbrooke, 1924, p. 50, and Montréal, 1920, pp. 41-42.

[5] S. s. du Canada, Ottawa, 1931, p. 137.

headline reads: *Communists of Dominion Join International,* we discover that at a convention held in the Labor Temple of Toronto, under the direction of delegates from Moscow, the communists of Canada chose to become affiliated to the Communistic International of Moscow. The soul of this convention was Kollaraw, the secretary of the International. What is more, socialism is said to have been responsible for the destructive strikes of the miners and steel workers in Nova Scotia, and of the car shop workers of Winnipeg. On occasions the red flag of socialism and of anarchy was hoisted, as happened during a parade on Labor Day in Montreal. As the counterpart to the password of the socialists, Father Simard suggested: "Catholics of the world over, let us unite to defend our religion, our country, our families, our good Catholic workers!"[6]

By 1929, Father Bissonnette could vividly describe how socialistic theories were being spread by weekly journals, books and leaflets. Sustained by secret funds, the equalitarian doctrine fascinates the worker and renders him dissatisfied with his lot. He then looks askance at true Christian social programs of which the Catholic syndicates are the guardians, and refuses to lend an ear to pontifical teachings.[7] The aim of the socialists is to group all such workers and lead them in a desperate war against capitalism and all who are opposed to their social theories.

That socialist attempts have produced disorder and anarchy was reported by Father Marcel-Marie Dugal, O.F.M. Socialism has been powerful to destroy; it can shake the bases of existing society but it is doubtful whether it would ever be able to build on its ruins a new order of liberty and justice. Little wonder, then, he continued, that so many socialistic procedures have failed wherever they have been introduced. Semler enumerated more than forty such attempts in North America since 1825 but each one more fruitless than the last.[8]

[6] S. s. du Canada, Sherbrooke, 1924, pp. 55-60.

[7] S. s. du Canada, Chicoutimi, 1929, p. 96.

[8] *Ibid.*, p. 65: Two excellent studies entitled *Utopias and the Philosophy of Saint Thomas* and *Utopie socialiste* have been made respectively by Sister M. Saint Ida Leclair of the Order of the Presentation of Mary (Washington: The Catholic University of America Press, 1941), and Mr. Arthur Saint-Pierre (Montréal: Ecole Sociale Populaire, 1913).

In 1920, Mr. André Fauteux reported the results of the socialistic regime in Russia after a three-year experiment. The harvest which once nourished a good part of Europe is now insufficient even for Russia; railroads and mines are in bankruptcy. Erlich, upon his return from a stay in Russia condemned the system in the following words:

> . . . the Russian bourgeoisie is ruined; but with it has equally foundered national industry to the great loss of the Russian proletariat, and to the great profit of German industry which is on the verge of replacing it. Bolshevism has engendered famine and starvation. . . . Individual liberty is abolished and every day hundreds of Russian laborers and intellectuals, whose only crime is not to think like the Bolshevists, are massacred without court procedure by Magyar and Chinese mercenaries. Besides scorning all notion of justice and right, socialism reduces to nothingness the talents and noblest passions of man. It suppresses talent, enthusiasm, intelligence, traditions and history.[9]

Again in 1927, Mr. Ernest Lapointe affirmed that the supposed liberation of the Russians is only fictitious. The governmental machine is still guided by a small number of leaders, absolute enough to have been able to suppress all liberties, notably those of speech and the press. A mere discharge of musketry promptly ended all tentative opposition.[10] Father M. A. Lamarche, O.P., also maintained that the socialist organization is essentially bu-

---

[9] S. s. du Canada, Montréal, 1920, p. 49: ". . . la bourgeoisie russe est ruinée; mais, avec elle, a sombré également toute l'industrie nationale, au plus grand détriment du prolétariat russe, mais, par contre, pour le plus grand profit de l'industrie allemande qui est en train de prendre sa place. Le bolchévisme n'a su engendrer que la famine et la disette. . . . Toutes les libertés individuelles sont abolies, et, chaque jour, des centaines d'ouvriers et d'intellectuels russes, dont le seul crime est de ne pas penser comme les bolcheviks, sont massacrés sans le moindre jugement par des mercenaires magyars et chinois. Le socialisme, outre qu'il méprise les premières notions de la justice et du droit confine, en dernier ressort, à la négation des talents et des plus nobles passions de l'homme. Il supprime le talent, l'enthousiasme, l'intelligence, le passé, les traditions, et l'histoire."

[10] S. s. du Canada, Québec, 1927, p. 355.

reaucratic and autocratic. According to Kalinine's report in the *Pravda* of June 19, 1930, similar inequality may be observed even in the ranks of Russian workers. Thus there still exists Russian proletariat and a higher stratum in this same proletariat.[11]

In line with their usual procedure, the followers of the Semaine Sociale endeavor to offer remedies for all critical situations. Thus at the 1936 assembly, Father Perrier insisted on the teachings of the Popes to nullify socialistic doctrine. Pope Pius XI, he said, advocates the reestablishment of "vocational groups"; the practice of justice, equity and charity in labor relations; the subordination of individual to general interests. The Church, therefore, calls for the collaboration of classes; repudiates violence, struggle, and opposition between employers and employees; demands a reform of morals as a means of realizing the Christian social order. Cardinal Villeneuve gave the French Canadians important directives in a commentary on *Quadragesimo anno*:

> The socio-economic world is seriously affected. Neither a levelling socialism nor a liberal capitalism can do anything save to destroy it. Only a doctrine of sensible, generous, just and charitable capitalism can set the world back on its hinges. This capitalism must remember the rights of all classes of society to an equitable distribution of wealth, a point which the State has the duty to enforce. But the State will remain powerless and inefficacious unless it favors the establishment of social institutions on which it can then rest, like a lever, as its focal point to raise all obstacles.[12]

---

[11] S. s. du Canada, Montréal, 1932, p. 338.

[12] S. s. du Canada, Trois-Rivières, 1936, pp. 335-337: "Le monde économico-social est gravement atteint. Ni le socialisme niveleur, ni le capitalisme libertaire ne pourront autre chose que l'achever. C'est la doctrine du capitalisme raisonnable et généreux, juste et charitable, qui peut remettre seul le monde sur son pivot. Ce capitalisme doit se souvenir des droits de toutes les classes de la société à une équitable répartition des richesses. L'Etat a pour mission de le lui imposer. Mais l'Etat restera impuissant et inefficace, à moins qu'il ne favorise la création des institutions sociales sur lesquelles il pourra ensuite s'appuyer, comme un levier sur son point d'appui, pour lever les obstacles."

To accomplish this renovation Pope Pius XI called all Christians to a methodical, organized, directed action controlled by religious authority. That this doctrine may penetrate the masses, something more than personal sanctification is required: Christian workers must be grouped and organized if they are to prosper and conquer.[13] Leo XIII's argument in *Rerum novarum* for the right to property as a means of maintaining peace was expressed by a Belgian politician in the smart formula: "Would you combat socialists? Increase the number of your proprietors."[14] And Mr. Médard Leduc admits that it is not only the abuses of capitalism that have forced the State to intervene in the life of individuals, but the improvidence of French Canadians as well. Therefore he recommends thrift as a remedy against socialism.[15]

In a course on *Socialisme et communisme* given in 1932, Mr. Joseph Barnard distinguished between socialism and communism. Socialism is a false and insidious doctrine based on the most complete scorn of all religious ideas; communism is the fatal limit of this first error but emphasized so furiously by its leaders that the result is nothing short of ridiculous.[16] The main difference between these two ideologies is that socialism does not attempt to apply all its errors at once; it goes half-way hoping thereby to attract sympathy. Nothing, on the other hand, stops communism; it goes straight to extremes and does not hesitate at absurdities.[17] These two ideologies, however, are similar in that they both deny the right of individuals to possess private property and confer this right on the community or on the collectivity.[18] Politically these two systems are also at odds. For the communist the socialist is too bourgeois, too conservative, too capitalistic. These two, however, in the opinion of Mr. Paul Fontaine, are "Siamese twins." They have the same materialistic conception of history, they make the same economic and social demands. They differ only in their method of action. The Comintern, the speaker goes on to say,

[13] *Ibid.*, 338.

[14] S. s. du Canada, Sherbrooke, 1924, p. 20.

[15] S. s. du Canada, Salaberry-de-Valleyfield, 1943, p. 61.

[16] S. s. du Canada, Montréal, 1932, p. 234.

[17] *Ibid.*, p. 248.

[18] S. s. du Canada, Sherbrooke, 1924, p. 52.

has its mystic, its dogma, its economics. Its prophets and saints are Lenin, Stalin, Boukharine and Trotsky. From the *Cahiers du Bolchévisme* Mr. Fontaine quoted the following: "He [Lenin] is a genial thinker, an incomparable leader, a true interpreter and follower of Karl Marx." And for Marx "man it is who creates God; religion is only the reflection of social economy, the opium of the people." Boukharine holds that religious beliefs will completely disappear with the entire disappearance of the antagonism of social classes. And so, as combat against religion is imperative, the abolition of the Church as an organization of religious propaganda must be undertaken.[19]

At the 1938 assembly, devoted to a study of *Divini Redemptoris,* Mr. Jean Penverne reported Marx as proclaiming that the happiness of a people demands the abolition of religion and Engels insisting on the absolute incompatibility of the two. The speaker added that not a few people, notably in France, claim a certain connection between communism and Christianity. In fact, one of the communists' favorite maxims is: "Christianity is communism" and by references to the Bible, to the supposed communistic state in which the early Christians lived, the communists attempt to prove their pernicious doctrine. If these communists were true Christians they would realize that apart from a few passages in the Bible favorable to community of goods for religious ends, the general spirit of the doctrine is opposed to it.[20]

The second false doctrine of communism is the denial of all civil authority. For the communist it is no better to obey man than God. In Lenin's words "parliamentarism is an instrument of falsity, of fraud, of odious babbling."[21] In his regime all men are absolutely equal. There is no authority established by God, since there is no God, and therefore no authority of parents over their children. The only authority that is recognized by communists comes from the collectivity.[22]

As to the family, communists hold that there is no such thing as an indissoluble marriage bond; woman is not attached to the

[19] S. s. du Canada, Québec, 1927, pp. 261-262.

[20] S. s. du Canada, Sherbrooke, 1938, 322.

[21] S. s. du Canada, Québec, 1927, pp. 262-263.

[22] S. s. du Canada, Sherbrooke, 1938, p. 56.

home; her task is to work in the factory. Let the State take care of her children. The consequences of these free unions or legal marriages, purely voluntary and dissolved at the will of anyone of the parties have caused alarm even in Russia, so much so that an attempt has been made to revert to the form of marriage more in conformity with the natural law.[23]

The school is dealt with in the same fashion. The right of education, it is claimed, is the prerogative of the State. There should be only one type of school directed by the State and the customary separation of sexes should be suppressed. In the words of Boukharine as reported by Mr. Fontaine, "the priests will be driven from all the schools." The press and private property suffer the same fate.[24] In communistic language, property is synonymous with theft for the simple reason that if property is allowed then equal distribution of goods becomes impossible.[25] Thus, Lenin is said to have emphasized the idea of a collectivized regimented economy.

Like socialism, communism spreads by means of persuasion and propaganda. But unlike socialism it makes use of violence. Lenin realized that "revolution is a very cruel and non-economical means of solving the question but history has found no other."[26] For Trotsky violence was something sacred, and the "costs of revolution are not useless expenses."[27] Besides, a revolution demands preparation, hence the peculiar communistic technique must be used drastically but efficiently. At the 1927 meeting of the Semaine Sociale, Mr. Paul Fontaine, legal advisor of the C.T.C.C., in his course on *La Menace communiste au Canada,* referred to the countries that had been affected at one time or another by communism: Hungary, Italy, Germany, France, and England. The communistic influence in England, the speaker claimed, has been manifest in the coal strikes of the time: there are seventy-five factory units and twenty communistic journals in England. The doctrine has spread to China, Egypt, India, South Africa, and

[23] *Ibid.,* p. 58.

[24] S. s. du Canada, Québec, 1927, p. 264.

[25] S. s. du Canada, Salaberry-de-Valleyfield, 1943, p. 176.

[26] S. s. du Canada, Québec, 1927, p. 264 cited from Lenine, *Sur la route de l'insurrection,* p. 29.

[27] *Ibid.,* cited from Trotsky, *La nouvelle politique économique,* p. 36.

Australia. The Third Red International has truly attempted to conquer the world.[28] But the countries like Russia, Mexico[29] and Spain, which have seen the workings of a communistic regime, pitilessly denounce the horrors of a Bolshevistic system.[30]

How has Canada fared? We find the same organization, the same propaganda, the same aspirations here as elsewhere. In 1927, communism had 4,000 followers. In the West, in Toronto, in Montreal, the ABC's of communism were being taught in several schools directed by foreigners. The communist party aims to consolidate labor organizations and at the same time to originate a struggle against capitalism; to dismiss present leaders and substitute revolutionary adepts; to take part in elections, in the political life of the nation and voice the demands of the working class; and finally to establish a proletarian dictatorship.

For the purposes of communist propaganda, Canada was divided into nine districts; nine branches of which were in the district of Quebec. Ontario headed the provinces in the number of its branches. Two journals, *The Workers* and a Jewish paper; a League of Young Communists organized in 1922 with two organs, *The Young Worker* and *The Young Comrade;* and a *Ligue d'Education des Unions* were other means of communistic propaganda.

All things considered, Mr. Fontaine believed that in Canada public opinion is not favorable to communism, on the contrary, the Canadian mind is generally sound; it affirms its principles of order and authority, is religious and believes in God and in the moral order. The powers expressive of public opinion are conservative; the press abhors revolution as interfering with the economic activity of the country. The provincial and federal parliaments are much more capitalistic than communistic. University folk are more intent on earning money than on seizing it from others by a forced sharing. Canadians are non-interventionists, rather they fear the State. It is significant to note that the *Congrès des Metiers et du Travail* of Canada refused to recognize soviet

[28] *Ibid.*, p. 268.

[29] A careful study showing the workings of the socialistic party in connection with education in Mexico was made by Sister M. Cecilia de Jesus Gaudreau, in an unpublished Master's Dissertation: *Mexico's Contribution to Rural Indian Education,* Catholic Teachers' College, Providence, R. I., 1943.

[30] S. s. du Canada, Sherbrooke, 1938, p. 25.

Russia, that it rejected a request of the government demanding the grant of credits to Russia for purchases in Canada; that one of its members was ostracized because he was a communist.

One must not conclude, however, that because the unions, public opinion, government, and the universities, are not in favor of communism, that the communist menace is non-existent in Canada. Mr. Fontaine for one, realized the dangers, especially the possibility that the misinformed may be enticed by visions of an earthly paradise. Hunger is a bad counsellor, hunger for bread and hunger for justice. The speaker, therefore, advised the rich to appease the two simultaneously.[31] Magistrate J. H. Lemay claimed that the best friend of communism is the employer who does not seem to understand that when he causes his employee to suffer from hunger he is preparing the victim to be exploited by agents from Moscow.[32] In fact, the power of communism is explained by the weakness of Christians.[33]

In 1937, Father M. A. Lamarche, O.P., referred to the decisions that had already been taken by the ensemble of the French Canadian people. Useless to say that they did not advocate communism.[34] Very different was the situation in the other provinces. Father Archambault tells of a communist leader in Toronto who obtained 44,148 votes at the municipal election of 1938. Two years previously, he had won 31,426 votes. In that same city one paper was spreading subversive communist ideas and the *Daily Clarion* paints Quebec in the most somber colors. About forty journals and periodicals published in Canada, a large number from the outside, tracts, pamphlets, theatrical performances, conferences and films pursue the same work of propaganda throughout Canada.[35]

In Russia, the pernicious results of communistic propaganda as reported in the Semaine Sociale are astounding. We have seen how the Semaine Sociale discussed Russia as a socialistic regime; the following text, however, refers to statements of Russia as specifically communistic. In 1927, Mr. Fontaine referred to the

[31] S. s. du Canada, Québec, 1927, pp. 268-272.
[32] S. s. du Canada, Montréal, 1932, p. 384.
[33] S. s. du Canada, Saint-Jean, 1942, p. 149.
[34] S. s. du Canada, Saint-Hyacinthe, 1937, p. 343.
[35] S. s. du Canada, Sherbrooke, 1938, pp. 26-27.

horrible massacres which annihilated the intellectual, social, and religious elite; to the fact that industries were being managed by the State to the detriment of Russian society. He also mentioned lower wages and higher cost of living, the absence of free press and syndicates, sordid habitations which favor immorality, legalized abortion, the deplorable state of public services. The speaker claimed that the number of unemployed at that time was more than a milion.[36] In 1938, moreover, Mr. Penverne stated that employment is the general rule.[37] In 1931, Father Eustache Gagnon, C.S.C., reported 175,000,000 Russian persons reduced to the lowest point of slavery.[38]

In brief, we find numerous references in the Semaine Sociale to the repudiation by the communist party of all that is held most sacred by humanity in general: God, future life, morality, respect for woman and child, respect for authority, the right to property, pity for the weak, and justice for all.[39]

At the 1938 assembly, Mr. Penverne, prominent lawyer of Montreal, gave a conference on *Le Communisme à l'oeuvre.* In it he reviewed the doctrine, method and results of this destructive regime. In the first six months of the religious persecution of 1929, four hundred twenty-three churches had been closed; one hundred fifty-six had been transformed into theaters or museums, thirty-eight into schools, fourteen into cooperatives, ten into veterinary centers, twenty-nine had been demolished, and one hundred seventy-one had been left unused. Three hundred seventeen additional churches had been demolished. Up to 1930, thirty-one bishops had been murdered, 1,600 priests and 7,000 monks. At the same time there were forty-eight bishops, 3,700 priests and 8,000 monks and sisters in prison. On August 6, 1935, the *Ligue Internationale contre la Troisième Internationale* published statistics in Geneva which indicated that 40,000 religious had been banished, arrested or killed. The speaker told of a certain Sobelson who was called by Stalin and asked to find a way to destroy the

---

[36] S. s. du Canada, Québec, 1927, pp. 266-267.

[37] S. s. du Canada, Sherbrooke, 1938, p. 348.

[38] S. s. du Canada, Ottawa, 1931, p. 96.

[39] S. s. du Canada, Montréal, 1932, p. 248; Trois-Rivières, 1936, p. 17; Saint-Hyacinthe, 1937, p. 268; and Saint-Jean, 1942, p. 150.

vermin infesting the inhabitants of the Kremlin. Sobelson's answer was: "The solution is simple. 'Collectivize' the vermin! That will be sufficient: half will perish and the other half will only have to pack up."[40] Boris Souvarine in his book on Stalin says that at the beginning of 1931 at least 5,000,000 peasants had been expelled from their homes and reduced to dire misery. For the winter of 1932 and the spring of 1933, American journalists at Moscow estimated that the number of deaths due to starvation had been from three to seven millions. The government then ceased to publish statistics.[41] Little wonder then that Lenin could say: "The millions of human lives that I need for my social experiment are not more precious in my sight than millions of guinea pigs."[42]

Bishop Desranleau, the last speaker of the 1938 meeting outlined an excellent program of activity to abolish communism:

> Communism is a monster. Let us keep away from it. It seeks our perdition, it wants to penetrate into our midst to destroy everything. . . . The government has given us just and energetic laws, let us use them. Let us practice charity towards its victims, but let us combat its projects, its enterprises, its methods, its ideas. And let us pray, let us pray a great deal: we shall conquer the godless only with the help of God.[43]

Among the remedies suggested by the Semaine Sociale to abolish communism is knowledge of its perversive doctrine. The common people must be made aware of this perverse doctrine even when it is camouflaged, as for instance, when communists say they are

---

[40] S. s. du Canada, Sherbrooke, 1938, pp. 332-334.

[41] *Ibid.*, p. 334.

[42] *Ibid.*, p. 83: Les millions de vies humaines qu'il me faut pour mon expérience sociale ne sont pas plus précieuses à mes yeux que des millions de cochons-d'Inde."

[43] *Ibid.*, p. 413: "Le communisme est un monstre. Gardons-nous-en. Il cherche notre perte, il veut pénétrer chez nous pour tout détruire. . . . Le governement nous a donné une loi juste et énergique, servons-nous-en. Faisons la charité à ses victimes, mais combattons ses oeuvres, ses entreprises, ses méthodes, ses idées. Et prions, prions beaucoup: nous ne vaincrons les sans-Dieu qu'avec le secours de Dieu."

fighting for democratic liberty. Again when they say they are defending the people against the injustices of capital, they lie. When they proclaim religious liberty, they lie even more boldly. In short, Catholic apostles must unmask communism.[44] The best way to ruin it, Canon Arsène Goyette claimed, is to maintain Christian civilization in all its integrity and intensify the practice of the virtues of faith, hope and charity. He then referred to the insistence of Pope Pius XI on detachment from the goods of this world and on Christian charity.[45] Father Emile Cloutier says that the only way to thwart communism is to reestablish among Christian peoples the communion of saints in all its sincerity and primitive fervor.[46] To listen to the teachings of the Church when its Bishops speak, was the advice of Canon Allaire.[47] Pope Pius XI not only condemned communism but reminded everyone of the strict obligation of combatting its propaganda and of remedying the abuses which provoked its incidence:

> But We cannot contemplate without profound sorrow the heedlessness of these who seem to make light of these imminent dangers and with stolid indifference allow the propagation far and wide of those doctrines which seek by violence and bloodshed and destruction of all society. Even more severely must be condemned the foolhardiness of those who neglect to remove or modify such conditions as exasperate the minds of the people, and so prepare the way for the overthrow and ruin of the social order.[48]

The remedy, in the words of Mr. Fontaine, the "ultimate remedy, the eternal remedy to abolish communism is the return of humanity to Him who said of Himself "I am the way, and the truth, and the life."[49]

Father Gauthier, an authority on the subject, believes that there is no actual danger of the incidence of communism in French

---

[44] *Ibid.*, p. 69.
[45] *Ibid.*, p. 355.
[46] S. s. du Canada, Joliette, 1935, p. 229.
[47] S. s. du Canada, Saint-Hyacinthe, 1928, p. 190.
[48] *Quadragesimo Anno, op. cit.*, p. 31.
[49] S. s. du Canada, Québec, 1927, p. 273.

Canada although there are some 22,000 women in factories militating in its favor. During a crisis of unemployment, he adds, the danger would be greater than before World War II because present-day communists no longer depend upon Moscow. Their policy is "Choose a critical period, one in which dissatisfaction is rampant, and act."[50] On the other hand, Mr. Saint-Pierre claims that there is no danger of a communist insurrection in French Canada. The actual number of communists in French Canada, he states, is insignificant as the last election proved. Like Father Gauthier, Father Archambault holds that Canada has not been delivered from the "claws of the monster" of communism.[51]

Individualism is another ideology prevalent in French Canadian thought though less obtrusive than communism. Father Lévesque declared that "we live in a century penetrated with individualism."[52] Precisely because egoism is so strong society is facing an extremely violent crisis, Father Charles-Omer Garant noted. Due to the fact that human reason has been given almost complete autonomy, man has become used to considering himself independent and free from all superior principle and has come to believe that his destiny depends solely upon his efforts.[53]

In the words of Mr. Bourassa, individualism has found in the Declaration of the Rights of Man its political formula and in the liberalism of the Manchester School its economic expression. In these two theories both the family and society are subordinated to individual egoism.[54] Canon Courchesne calls liberalism and socialism rival brothers of the same revolutionary principle: both showing traits of resemblance which indicate their common origin. For liberal individualism, society is non-existent. For socialistic individualism to attain absolute equality individuals are all reduced to a state of annihilation.[55]

---

[50] Interview with Father Lorenzo Gauthier at the Ecole Hippolyte, September 27, 1944.

[51] Interview with Mr. Arthur Saint-Pierre at the University of Montreal, August 22, 1944, and *L'Action Catholique,* Québec, September 30, 1944.

[52] S. s. du Canada, Joliette, 1935, p. 309.

[53] S. s. du Canada, Saint-Hyacinthe, 1937, p. 265.

[54] S. s. du Canada, Montréal, 1923, p. 280.

[55] S. s. du Canada, Trois-Rivières, 1925, pp. 88-89.

Among the characteristics that Professor Montpetit notes as peculiar to French Canada he mentions individualism, especially that lack of solidarity, congenital so to say, which cannot be eradicated,—"plus résistant qu'entreprenant."[56] In 1941, His Excellency Msgr. Ildebrando Antoniutti, Apostolic Delegate of Canada, maintained that exalted individualism in the religious sphere has engendered the disorganization of the Christian family resulting in a breakdown which has made man the sole author of his credo and of all his errors. In the social order, individualism has been responsible for the many disorders allied to that liberalism.[57]

The opposition of the Semaine Sociale and of its followers to the theory of liberalism may be deduced from the fact that many courses were given in an endeavor to point out its perversity. In 1920, Msgr. Paquet stated that the Liberal school based its laissez-faire policy on the rationalistic principle that the nature of man is free from original imperfection and that social progress is consequent upon absolute liberty.[58] In 1927, Mr. Paul Fontaine summarized the dogmas of the Liberal school: misery is the ransom of progress; everything will function well eventually; natural laws correct their own faults.[59] The following year Mr. Montpetit reviewed the optimistic hypotheses of the physiocrats: economic laws if observed will create peace, harmony and prosperity, provided that man does not interfere and personal interest is the norm of human activities.[60] Thus, the Liberal school rejects the regulation of labor by law, to determine minimum wages, and measures to regulate production and reduce competition.[61]

Furthermore, economic liberalism has justified the worst abuses. According to its principles, the enterprising, audacious individual may use any means whatever to attain wealth. The race for money has given rise to that immoderate, inhuman, totalitarian capitalism

[56] Edouard Montpetit, *Le Front contre la vitre* (Montréal: Editions Albert Lévesque, 1936), p. 47.

[57] S. s. du Canada, Québec, 1941, p. 198.

[58] S. s. du Canada, Montréal, 1920, p. 69 and Montréal, 1932, pp. 65-66.

[59] S. s. du Canada, Québec, 1927, p. 260, and Trois-Rivières, 1936, p. 334.

[60] S. s. du Canada, Saint-Hyacinthe, 1928, p. 263, and Sherbrooke, 1938, pp. 38-39.

[61] S. s. du Canada, Ottawa, 1931, p. 136.

which concentrates all the economic and political power of a nation in the hands of a few and submits the common good to the interests of a minority.[62] The consequences have been disastrous in placing on the same footing man and nothingness, the God of light and the Prince of darkness, the Author of all perfection and the propagator of all perversity.[63]

For the protagonist of liberalism wealth constitutes an end in itself. In the domain of business, economic liberalism has begotten anarchy and has led fatally to the destruction of the weak by the strong and the establishment of an oppressive economic dictatorship over society, the ruling class included. A directed economical regime should be substituted to this rule of anarchy and dictatorship.[64] As stated by Pius XI: "Free competition and still more economic domination must be kept within just and definite limits, and must be brought under the effective control of public authority, in matters appertaining to this latter's competence. The public institutions of nations must be such as to make the whole of human society conform to the common good, i.e., to the standard of social justice."[65]

The first reference made to racism as a perversive ideology may be found in the 1938 reports of the Semaine Sociale. Father Gonzalve Poulin, O.F.M., Professor of Social Economy at Laval University, declared that the racist order is the result of "laïcisme" and naturalism. That form of racism which places the salvation of a people in blood kinship is in opposition to Christ's doctrine proclaiming the necessity of Revelation and of grace for the salvation of humanity. When Rosenberg carried his racial pride to such a limit as to write: "the Nordic blood represents the thought and mysteries which have conquered the ancient sacraments," he ignored the mystery of the fecundity of the Blood of Christ in the redemption of man and was thereby hostile to Revelation. He denied the transcendency of the human person and estab-

---

[62] S. s. du Canada, Salaberry-de-Valleyfield, 1943, pp. 14-15.

[63] *Ibid.*, p. 37.

[64] S. s. du Canada, Montréal, 1932, p. 281.

[65] *Quadragesimo anno, op. cit.*, p. 30, and S. s. du Canada, Trois-Rivières, 1936, pp. 328-329.

lished a fictitious order on the oppression of souls and of interior liberties.[66]

At the 1940 meeting of the Semaine Sociale, Father Arthur Caron, O.M.I., Vice Rector of the University of Ottawa, gave an excellent course on *Le racisme*. He remarked at the outset that there exists an element which plays a preponderant role in the matter of racism, and that is collective and racial egoism. Profoundly rooted in the past, it has manifested itself in recent years in a most dynamic, virulent, and brutal form.[67] He defined the word "race," however, in much the same terms that Dr. Cooper, prominent anthropologist of Catholic University, uses: "a large group of people with similar physical characteristics that are hereditary."[68] Father Caron then described the early racial sociological theories of Aristotle, of the Romans and Spaniards. These theories were put into definite form by Gobineau and Lapouge and received favorably in Germany by Chamberlain, Rosenberg, Bergmann and Günther. For the leaders of the Third Reich, racism was no longer a simple school hypothesis or an armchair speculation; it was a credo whose dogmas were not to be disputed. The fundamental dogma of racism is the dogma of blood to which racists assign such value as to make it the supreme criterion of an undisputed primacy. Race or blood is the ultimate norm of morality, of politics, of law, and of religion. The speaker justly claimed and proceeded to explain how racism is anti-scientific in its origin, anti-human, anti-social and anti-Christian in its consequences. He concluded with the hope that French Canadians be preserved from similar poisons but reminded his hearers of an article in one of the current dailies which exalted the humanism of blood on par with the humanism of culture. Humanism is not in the blood or of the blood; it is in man and of man; it is in thought and culture; it is in life and in the ideal that we derive from it; it is in Revelation and in the Church. That is the type

---

[66] S. s. du Canada, Sherbrooke, 1938, p. 132.

[67] S. s. du Canada, Nicolet, 1940, p. 122.

[68] Course in Anthropology given at Catholic University by Msgr. Cooper during the term 1943-44.

of humanism that should be defended, cultivated, preserved, as it is befitting a people of Latin and Catholic tradition.[69]

To summarize, one may say that an intensive consideration of the respective effects of these perversive ideologies will encourage the application of the proposed remedies to safeguard the rights of the individual against socialism and communism, the common good against individualism and liberalism, and the Christian spirit against racism. Hence, the Semaine Sociale in particular and the French Canadians in general are intent on collaborating to combat the pernicious "ism's" so destructive of French Canadian traditional and social institutions.

---

[69] S. s. du Canada, Nicolet, 1940, pp. 124-144. In the proceedings of the Semaine Sociale there is one disparaging remark made about Negro women displaying systematic corruption in connection with the movies "à bas étage." S. s. du Canada, Chicoutimi, 1929, p. 90.

CHAPTER XI

The Semaine Sociale and Christian Reconstruction

The Semaine Sociale, faithful to its mission of diffusing the social teachings of the Church, has taken the lead in stating means of remedying the evils of contemporary society and of restoring the present social order to normal conditions. These include the reform of morals and of institutions, Catholic Action, specialized movements, personalist action and widespread use of various supernatural aids. Hence, this Catholic sociological institution devoted its 1944 sessions to the study of *La Restauration sociale*. In accordance with the recommendation of Pope Pius XII's radio message of Christmas, 1942, the collaborators of the Semaine Sociale outlined a program based on his decisive charter.

At their 1942 meeting, Archbishop Charbonneau of Montreal reminded his audience of the true plan of social reconstruction advocated by Pius XI and adapted to present circumstances; that morals and institutions be reformed; that a return to the precepts of the Gospel should be effected; and that the virtues of moderation and detachment, of justice and charity should be practised.[1] Accordingly Bishop Forget insists that only a reform of morals is capable of maintaining public order, peace and tranquillity in society against the assaults of revolutionists. Without such reforms, Pope Pius XI claimed all efforts will be futile.[2] The same idea was expressed by Cardinal Villeneuve when he preached "total renewal" to the 1938 audience of the Semaine Sociale,—a renewal having its source in the soul, thereby transforming not only the inner life of the individual but also professional and economic life of society.[3] Dom Crenier, O.S.B., recommends a return to Christian morals by detachment from the goods and pleasures of this world.[4] Father Archambault cites Mr. Arthur

[1] S. s. du Canada, Saint-Jean, 1942, p. 33.
[2] *Ibid.*, pp. 209-210.
[3] S. s. du Canada, Sherbrooke, 1938, p. 34.
[4] *Ibid.*, p. 151.

Hays Sulsberger, President of the New York Times, as upholding the moderation proposed by Pope Pius XI, defining it as a form of self-conquest and endeavoring to stress its necessity, saying, "We have more to do than to conquer the Germans and the Japs. We have another fight to win, another frontier to conquer, . . . and that, a spiritual frontier. . . . For the arduous days that lie ahead, may the new social order, imposed by war, bring us that spiritual renewal which will give our democracy permanent bases."[5]

To effect this reform of morals, the followers of the Semaine Sociale believe, the practice of justice and charity is indispensable. Canon Comtois differentiates between justice and charity: in that justice grants something to another, it resembles charity; it differs from charity in that the latter gives to another something which does not belong to him, while justice gives him a good which already belongs to him.[6] Father Gonzalve Poulin, O.F.M., speaks of charity as the love of God and men. In a more restrictive sense it means: benevolence towards others without outside pressure, almsgiving for instance. Justice determines under certain circumstances and according to general rules what is due an individual while conscience and a particular judgment determine the role of charity.[7]

To the members of the 1935 assembly of the Semaine Sociale, Father Emile Cloutier emphasized the fact that charity is the essence of Christianity, that without it there is no true spirit of Christ even if one has faith enough to "move mountains." With charity, the speaker claimed, one has every virtue: justice, honesty, devotedness, generosity, self-abnegation, and self-sacrifice. Charity fosters apostleship, zeal for the salvation of souls, passion for good, and helpfulness towards little ones.[8]

It seems to be the general attitude of the followers of the Semaine Sociale that social justice and charity are capable of solving all social conflicts. Thus, Senator Thomas Chapais could

---

[5] S. s. du Canada, Salaberry-de-Valleyfield, 1943, p. 12.

[6] S. s. du Canada, Trois-Rivières, 1925, p. 39; Saint-Jean, 1942, p. 187; Montréal, 1920, pp. 196-197; Ottawa, 1922, p. 38.

[7] S. s. du Canada, Sherbrooke, 1938, p. 133.

[8] S. s. du Canada, Joliette, 1935, p. 229.

say in 1921 that French Canadians have always loved justice and have given ample proof of this in their attitude towards the minorities in their Province. These small groups are treated as if they were brothers. The respect and sympathy accorded them are manifestations of the spirit of justice and charity still prevalent among French Canadians.[9] Again, Senator Chapais insisted that if employers and employees are inspired with charity and justice the most perfect order and the most fruitful harmony will result in the industrial world.[10] In 1922, Mr. C. J. Magnan was no less emphatic about the need of charity in present-day society. At that time he was able to add that the Province of Quebec enjoys enviable social conditions. Peace reigns, strikes are few and the relations between capital and labor are not strained. Here charity takes on different forms: it leaves no suffering unrelieved, no affliction uncomforted, and no misery unassisted.[11] In 1925, Father Archambault told his hearers that justice no longer played in French Canada the essential and fundamental role which had formerly been assigned to it. Among the causes that brought about this tendency he listed: greed for gain, desire for pleasure and cupidity in general.[12] Father Eugène Tremblay holds that justice without charity is hard and cold,[13] and Cardinal Villeneuve affirms that justice will never be sufficient unto itself.[14]

At the 1936 meeting, Mr. Wilfrid Gariépy, Federal Deputy of Trois-Rivières, declared that conditions in the world in general will be ameliorated only when truth will take its place in society, when minds will be imbued with Christian principles and hearts orientated by justice and charity.[15] Canon Goyette avers that charity can bar the way to communism. He calls it the queen of virtues. God, he adds, demands that it reign fully in the heart of the rich; that it watch over Princess Poverty as Saint Francis of Assisi once said.[16]

[9] S. s. du Canada, Québec, 1921, p. 431.
[10] *Ibid.*, pp. 432-433.
[11] S. s. du Canada, Ottawa, 1922, pp. 309-310, and Montréal, 1932, p. 392.
[12] S. s. du Canada, Trois-Riviéres, 1925, pp. 27, 30.
[13] S. s. du Canada, Sherbrooke, 1938, p. 187.
[14] *Ibid.*, p. 383.
[15] S. s. du Canada, Trois-Rivières, 1936, p. 282.
[16] S. s. du Canada, Sherbrooke, 1938, p. 358.

As evidence of the importance of justice in social relations, the Semaine Sociale selected that virtue as the subject for its 1925 meeting. Mr. Leo Pelland began his course with Saint Thomas' definition of justice: "a permanent and perpetual disposition of the will which forces us to grant to each one his due."[17] Canon Courchesne explained the types of justice. General justice is the virtue opposed to individualistic egoism; Saint Thomas had called it legal justice and today Catholic sociologists have agreed on the name social justice. By distributive justice civil authority gives each one his due according to his social value and needs and consequently according to his rights. Justice is commutative when it forces individuals to respect mutual rights in exchange and in all similar relations.[18] Objectively, according to Mr. J. A. Trudel, professional justice is the "ensemble of the duties of state to which the professional man is bound."[19] Father Marchand specified how justice can be violated and offered remedies for such ills.[20] Of the many effects of justice Father Stanislas, O.F.M., mentions peace among nations, understanding between ruler and ruled, fraternity between employers and employees; happiness in the home; respect for contracts, honesty in business and exchange, triumph of innocence over brute force, of right over ambition and cupidity.[21]

At the 1944 meeting in Ottawa, various speakers declared that the Christian principles of justice and charity must be practiced before the social order can be restored. A letter from Bishop Vachon read at this meeting told the audience that if the post-war decisions and actions of those presiding over the destinies of nations are not directed by principles of justice and charity, peace and happiness cannot be lasting.[22] At the same meeting Mayor Stanley Lewis of Ottawa in the first address ever given at the Semaine Sociale in English declared emphatically that charity is the greatest need of the day. The commandment "Love thy neigh-

---

[17] S. s. du Canada, Trois-Rivières, 1925, p. 54, and Ottawa, 1922, p. 34.
[18] *Ibid.*, pp. 90-91.
[19] *Ibid.*, p. 142.
[20] *Ibid.*, pp. 181-188.
[21] *Ibid.*, pp. 21-22, 354, and Montréal, 1920, p. 94.
[22] S. s. du Canada, Ottawa, 1944, p. 11.

bor as thyself" must be practiced for better living.[23] Msgr. Cyrille Gagnon also affirmed that it is by the Christian spirit and the faithful practice of justice and charity that a spiritual renovation will be accomplished.[24] Chief Justice Rinfret, another speaker at this meeting, stated that the necessity of reform is self-evident. He advocated the preparation of a program of reconstruction in accordance with the spirit of justice and Christian charity.[25] Again, in the closing speech of this session, Msgr. Chartrand roused his audience with "Let us work for a better order! Let us imbue our lives with a Christian spirit of justice and charity."[26]

Education, as was indicated in the chapter on that subject, should bring about the reform of morals advocated by the Popes and the Semaine Sociale. As early as 1920, Father Archambault told how the promoters of Catholic social doctrine were amazed at the number of employers and employees ignorant of the rudiments of the social doctrine of the Church.[27] In the 1929 closing speech Bishop Lamarche begged the youth of French Canada to become cognizant of social questions.[28] Bishop Desranleau insisted that the French Canadians find a remedy to cure their "mal d'ignorance" and invited them to study the social doctrine of the Catholic Church.[29] Archbishop Charbonneau, too, perceived the expediency of Catholic social education and lauded the tireless propagandists of the Semaine Sociale.[30]

Mr. Albert Rioux, speaking at the 1944 meeting, stated that the basis of social reconstruction is the formation of youth. This is the task of religious and national education. After having demonstrated that this double education should take place at different levels of social life, he deplored the fact that many millions of young people leave school after the eighth grade.[31] He further

---

[23] *Ibid.*, p. 32.
[24] *Ibid.*, pp. 242-246.
[25] *Ibid.*, p. 199.
[26] *Ibid.*, p. 271.
[27] S. s. du Canada, Montréal, 1920, p. 14.
[28] S. s. du Canada, Chicoutimi, 1929, p. 317.
[29] S. s. du Canada, Sherbrooke, 1938, p. 414.
[30] S. s. du Canada, Saint-Jean, 1942, p. 33.
[31] S. s. du Canada, Ottawa, 1944, pp. 129-133.

remarked that one should master his own language before studying a foreign idiom and told of an Anglo-Canadian complaining: "French Canadians give me no opportunity to learn their language, they always speak to me in English."[32] National education, he claimed, should be grafted on religious formation. He recommended post-academic teaching for the 300,000 young men who idle away their leisure moments after they have left primary school. Moreover, he maintained that there should be two hundred thirty intermediate schools and a travelling library for the sons of farmers, for French Canadian education should bring one nearer the land. The formation of the young girl is also important, in Mr. Rioux's opinion. He saw a diploma in stenography in the home of a colonist and questioned its appropriateness.[33]

Besides a reform of morals the Semaine Sociale, in keeping with the teachings of the Popes, demands a reform of institutions. First and foremost is the renovation of the family. In the words of Judge Tremblay, the moral conditions of the family depend upon the good will of parents and children and of their submission to natural and divine laws. A supernatural renovation is urged to restore the Christian ideal of marriage as willed by God Himself. Property is a factor of social peace and the slum is truly the most powerful agent of family demoralization. For economic security, better living conditions, for the determination of wages and family allowances, families must look to the activities of statesmen. Housing projects like those submitted by the *Union économique d'Habitations* of Montreal and the *Conseil supérieur de la Coopération* of Quebec result in the construction of homes accessible to wage-earners of average income.[34]

Father Archambault insists on the important role that the members of Catholic Action groups could play in the restoration of the French Canadian family. The service of preparation for marriage launched by the J.O.C. and that of family orientation help to guarantee true Christian homes. Again, Catholic Action would protect the family against divorce, immorality, sensuality and

---

[32] *Ibid.*, p. 132.
[33] *Ibid.*, p. 133.
[34] *Ibid.*, pp. 206-229.

similar dangers. It would also defend the rights of parents especially those pertaining to education.[35]

In 1942, the Franciscan Fathers founded the *Institut Familiale,* an organ of documentation and family apostleship, of coordination and collaboration.[36] It aims to serve the home by educating parents and children, by fostering collaboration with teachers. Its chief means of action include: study clubs, library, journals, forums, films, courses on family problems. Helpful also are such other activities as: family clubs, parents' schools, parent-teacher associations, school of family education, assistance to the family, family service, *Ligue Ouvrière* and *Ligue Indépendante catholique.*[37]

Father Gonzalve Poulin, O.F.M., suggested January 1944 in an article in *Relations* the founding of a *Conseil supérieur du bien-êtres des familles.* Such an organization is important to group existing family associations, to consolidate the activities of all those interested in the well-being of the family, to defend and promote its interests in the political field. The task would consist in elaborating a family program appropriate to Quebec, a true charter of the French Canadian family. Father Archambault believes such a council is necessary for the protection and progress of the family in the province of Quebec.[38]

Finally, the stabilization of the family, Mr. Hermas Bastien claims, presupposes an extensive policy of agricultural expansion supplemented by prudent, audacious, political measures allowing a greater possibility for the instauration of small-size industries.[39] That the heads of families may receive sufficient resources, taxes, social obligations, allocations, and pensions should be adjusted with a view to favoring not the individual but the family.[40]

---

[35] Archambault, *Pour restaurer la famille* (Montréal: Ecole Sociale Populaire, 1944), pp. 24-25.

[36] *La Famille,* VIII (1945), p. 524: *La Famille,* a journal of family affairs, is one of the most practical periodicals on the subject in French Canada.

[37] Archambault, *Pour restaurer la famille, op. cit.,* p. 21.

[38] *Ibid.,* p. 29. For the first time in Canada a *Semaine nationale de la Famille* was held in January, 1945.

[39] S. s. du Canada, 1938, Sherbrooke, p. 48.

[40] Archambault, *Pour un ordre meilleur, op. cit.,* p. 16. Father Jean-de-Brébeuf Laramée, O.F.M., is at present engaged at the Catholic University in a scientific study on *L'Autorité dans la famille canadienne-française.*

The Semaine Sociale proposes for the reform of the present economic order in French Canada the organization of corporations as advocated by Pope Pius XI in *Quadragesimo anno* and in *Divini Redemptoris*. Cardinal Villeneuve's declaration is emphatic: "Il nous faut faire du corporatisme à plein"; Father Archambault was a pioneer in recognizing its necessity. As early as 1920, he reminded professional associations of their obligation to possess a spirit in conformity with the principles of the Gospel.[41] Many collaborators[42] of the Semaine Sociale agree to the expediency of corporations resting on justice and charity for the restoration of peace among the classes, for the prosperity of economic life and for the restoration of the moral health of society. A few speakers of the Semaine Sociale, namely Father Philippe Perrier,[43] Father Lorenzo Gauthier,[44] Mr. Georges-Henri Saint-Cyr,[45] Mr. Gérard Filion,[46] and Father Archambault[47] recommend a similar institution for the agricultural class.

At the 1944 Ottawa meeting of the Semaine Sociale, Father Archambault recalled how attempts at corporations in France, Holland, England, the United States, Belgium and Switzerland have met with promising success. He mentioned in particular the citrus fruit and coal industry of the United States, the clock-making industry of Montreal and construction in Saguenay.[48] In Canada the system functions under the name of Industry Councils. The plan proposed by Philip Murray, President of the C.I.O., to establish industrial peace in the United States is no other than

[41] S. s. du Canada, 1920, p. 13.

[42] At one time or another we find in the proceedings of the Semaine Sociale the following expressing their opinion in favor of establishing corporations in French Canada: Archbishop Charbonneau, Fathers Philippe Desranleau, Emile Cloutier, Lorenzo Gauthier, C.S.V., Adrien Malo, O.F.M., Eugène Tremblay, Philippe Perrier, C.O. Garant, J. B. Desrosiers, S.S., G. Sauvé, O.M.I., Senator Gouin, Messrs. Maximilien Caron, Alfred Charpentier, Omer D. Paulhus, Léopold Richer, Jean Bruchési, and Firmin Létourneau.

[43] S. s. du Canada, Rimouski, 1933, p. 261.

[44] *Ibid.*, p. 301.

[45] S. s. du Canada, Trois-Rivières, 1936, pp. 137-138.

[46] S. s. du Canada, Ottawa, 1944, pp. 99-113.

[47] *Ibid.*, pp. 23-24.

[48] *Ibid.*, p. 28.

the corporative system. He himself once declared that he had found inspiration in *Quadragesimo anno*. Bishop Haas is also an advocate of corporatism.[49]

In the thinking of the Semaine Sociale a reform of institutions cannot be effected without a Christian renovation of politics. In the words of Msgr. Gagnon, the State must pass laws favorable to the weak and poor. Again, Mr. Victor Chabot, C.R., insists that corporations can be organized only with the help of sound social politics.[50] But in French Canada, Mr. Gérard Filion claims, social legislation should consider the rights and traditions of the Province of Quebec, should take into account the autonomy of the respective provinces. Socialistic measures which inevitably lead to socialism should meet with the disapproval of the governing body[51] for they accustom people to rely on the State alone for the cure of all evils. The same speaker insists that each time the State intervenes in the social domain, it does so at the expense of personal liberty. It is Mr. Charpentier's belief that once industries are organized into "orders" capital will no longer dominate politics. On the contrary, industry will be controlled by "vocational groups."[52] The State then, faithful to its supplementary role, will exercise only an ultimate control. Judge Tremblay, in referring to family allowances, points out the defects of the present Federal legislation and attributes to the measures, "an originality of which Canada has no right to be proud." He concludes that "Politics must have reasons that reason cannot explain." The fearless Eugène L'Heureux, without advocating the suppression of the Senate and Legislative Council would accept their suppression very willingly to free the government from certain parasites whose influence is often pernicious. He recommends in their place economic councils composed of competent, patriotic, Catholic-minded social thinkers.[53]

Father Emile Cloutier at the 1932 assembly reminded his audience of Pope Pius XI's hope of seeing established on an inter-

---

[49] Archambault, *Pour un ordre meilleur, op. cit.*, pp. 46-47.
[50] S. s. du Canada, Saint-Hyacinthe, 1937, p. 291.
[51] S. s. du Canada, Ottawa, 1944, pp. 105-106.
[52] *Ibid.*, p. 124.
[53] S. s. du Canada, Montréal, 1932, p. 287.

national plan groups analogous to those recommended on a national level. Such institutions would contribute much to that justice and charity which the Master of human societies imposed as a life rule upon nations as well as upon individuals.[54] To the 1943 Valleyfield meeting, Professor Adelard Leduc recommended a scheme for international solidarity constructed according to the cherished plan of Pope Pius XII. To render such a plan effective, the Pope repeatedly insists on a spirit of collaboration and solidarity, of temperance, and true understanding, on a return to Christian morality as a norm of international life.[55] In the opinion of Mr. Charpentier, social reconstruction must also take into account international relations. An institution similar to the International Bureau of Labor and to the International Conferences of Labor might suggest adequate solutions by way of recommendations or agreements.[56]

The Semaine Sociale next advocates Catholic Action as a means of Christian reconstruction. In fact, the social week of 1941 was devoted entirely to its discussion. Although Catholic Action is as old as Christianity it has been given a new impetus under Popes Pius XI and XII. Pope Pius XII defined it as "the collaboration of laymen in the apostolate of the hierarchy."[57] Canon Wilfrid Caillé, director of Catholic Action in the diocese of Joliette, quoted Civardi's definition: "The organization of Catholic Laity, consecrated to the apostolate in aid of and in direct dependence on the hierarchy, in view of the triumph of the Kingdom of Christ, in individuals, in the family, and in society at large."[58] By popularizing the expression "Catholic Action," Pope Pius XI wished to emphasize a modern form of lay apostolate. Indeed, he invited lay people of all classes without distinction of sex or age.[59] The Apostolic Delegate, His Excellency Ildebrando Antoniutti, called

---

[54] S. s. du Canada, Montréal, 1932, pp. 267-268.

[55] S. s. du Canada, Salaberry-de-Valleyfield, 1943, pp. 209-210.

[56] S. s. du Canada, Ottawa, 1944, pp. 127-128.

[57] S. s. du Canada, Québec, 1941, pp. 61-62.

[58] *Ibid.*, p. 67: ". . . l'organisation du laïcat catholique vouée à l'apostolat auxiliaire de la hiérarchie ecclésiastique et sous sa dépendance directe pour le triomphe du règne du Christ dans les individus, dans les familles et dans les sociétés."

[59] *Ibid.*, p. 158.

Catholic Action a work of charity, devotedness and sacrifice.[60] Father Gauthier asserted that it is "the proper ground for collective action."[61] Cardinal Villeneuve declared that Catholic Action by sowing justice, charity, and the evangelical virtues in modern life will thereby purify it.[62] In the words of Senator Gouin, Catholic Action aims directly to rechristianize not only individuals but institutions and social milieus by the organization of a collective and official apostolate.[63] Father Archambault ended the opening address of this gathering by quoting Cardinal Pizzardo:

> Catholic Action is the viaticum that Divine Providence brings to modern societies and to the Church of the twentieth century through the intermediary of the Vicar of Jesus Christ. It is the answer of the Popes to the cry of love of the Sacred Heart and is intended to awaken society from its present lethargy and lead it back to Christ.[64]

There are various means employed by Catholic Action to bring about the rechristianization of modern world. These are given due emphasis by the Semaine Sociale. In 1932, Father Lévi Côté, O.M.I., indicated the spiritual renovation of lay apostles evidenced in numerous spiritual exercises and laymen's retreats.[65] Father Lévesque reminds his audience that to mind one's business in Catholic Action is not good policy. "Had the Son of God chosen to mind his business," he adds, "He would not have left heaven to come to our poor planet. If the Twelve had been content to mind their business they would not have overrun the world to plant the cross and regenerate men in the Blood of Christ."[66] At

---

[60] *Ibid.*, p. 197.

[61] S. s. du Canada, Trois-Rivières, 1936, p. 380.

[62] *Ibid.*, p. 340.

[63] S. s. du Canada, Québec, 1941, p. 249.

[64] *Ibid.*, p. 24: "L'action catholique est le viatique que, par l'intermédiaire du Vicaire de Jésus-Christ, la divine Providence apporte aux sociétés modernes et à l'Eglise du XXe siècle. Réponse des Pontifes au cri d'amour du Sacré-Coeur pour réveiller notre société, si somnolente et si froide, et la conduire au Christ."

[65] S. s. du Canada, Montréal, 1932, p. 353.

[66] S. s. du Canada, Joliette, 1935, p. 317.

the 1941 meeting of Quebec, Canon Caillé gave an example of true Catholic Action in practice. In a certain parish, cheap Protestant bibles were being sold from house to house. The following Sunday the Pastor announced that the Jocists and Jacists would go to collect these same books. This is genuine Catholic Action, that is to say, a collective activity, operating not upon the personal whim of an individual but under delegated authority.[67] Father M. A. Lamarche, O.P., also cites fields of Catholic Action. Thus when an investigation is put under way, Catholic Action does not shrink from the difficult task of collecting statistical data, facts and documents. Again for the propagation of a journal, Catholic Action is not content with expounding its value; it tries to persuade each buyer by going from house to house. For the organization of leisure-time activities, it does not merely philosophize on the expediency of such measures; rather it sets to work to open public libraries, parochial movie-houses or to organize sports.[68]

The *Institut Pie XI* founded in 1937 by Archbishop Gauthier is the school of Catholic Action and of religious sciences at the University of Montreal. It is annexed to the Faculty of Theology and is an answer to the demand of Pope Pius XI to diffuse the sacred sciences in general and pontifical documents in particular. Its program includes courses in Catholic Action, the social doctrine of the Church, dogmatic and moral theology and other religious sciences. In short, the Institute is a preparatory school for Catholic Action.[69]

Now, to perform this sort of work special qualities are necessary. Most Reverend Ildebrando Antoniutti makes the following indispensable to the vitality and efficacy of Catholic Action: the sound interior formation of its members and the perfect organization of its exterior activities.[70] In the words of Father Côté, the apostle of Catholic Action must possess sufficient knowledge of religion, be convinced of the importance of Catholic doctrine and have a sincere desire for growth in the supernatural life.[71] Father

---

[67] S. s. du Canada, Québec, 1941, pp. 64-65.

[68] S. s. du Canada, Saint-Hyacinthe, 1937, p. 351.

[69] Interview with Father Desrosiers, Director of the Institut Pie XI, September 27, 1944.

[70] S. s. du Canada, Québec, 1941, p. 196.

[71] S. s. du Canada, Montréal, 1932, p. 360.

Lévesque, in a brilliant study on Catholic Action as the agent of social restoration, enumerates four qualities that should be developed in lay apostles: science, prudence, strength and union.[72]

In the words of Mr. Léo Pelland, the good pursued by Catholic Action is both religious and moral. In fact, Catholic Action has no other task than to imbue souls with the true spirit of Christ; to extend the reign of Christ to all private, public, national and international relations; to pursue the conquest of souls and the Christian restoration of society; to defend religion, its interests and liberty, the sanctity of marriage and the family; to combat *laïcisme* and do away with neutrality in the school; to assure the observance of Sunday and holydays; to contribute to an extensive diffusion of the principles of faith and Christian doctrine, to the expansion of Christian ideas; and to spread the knowledge of the Gospel.[73]

The results of a study to measure the extent of Catholic Action in Canada were given in 1941 by Canon Chamberland, former Director of Catholic Action in the Archdiocese of Quebec. Reports give evidence of its establishment in fifteen dioceses, the earliest in 1933. Societies as general organs of Catholic Action for adults and youths were found in most dioceses. Nine have a diocesan committee of Catholic Action. Very few dioceses have a written constitution.[74]

To show the necessity of Catholic Action, Father Malo reported on the findings of the Jocists relative to the moral life of 2,190 young workers from sixteen to twenty-five years of age living in seventy-two different parishes:

744, that is, 34% possess a religious training sufficient to explain and defend their religion;
338, that is, 15% have remained fervent Catholics;
957, that is, 44% have kept the religious practices of early school days;
408, that is, 19% are luke-warm Catholics;
487, that is, 22% no longer practice their religion;
363, that is, 17% have a priest as advisor;

[72] S. s. du Canada, Sherbrooke, 1938, p. 405.
[73] S. s. du Canada, Québec, 1941, p. 159.
[74] *Ibid.*, pp. 130-135.

875, that is, 40% are afraid of the priest;
679, that is, 31% have made a layman's retreat.[75]

What Dr. Louis-Philippe Roy calls *Apostolat spécialisé* constitutes an effective means of Catholic Action. He distinguishes between specialized apostolate, as being the idea, and Catholic Action as being the incarnation of the idea, that is, its passing into practice.[76] Pope Pius XI insists on specialized movements as the preferred if not the exclusive, method of Catholic Action.[77]

The J.O.C., as a specialized movement for youth, is by far the most wide-spread in French Canada. In 1943, the Canadian J.O.C. published a worth-while post-war plan which read as follows:

1. Work for all, that is, no more unemployment;
2. Woman in the home, man in the mill;
3. Work given to men rather than to women;
4. Demolishing of slums and constructing of healthy and comfortable housing quarters;
5. Family legislation allowing youth to prepare for the future;
6. Professional orientation for all, even in school;
7. Rehabilitation of soldiers.[78]

Furthermore, the J.A.C. and J.E.C., discussed earlier, accomplish in their respective milieus what the J.O.C. does among the work-

[75] *Ibid.*, pp. 87-88: "744, soit 34 p.c., possèdent une formation religieuse suffisante pour expliquer et défendre leur religion: 338, soit 15 p.c., sont demeurés des catholiques fervents; 957, soit 44 p.c., ont gardé à peu près les pratiques religieuses de leur vie scolaire; 408, soit 19 p.c., sont des catholiques tièdes; 487, soit 32 p.c., ne pratiquent plus ou presque plus leur religion; 363, soit 17 p.c., ont un prêtre pour confident; 875, soit 40 p.c., ont peur du prêtre; 679, soit 31 p.c., ont fait une retraite fermée."

[76] *Ibid.*, p. 95.

[77] S. s. du Canada, Trois-Rivières, 1936, p. 380.

[78] Archambault, *Pour un ordre meilleur, op. cit.*, pp. 15-16: 1. un plan de travail pour tous, c'est-à-dire plus de chômage; 2. La femme au foyer, l'homme à l'usine; 3. Le travail donné à l'homme de préférence à la femme; 4. Démolition des taudis et construction de logements sains et confortables; 5. Une politique familiale qui permettra aux jeunes de préparer leur avenir; 6. Orientation professionnelle pour tous, dès l'école; 7. Réhabilitation des soldats.

ing population. The *Ligue ouvrière catholique,* L.O.C., an adult association, is concerned particularly with the restoration of the wage-earning family. To that effect it prepared what Father Archambault calls one of the best programs of family restoration.[79] The *Ligue indépendante catholique,* L.I.C., aims to spread Christian principles among the bourgeoisie. Finally, the *Ligue agricole catholique,* L.A.C., assumes the responsibility of protecting the rural domain from urban contamination and of spreading a knowledge of the benefits of rural life.[80]

The Semaine Sociale recommends personalist action[81] before concerted activity as a primary means to bring about Christian reconstruction. Thus in 1931, Father Carmel, C.SS.R. declared that the least activity undertaken secretly for the reign of Christ, accomplishes more for humanity than all the discussions of legislators and all the laws of potentates who fail to act.[82] In 1940, Mr. Ernest Forest, public notary, ended his course on *Le vrai chrétien* by asserting that the first duty of a Christian is his personal sanctification. Only when thus strengthened may he reach his neighbor through the various means which the Church offers him to work for restoration in Christ.[83] Father Archambault expressed the same idea when he quoted the late Msgr. Johnson "Better men for better times."[84] No less impressive are Father Garrigou-Lagrange's words: "The world needs, not so many philosophers and sociologists but saints, men who are the living image of the Savior among us."[85] Mr. Forest alludes to Saint Louis on his throne, to Saint Benoit Labre on his stump-bed, to Saint Theresa's hidden life and to Brother André's humility. These saints truly lived the Gospel of Christ.[86] In 1943, Msgr.

[79] For the detailed program see Archambault, *Pour restaurer la famille, op. cit.*, pp. 26-28.

[80] S. s. du Canada, Québec, 1941, p. 105.

[81] This concept is well explained by Paul H. Furfey in *Fire on the Earth* (New York: Macmillan Company, 1936), pp. 92-97.

[82] S. s. du Canada, Ottawa, 1931, p. 299.

[83] S. s. du Canada, Nicolet, 1940, p. 41.

[84] S. s. du Canada, Ottawa, 1944, p. 31.

[85] S. s. du Canada, Nicolet, 1940, p. 38.

[86] *Ibid.*, pp. 38-39. For an intensive study of social action of twenty-five saints and beati who died since January 1, 1835, see Mary Elizabeth Walsh, *The Saints and Social Work* (Silver Spring: The Preservation of the Faith, 1937).

Wilfrid Lebon commented on the heroism of the Canadian martyrs, and showed how temperance, because it insures moderation in all human activities, is closely linked with the noble thoughts and heroic actions of saintly men and women.[87] At the 1938 assembly, Canon Goyette gave concrete examples of charitable actions performed by a Saint Jean de Dieu, a Saint Gregory and a Saint Elizabeth of Hungary.[88]

The ordinary means to personal sanctification, in the words of Father Gauthier, are frequent reception of the sacraments, meditation, the liturgy, daily labor, voluntary poverty, obedience and chastity.[89] Among other means, the work of the Saint Vincent de Paul Society and the layman's retreat have already been mentioned in the discussion on the Church. For total Christian renovation the laymen's retreat is particularly recommended by Father Gauthier,[90] Canon Harbour,[91] and Judge Arthur Laramée.[92] Again the Semaine Sociale, represented by Father Gustave Lamarche, C.S.V., stresses the necessity of a deep interior life to better social conditions.[93] In 1941, Father Francis Goyer, S.S.S., reminded his audience that the soul of the apostolate is interior life, that triumphs are above all the results of prayer and union with God.[94] At the 1943 meeting Mr. Leduc told of Lyautey, marshal of France who once visited the Oblates of Sion in Lorraine and addressed them as follows:

> My dear monks, your life, your rules, your prayer, your sacrifice are as necessary, as fruitful, as great as any creation in this world. There is an equilibrium, an order of life. With action there is meditation, with exterior effort there is interior aspiration. . . . Life would be an incoherent folly if spirituality did not rule it.

---

[87] S. s. du Canada, Salaberry-de-Valleyfield, 1943, pp. 194-196.
[88] S. s. du Canada, Sherbrooke, 1938, pp. 360-361.
[89] S. s. du Canada, Nicolet, 1940, p. 215.
[90] S. s. du Canada, Nicolet, 1940, pp. 218-219.
[91] S. s. du Canada, Saint-Hyacinthe, 1937, pp. 281-282.
[92] S. s. du Canada, Joliette, 1935, p. 308.
[93] *Ibid.*, pp. 241-247.
[94] S. s. du Canada, Québec, 1941, p. 223.

Without men like you, men like me would be nothing. . . .[95]

The Semaine Sociale is well aware that only supernatural means can bring a reform of society. Hence, we find in the reports of the proceedings numerous references to the aid of revelation, to the power of the Eucharist and the social role of Christian virtues. Mr. Forest emphasized the need of an honest return to the doctrine of the Gospel,[96] Canon Harbour referred to the Gospel as the remedy for present social evils,[97] Cardinal Pacelli, as Papal Secretary of State, advocated Catholic social doctrine as the criterion and key for the real solutions of current problems;[98] Bishop Deschamps directed the French Canadians to the social wealth contained in the Gospel;[99] Father J. C. Tremblay insisted that the social action of the Church of Christ, benevolent yesterday is benevolent today and will be so to-morrow;[100] Mr. Paul Grenier affirmed that the true formula for all social regenerations can be found in the Book of Truth, that is in the Gospel;[101] and finally Bishop Desranleau voiced a return to the Gospel as the infallible means of reestablishing order in the world.[102]

The power of the Eucharist was stressed by Father Louis Tardiff, S.S.S., when he declared that this Sacrament is a source of especial benefits for the individual and for society. It enlivens faith, curbs pride, weakens concupiscence, sustains hope of immortal goods. But the Eucharist does even more for society. It reestablishes equilibrium among the various classes by the suppres-

[95] S. s. du Canada, Salaberry-de-Valleyfield, 1943, pp. 212-213: ". . . petits moines, votre vie, vos règles, vos prières, votre sacrifice, sont aussi nécessaires, aussi féconds, aussi grands, que n'importe quelle création ici-bas. Voyez-vous, tout est équilibre, tout est ordre. A côté de l'action, il y a la méditation. A côté de l'effort extérieur, il y a la vie intérieure. . . . La vie ne serait qu'une folie incohérente si la spiritualité ne la règlait pas. Sans des hommes comme vous, des hommes comme moi ne seraient rien. . . ."

[96] S. s. du Canada, Nicolet, 1940, p. 26.

[97] S. s. du Canada, Saint-Hyacinthe, 1937, p. 284.

[98] S. s. du Canada, Montréal, 1932, p. 8.

[99] *Ibid.*, p. 391.

[100] S. s. du Canada, Chicoutimi, 1929, p. 282.

[101] S. s. du Canada, Québec, 1927, p. 365.

[102] S. s. du Canada, Sherbrooke, 1938, p. 20.

sion of arrogance, unkindness and fraud in the powerful; of envy, sedition and revolt in the less fortunate. In a word, it firmly unites all Christians in charity.[103] At the 1940 assembly, Msgr. Antonio Camerand, Vicar General of the diocese of Nicolet, declared that families and society will experience peace and happiness only when every one will have met at the altar-rail.[104] Clémençeau on one occasion told Catholics: "If you were what you should be, the face of the world would be changed."[105]

The Semaine Sociale also emphasizes the social role of the virtues. Father Poulin insists on the need for charity to compensate for the insufficiencies of justice and to supplement the imperfections of the social order.[106] In the opinion of Msgr. Gagnon, fraternal charity is the true remedy for that egotism which dries the hearts and poisons social life.[107] Father Lévesque refers to justice and charity as establishing a sort of *connaturalité* with the common good and benevolence towards one's neighbors.[108] In the words of Mr. Pelland the effect of charity is nothing else than peace, that is to say, tranquillity of order, perfect harmony among all peoples in all things.[109]

In brief, the Semaine Sociale has stressed all the natural and supernatural means offered by the Church to effect the reform of morals and institutions recommended by the Popes. For concerted action, the representatives of the Semaine Sociale have advocated specialized movements in connection with Catholic Action. Nor did they minimize that personalist action which requires, as a preliminary, personal sanctification. To better social conditions, they also recommend works of mercy and for spiritual renewal advocate retreats and growth in interior life; for better relations among the various classes of the social order, the Semaine Sociale insists on the power of the Eucharist, on the social teaching of the Gospel and the social role of the virtues of charity and justice.

---

[103] S. s. du Canada, Montréal, 1920, pp. 143-144.
[104] S. s. du Canada, Nicolet, 1940, p. 208.
[105] *Ibid.*, p. 40.
[106] S. s. du Canada, Sherbrooke, 1938, p. 135.
[107] S. s. du Canada, Ottawa, 1944, p. 246.
[108] S. s. du Canada, Joliette, 1935, p. 315.
[109] S. s. du Canada, Québec, 1941, p. 170.

CHAPTER XII

General Summary and Conclusions on the Social Thought of the Semaine Sociale

From the foregoing study of the social thought of the Semaine Sociale the writer has tried to discover the position that the collaborators of the Semaine Sociale have taken relative to major social problems of French Canada and the action they have emphasized to help solve these peculiar problems. These will be summarily reviewed in this final chapter. Now and then, the writer will pass judgments, give opinions and arrive at conclusions from the evidence found in the reports of the Semaine Sociale. The general summary will follow the order of the study, preceded, however, by a definition of Sociology in the light of the teachings of the Semaine Sociale.

The term *Sociology* in Canada has not been subjected to that minute analysis which has given rise to endless discussions among American sociologists. The conception of sociology used in French Canada is the ordinary Catholic one, not the conception of American materialists. The few works of a purely scientific nature produced in French Canada have occasioned casual criticisms on the part of French Canadians. Some declare that the Semaine Sociale is too exclusively philosophical; others argue that it is more theoretical than practical. On the other hand, when an effort was made by social science students of Laval University to apply to Quebec City some American concepts, Burgess' concept of concentric zones for instance, the scientific workers were taunted by another group who emphatically asserted that these sociologists had the circles fit Quebec City and not Quebec City the circles.

The Semaine Sociale never claimed to use only empirical methods; it aimed rather to diffuse the social doctrine of the encyclicals and of the Catholic Church while basing its teachings on philosophy and theology. In giving directives it has in no way repudiated its primary aim. If an attempt were made to formulate a definition of sociology in the light of the teachings of the Semaine Sociale, it seems that this definition would apply only to a Catholic sociology. To the French Canadian elite of the Semaine Sociale, sociology is a practical discipline, based on sound philosophy and theology, which studies the doctrine of the social encyclicals and examines the data on social problems in the light of the social teaching of the Church. For instance, the study of criminology would not be included in French Canadian sociology, for crime, in the opinion of several followers of the Semaine Sociale, does not reach large enough proportions to constitute a major social problem.

The fact that French Canadians have sponsored many movements appears paradoxical in view of their decidedly individualistic nature. Still the French Canadian is willing to restrain his own tendencies for what he considers necessary to preserve the integrity of his traditions and customs. Thus the *Société Saint-Jean-Baptiste* (1834) has been and still is a most important safeguard of national and religious interests. The feast of Saint John Baptist is truly their national feast-day and is usually observed by demonstrations accompanied by speeches lauding the sacredness of their religion, traditions and of the French language.

Again, one would not expect such institutions as the *patronage* and *foyer* to take root as early as 1880, at a time when French Canadians strongly held to the integrity of the family. The clergy, in the person of Father Henri Gauthier, was even concerned over sporadic cases of homeless working girls—exceptions to the general rule—on the ground that in French Canadian practice of charity, no one should be exposed to temptations: spiritual values have always been a major concern with French Canadian people.

Although in French Canadian thought woman's place is in the home, Mrs. Béique and Mrs. Gérin-Lajoie, without neglecting their household duties, launched in 1907 the *Fédération nationale de Saint-Jean-Baptiste,* which has won the recognition and approbation of the episcopacy. Quite different from the concept of the retiring, shy, timid French Canadian woman is the picture of these reformers who exposed themselves to criticism and ridicule to fight the good cause, particularly in uprooting the evils related to alcoholism.

Meanwhile, a few prominent thinkers of French Canada were

considering how the social teachings of the Popes could be brought to employers and employees. Accordingly, Father Archambault, wide-awake to contemporary social problems, founded, in 1920, the Semaine Sociale with the express purpose of forming an elite that will in turn diffuse Catholic social doctrine and apply Christian principles to French Canada proper.

In the reports of the Semaine Sociale we hear what the French Canadians say about themselves. Here we find them speaking not as a sophisticated group but as one having intimate relations with one's own, that is, as a we-group. They discuss their problems, unmask their faults and deficiencies, propose their solutions and plan for their future; in other words, they take things into their own hands. Should, at any time, an attempt be made to do away with old French laws, the writer believes that Taschereau's "Hands off Quebec;" would be voiced anew and such measure surely meet with outright opposition. The French Canadians as a group feel that they can attend to their own peculiar problems. Although they may appear a "queer" people to some spectators, they are proud to "bear witness" to the world, particularly in diffusing through twenty-five successive years, point by point, the doctrine contained in the social encyclicals. The disciples of the Semaine Sociale are proud of their attainments but feel the urgency of remaining on guard, ever ready to resist the forces that would attempt to materialize and denationalize their country. The Semaine Sociale is protected from political prejudices by its doctrine based on a philosophy commanded by the exigencies of reason and not on novel hypotheses. Moreover, each course is a realistic and scholarly study; when such reports fall into the hands of persons with receptive minds, they sow seeds of social movements.

Thus, the writer has gathered that the Semaine Sociale has become part of the intellectual and moral landscape of French Canada. Each year it projects its light on a social problem of vital interest. The reports of its proceedings are a source of information and inspiration, and contain important principles of social education. The perusal of these volumes awakens one to the fact that Catholicism is a social religion. Each new subject, property, family, profession and State has been presented in the light of Catholic doctrine and submitted to the rigorous judgment of truly Christian morality.

Again, by its practice of decentralization the Semaine Sociale utilizes the talents which might otherwise have remained buried in the different regions and invites the elite to engage in intellectual work and research. The Semaine Sociale is probably more appreciated in small than in large cities, due to the fact that its meeting in a small center may be the principal intellectual event of the year. The writer hopes that the ambulatory University will one day hold its sessions in some city of one of the Maritime Provinces. Furthermore, the acquaintances made at the meetings of the Semaine Sociale constitute a no less marked advantage. The exchange of ideas between practitioners and theorists is beneficial. The exposition of their methods, results, failures and successes furnishes valuable sources of information on the one hand, and prevents useless groping on the other.

There is evidence throughout the existence of the Semaine Sociale of an intimate relation between the clergy and the laity. The diocesan clergy, large numbers of religious orders and lay-professions have been represented, at one time or another, by their respective members and have maintained close contact with the organization. During the first decade of the Semaine Sociale the outstanding contributors were its inaugurators and immediate followers. The second decade saw an expanding body of workers inspired by the zeal of the early contributors.

Today, the Canadian Semaine Sociale has reached its maturity. It has several really outstanding achievements to its credit: the inauguration of courses in sociology at the University of Ottawa, the stimulation of corporative and cooperative endeavors and the promotion of the labor movement and of colonization. It has made considerable progress in stimulating and formulating public opinion as shown in the second chapter of this study. More important still: it has succeeded in introducing the theoretical and practical social teachings of the Popes into the study of the French Canadian social problems. This Catholic Sociological University is in all likelihood destined to exert a profound influence on the future of French Canada.

Among the followers of the Semaine Sociale we find noted political leaders, all of them active supporters of French Canadian rights and astute observers. But no figure compares with that ideal Prince of the Church, Cardinal Villeneuve, who occupied the rostrum of the Semaine Sociale thirteen times to explain, comment on or emphasize some particular point of social doctrine. Three prominent bishops, members of the General Commission, have propagated Catholic sociology by word and pen. Rectors of universities, pastors, the Chief Justice of the Supreme Court, a senator, statesmen, judges, lawyers, professors, union leaders and social workers have shaken the customary apathy of French Canada to intellectual pursuits and have given an impetus to social education at least among the professional elite.

The relative freedom which the Church enjoys in French Canada today is remarkable and arouses wonder in outsiders. But it must not be forgotten that it has been obtained only through persevering insistence on the part of the Clergy and faithful alike. Instead of turning their energies to the controlling of industries, the Semaine Sociale maintains that the French Canadians for centuries have chosen to defend what they hold to be their most sacred rights: their language, traditions, culture and religion. This, in the opinion of the writer, is one way of accounting for their backwardness in directing industries; in this economic age, they have remained non-materialistic. Spiritual values still hold the prominent place in French Canadian thought. Rather than inquire into how many industries the French Canadians control, the Semaine Sociale is more concerned with the number of Catholics who have remained faithful to their religious practices. The study made by the J.O.C. in 1941 is only one evidence of the importance French Canadians attach to spiritual values. Again, a politician or a professional who incurs the displeasure of the Church must bear with ostracism of one kind or another. Although the Church in French Canada appears to be less influential today than it was in earlier times, its prestige is still great, as the case of former Mayor Bouchard of Saint-Hyacinthe testifies. To the clergy, French Canadians owe the maintenance of family ideals, their firm hold on the soil where factory roofs do not shut out the sky, their scorn for the dollar-chasing activities of their English-speaking neighbors, and above all their *survivance.* Thanks to the clergy again, these same English-speaking neighbors have not interfered with the French Canadian pattern of life.

All open-minded French Canadian intellectuals, cognizant of the crisis that the family is facing in other countries, realize that the French Canadian family, although winning world-wide admiration by its stability, fecundity, and morality, is menaced by evils common to the world in general and by perils characteristically Canadian. It must not be assumed that French Canadians are completely sheltered from such modern and universal problems as depopulation, alcoholism, woman labor and the exodus from the farm. The fact that divorce is not recognized in the Province of Quebec, indicates that French Canada is less affected by this plague than are other countries. The Semaine Sociale expresses great concern relative to feminism. Msgr. Gagnon emphatically denounces its excesses and shows its implications on family life. Only lately have women students been on the increase at the University of Montreal, especially in the Social Science School.

Although depopulation is on the increase, French Canadians still have a comparatively high birth rate. The wealth of French Canada lies in human capital, referred to as the "Canadian miracle," and making possible their survival. Many French Canadian social thinkers consider the problem of the family to be the critical problem of French Canada not so much because of its demoralization but because it reflects a rising tendency to turn to pleasure, to an easy life and to a search for personal satisfactions. From the very outset, alcoholism has found a stern adversary in the clergy; the campaign of thirty years ago forced the government to declare prohibition. The experiment proving unsuccessful, it was shortly replaced by the *régie provinciale*. Under this system the State receives the revenues. Naturally, to increase this income it multiplies taverns. Protests from the episcopacy are many, but on the whole the ravages of alcoholism in the Province as compared with those of other provinces are not startling.

The Semaine Sociale holds that industrialism has revolutionized the former patriarchal type of French Canadian family and substituted in its stead party politics and a wage system in urban centers—both of these fatal to family solidarity. In urban centers, slums with their disorganizing factors have taken the place of the farm house where large families could once thrive. On the other hand, those aids given to the French Canadian family in the form of maternity care, relief and assistance, education and domestic science schools are timely. Concerning the recent Family Allowance Law, many Church leaders think it is a good step in the right direction. Naturally, they say, it is not perfect.

The French Canadian province has made progress in spite of handicaps of all sorts. Material progress may not have followed the momentum of those countries principally imbued with economic and plutocratic ideals, but French Canadian standards of eternal values have remained active in both their social and economic life. Because of this attitude towards material goods, French Canadians impress the writer as a very contented people. Who can find today a group of workers less inclined to class-struggle, more respectful of legitimate authority, less enthralled by atheistic materialism? Brought up in the love of God, in the practice of religion, respect for order, fidelity to duty, the French Canadian referred to in the Semaine Sociale constitutes a modest, happy, quiet, contented individual.

Until the appearance of the social encyclicals, urban parts of French Canada had been under a decidedly capitalistic regime. When working conditions became deplorable, the State acted as the "providence of the workingmen" and intervened by legislation. The Semaine Sociale holds that this intervention should be undertaken jointly with the Church. It warns French Canadians against the present tendency to amplify the role of the State and exaggerate its functions. The State should not become a bureau of benevolence, an automatic distributor of pensions, grants and subsidies but a moderator safeguarding order and peace, assuring a family economy, and preserving religion.

Cardinal Villeneuve denounces "mental urbanism," that is, the mentality which prompts rural dwellers to adopt the ideologies, the fashions and ways of life of urban centers, and induces them to abandon the soil for city dwellings. Attempts have been made to ruralize those country schools, convents and colleges which are responsible for the creation among the country youth of what the Cardinal calls "mental urbanism."

It is difficult to grasp the true meaning of patriotism as found in French Canadian thought. True, French Canadians appear to many to be little concerned with affairs outside their own province yet their representatives are among the most active in the Federal Parliament. They call themselves Canadians; the other nationalities are for theim either Anglo-Canadians, Irish-Canadians or Scotch-Canadians. Many French Canadians feel an obligation towards neither England nor France, but towards Canada only. Still the French Canadian group seems to offer the greatest resistance to a strong national unity and have been a source of both wonder and aggravation to the other provinces. Some believe that the danger of assimilation has disappeared, that the French Canadians are masters of their destiny; others hold that the fight for their rights is still in full swing, that there will be no end to this struggle. It seems to the writer that they have been constantly on the alert to preserve at all costs their customs, language and religion. Because subtle and important differences exist between the French Canadian and Anglo-Canadian they have remained notably indifferent towards each other, though without marked misunderstandings among themselves. The conflict appears to be more an imperial than a provincial problem.

The French Canadian feels the necessity of knowing English for business transactions, especially in Montreal. The question of bilingualism seems to work only one way. The Anglo-Canadians will not learn French and the situation appears alarming to Msgr. Perrier because today even the elite converge toward English. Others believe, and rightly so, that if English becomes widely used so as to supplant French the fault will lie wholly with the French Canadians themselves.

The Semaine Sociale is not opposed to capitalism as such but condemns hyper-capitalism, an economic dictatorship, that concentration of power into the hands of a financial oligarchy, that regime which does not discriminate between material and spiritual values, which disturbs acquired equilibrium without substituting a new one in its place, which confuses the power of impulsion with the power of direction.

Due emphasis is given to conditions of labor in French Canadian social thought. For the observance of Sunday rest in particular, the Semaine Sociale went to all lengths: the *Ligue du dimanche* headed by Father Archambault and Msgr. Lapointe undertook to put lukewarm Catholics in step with genuine French Canadian

Catholics who consider Sunday profanation a national crime. Again, the Semaine Sociale and its followers insist on the abolition of labor among married women. They are convinced that the woman's place is mainly in the home and hold that unemployment would be reduced if the respective sexes resumed their normal place in life.

Among the solutions proposed to better economic conditions, the Semaine Sociale stresses the cooperative movement. Though the French Canadians were slow in adopting this procedure of buying and selling on a large scale, today they are making up for lost time. They have developed cooperatives of all types and established a *Conseil supérieur de la coopération* to spread the doctrine of cooperation and thus coordinate this movement. French Canadians have faith in this form of enterprise, thinking it is destined to give them the social and economic independence they need to continue their march towards a higher destiny. The *Caisses populaires,* the first real attempt at cooperation, constitute a very powerful cooperative institution in French Canada. Foreigners from Costa Rica, Argentina, and other countries of South America and the United States, have come to study its functioning. By means of cooperatives French Canadians have attained powerful economic and social standing and have helped destroy the myth of their fatal economic inferiority. This movement alone can save French Canada; it is the only remedy for its economic ills and the only protection against socialism and with this the writer fully agrees. Quite significant is the fact that in several of these cooperative movements, we find both French and English groups. Let those who still believe that "nothing good can come out of French Canada" consider the message sent out by French Canada to the four corners of America: "Cooperation is Christian charity in activity." Survival is their aim, cooperation their means. French Canadians realize that without union a people will perish, that a nation divided against itself enriches its neighbors.

The Catholic labor unions in French Canada have achieved remarkable results. For their insistence on the idea 'Catholic' and 'national' they have incurred the antagonism of non-Catholic employers. The number of members is, none the less, on the increase. Although handicapped by not being able to resort to means that would not be in accordance with the dictates of a doctrine more austere than that advocated by non-Catholic groups, their expansion has been notable. One characteristic of the Catholic syndicate is the presence of a chaplain at its meetings and the expression of his opinion in the various decisions. The tenet of French Canadians concerning unionism is commonly stated as "free syndicates in organized profession." Msgr. Eugène Lapointe was a pioneer in the establishment of Catholic syndicates in Chicoutimi and thence they spread to all sections of the Province. The able Vicar General has left to French Canadian posterity associations which aim to establish social peace and justice, awaken a reverence for moral worth, in a word, emphasize spiritual values. It was fortunate that French Canadians were so organized at a time when neutral unions with socialist tendencies were attempting to enlist Catholics and non-Catholics alike. Father Albert Fortin, under the pseudonym Aubert du Lac, has shown in *L'Oeuvre d'une élite* how the *Cercle d'Etude des Ouvriers* has helped to spread labor unions principally in Quebec City. The Semaine Sociale would make these Catholic syndicates form the basis for the establishment of corporative organizations as advocated by the social Popes, and insists on the immediate establishment of such a corporative system whose role would be to place economy at the service of man rather than man at the service of economy. French Canadian thinkers, like Professors Caron and Minville, who have studied the question, conclude that only a corporative institution can establish and restore society on more humane and more Christian bases than those of present-day capitalism.

The Semaine Sociale has long recognized that colonization in French Canada should be a permanent and national institution: it is a question of extinction and survival. Present colonizing policies are inadequate. Cooperating with the State, the clergy have multiplied diocesan societies of colonization to prepare and coordinate the work in a given region, to organize aids for needy colonists and to choose the best persons for the various centers of colonization. To the Church in French Canada, colonization is a question of vital importance and for that reason she feels it should be a permanent and national institution. If in fifty years all lands in the Province of Quebec will be occupied, in the opinion of a prominent economist, where then will French Canadian sons build their homes? Would Canada then become the Canada of the French Canadians or a Canada of one nation?

When we consider that for eighty years French Canadians were without adequate schooling facilities, instead of minimizing their accomplishments in education we are prompted to admire the excellent system of instruction operating in French Canada today. The *Conseil de l'Instruction publique,* with its Catholic Committee comprising the bishops of all the Province and an equal number of laymen, its Protestant Committee attending to Protestant education, and a Jewish Committee for Jewish schools, forms a regime of confessional schools under the direction of a committee independent of politics. And such a system, which also operates in some of the other Provinces, is unique in the Western Hemisphere. In French Canada the Catholic majority concedes to the non-Catholic minority absolute authority over its school system, and provides for its use a generous proportion of school taxes. The anti-French and anti-Catholic propagandists who have branded the Province of Quebec as narrow-minded and intolerant, may well consider such a situation in which an entire people give proof of scrupulous respect for the rights of minorities. Mr. Omer Côté, Minister of the Provincial Government, is charged with providing the necessary funds to the Council. Under such a regime French Canadian schools have remained confessional and progressive. Fifteen years ago, the *sous-ministre* of New Brunswick, Mackay admitted that Quebec was ahead of them in educational progress by a century. What would he say today?

All down their history French Canadians have been thundering against neutral schools. To this day the teaching of religion has occupied a place of honor in education and will continue to do so if we are to judge from Mr. Omer Côté's statement at the meeting of the *Alliance des professeurs de Montréal* on February 1, 1945, "Il n'y a pas trop de religion dans nos écoles." In agreement with many others he is, in fact, convinced that there is not nearly enough. It is the writer's belief that the French Canadian system of education is not inferior to that of other countries because it is based on Christianity. The other provinces have not failed to recognize the interesting variety of schools: agricultural and technical. Even the school of domestic science is well represented. The numerous classical colleges furnish that culture, the loss of which some Americans at present deplore, that culture, which in past years, the wealthiest sought in Europe. French Canadians are well aware of the incalculable services rendered by religion to their young. They know that most sound thinkers today demand religious teaching in the school, be they of England, the United States or other provinces of Canada.

One does not see in French Canada long lines of children waiting to be admitted to a movie-show. The Province of Quebec has a law forbidding the admission of children under sixteen years of age unless the movie be free of charge and given in an educational institution. A Bureau of Censorship prohibits the presentation of immoral and anti-religious films.

Even though the Catholic press has not the circulation of the neutral *La Presse* especially among the masses, it is considered by the Semaine Social to be an important agent of education. There has been a remarkable purgation in recent years of what was once called the "yellow press." The detailed narration of crime has practically disappeared. When one is asked why one buys *La Presse,* the answer is frequently: "My wife wants to read the Dupuis ads."

The radio, too, is considered an important means of education. Recently, its programs aroused the attention of the *Conseil de l'Instruction publique*. It was decreed at the last meeting of the Catholic Committee to write to the various radio stations to demand the exclusion of programs which vulgarize the French language and thus exert an objectionable influence on the language of young people. The French Canadian elite is intent on keeping intact the elegant French speech of the clergy, the legal profession and the journalist which is none other than the so-called "Parisian" French. Definitely, if imperceptibly, all avenues of education are under the watchful eye and care of the Church.

In French Canada, as early as 1894, Mr. Joseph Royal had indicated the false maxims of socialism; in 1901, Father Lortie had exposed its dangers and in 1914 Professor Saint-Pierre had condemned it. The Semaine Sociale preceded *Divini Redemptoris* in expounding the pernicious tenets of communism and was subsequently confirmed in its attitude by that encyclical. Some speakers made a closer identification between socialism and communism than others did, but after 1932 they abandoned calling Russia socialistic; unanimously they spoke of the Communistic regime of Russia. Throughout the Province, communism has made little progress, precisely because its atheism jars the religious sentiment of the population. In the Province of Quebec, the *loi de cadenas,* which authorized the closure of communistic sources of propaganda, shows what a people can do in the face of foreign elements of disorder. The Federal law proscribing communistic organizations within Canada aided considerably.

Individualism, common also to most peoples today, seems to be a defect of French Canada. We see this not so much in actual practice but in a certain disinterestedness in the lot of others, a negative attitude towards unknown neighbors. To combat the evils of liberalism the Semaine Sociale has stressed the establishments of corporative organizations as advocated by the social Popes. Racism has been condemned as unworthy of children of the same Father.

Rarely does French Canadian social thought fail to propose remedies for existing abuses. The French Canadian facility for adaptation is evident when we consider the rapidity with which institutions were founded as new needs arose,—institutions which have aroused the admiration of outsiders, for the prosperity they enjoy and the influence they exercise on their people. As soon as a need is felt, or an abuse takes root, or a reform becomes urgent, there arises an organ, an initiative which gains momentum, accomplishes its beneficial role and works for better social conditions.

Religious influence in French Canada exerts a preponderant action in all the phases of society, in all its activities, not only in those specifically religious but also in social, civil and political activities. The French Civil Code, which continued to rule domestic and civil life after the English Conquest, is in part responsible for the conservatism of French Canada. It is constantly being adapted to present local conditions, the law-makers, however, guarding and defending it with continuous vigilance. The disciples of the Semaine Sociale are convinced that their Catholic and French civilization is superior to that of their neighbors and that while more human it is also more divine. Up to now, they hold, this situation has allowed French Canadians to survive. They are now beginning to go ahead and even surpass others. Mr. Côté's speech confirms this stand.

In the thinking of the Semaine Sociale, Catholic Action, in the hands of specialized apostles, can solve serious contemporary problems and enrich life with Christian ideals. Because "the world is dying of ignorance of truth" and action dominates the Semaine Sociale, Father Archambault and his collaborators have undertaken the arduous task of "bearing witness." They appear to the writer as a "spectacle to men and angels," a cultivated group solving social problems in a Christlike fashion and maintaining public morality. Favoring a technique of non-participation, induced to weigh Christian social values against materialistic policies of other nationalities, they present a living example of Catholic faith.

As it has been pointed out in the chapter on Christian Reconstruction, justice and charity, two essential elements of moral and social greatness, are the heritage of French Canada in general. A nation without these is bound to decay. French Canada has survived and has preserved something of the faith, aspiration and idealism of its forefathers. The French Canadian loves justice, as his attitude and respect towards minorities in his Province testify. Charity, too, finds expression in multiple ways especially in works of mercy. The writer believes that if French Canadians continue to practice these fundamental virtues, they will redeem their apparent weakness and relative inferiority and may look to the future with light heart and hopeful cheer. In normal times, French Canadians appear as a model of order, probity and social peace, a people attached to their birthplace and country, determined to survive with their language, their traditions, and their religion. They remain a great people because they are a truly religious people. The Semaine Sociale has recognized a manifestation of God's richness in the diversity of peoples, has brought to light the endeavors of the French Canadian to maintain that diversity, to perpetuate the virtues and qualities of the French soul and its civilizing influence. In a word, it has brought to light the past and present conditions and accomplishments of a great people that has exemplified the saying: "In necessariis unitas, in dubiis libertas, in omnibus caritas."

SELECTED BIBLIOGRAPHY

Primary Sources

Comptes rendus des Semaines Sociales du Canada. Montréal: Ecole Sociale Populaire.

I. Montréal, 1920 (Encyclique *Rerum novarum*)
II. Québec, 1921 (Le Syndicalisme)
III. Ottawa, 1922 (Capital et travail)
IV. Montréal, 1923 (La Famille)
V. Sherbrooke, 1924 (La Propriété)
VI. Les Trois-Rivières, 1925 (La Justice)
VII. Québec, 1927 (L'Autorité)
VIII. St-Hyacinthe, 1928 (Le Problème économique)
IX. Chicoutimi, 1929 (La Cité)
X. Ottawa, 1931 (L'Etât)
XI. Montréal, 1932 (L'Ordre social chrétien)
XII. Rimouski, 1933 (Le Problème de la terre)
XIII. Joliette, 1935 (L'Education sociale)
XIV. Les Trois-Rivières, 1936 (L'organisation professionnelle)
XV. Saint-Hyacinthe, 1937 (La Coopération)
XVI. Sherbrooke, 1938 (Pour une société chrétienne)
XVII. Nicolet, 1940 (Le Chrétien dans la famille)
XVIII. Québec, 1941 (Action catholique et action sociale)
XIX. Saint-Jean, 1942 (La Démocratie)
XX. Valleyfield, 1943 (La Tempérance, règle de vie)
XXI. Ottawa, 1944 (La Restauration sociale)

Books

Almanach du peuple. Montréal: Librairie Beauchemin, 1943.

Allaire, J. B. *Dictionnaire biographique du Clergé canadien-français.* Montréal: Imprimerie du "Devoir," Vol. III, 1911.

———. *Dictionnaire biographique du Clergé canadien-français.* Québec: Imprimerie l'Action Sociale Ltée, 4e supplément, 1918.

———. *Dictionnaire biographique du Clergé canadien-français.* Montréal: Imprimerie De LaSalle, 3e complément, 1930.

———. *Dictionnaire biographique du Clergé français.* Saint-Hyacinthe: Imprimerie du "Courrier de Saint-Hyacinthe," Vol. VI, 1934.

Angus, H. F. *Canada and Her Great Neighbor.* Toronto: The Ryerson Press, 1938.

Annuaire général de l'Université Laval pour l'année académique 1943-1944. Québec: L'Action Catholique, 1943.

Archambault, Joseph-Papin. *Esquisses sociales.* Librairie d'Action Canadienne-Française, Ltée, 1930.

———. *Pour un catholicisme conquérant.* Montréal: Ecole Sociale Populaire, 1933.

———. *La Question sociale et nos devoirs de catholiques.* Montréal: Ecole Sociale Populaire, 1917.

———. *La Restauration de l'ordre social d'après les encycliques Rerum novarum et Quadragesimo anno.* Montréal: Ecole Sociale Populaire, 1932.

———. *Les Syndicats catholiques: une digue contre le bolchévisme.* Montréal: Editions de La Vie Nouvelle, 1919.

Armstrong, Elizabeth H. *The Crisis of Quebec, 1914-18.* New York: Columbia University Press, 1937.

Aubert du Lac. *L'Oeuvre d'une élite.* Québec: Editions de L'Action Sociale Catholique, 1918.

Barbeau, Marius. *Québec Where Ancient France Lingers.* Toronto: The Macmillan Company of Canada Limited, 1936.

Barbeau, Victor. *Mesure de notre taille.* Montréal: Imprime au "Devoir," 1936.

Bergeron, Jean. *L'Agriculture et l'Eglise; deux amies intimes d'origine divine.* Québec: Jean Bergeron, 1943.

———. *Loi morale et pain quotidien.* Montréal: Editions Albert Lévesque, 1932.

Bernier, Adrien. *The Schools of Sainte-Anne-de-la-Pocatière.* Québec: Louis-A Bélisle, 1942.

Bilodeau, Georges-Marie. *Le vrai remède.* Québec: L'Action Sociale Limitée, 1931.

Biographies canadienne-françaises. Ottawa: J. A. Fortier, 1920.

Les Biographies françaises d'Amérique. Montréal: Les Journalistes associés, 1942.

Bovey, Wilfrid. *Canadien: A Study of the French Canadians.* London: J. M. Dent and Sons Ltd., 1933.

———. *The French Canadians Today.* J. M. Dent and Sons Ltd., 1939.

Bracq, Jean C. *The Evolution of French Canada.* New York: The Macmillan Company, 1926.

Brady, Alexander. *Canada.* New York: Charles Scribner's Sons, 1932.

Bruchesi, Jean. *Histoire du Canada pour tous.* Tome II. Le Régime anglais. Montréal: Editions Albert Lévesque, 1935.

———. *Histoire du Canada pour tous.* Tome I Le Régime français. Montréal: Editions Albert Lévesque, 1936.

Chagnon, Louis. *Directives sociales catholiques.* Montréal: L'Action Paroissiale, 1937.

The Canada Year Book. Ottawa: James A. Mackinnon, 1942.

The Canadian Parliamentary Guide. Ottawa: Syndicats d'oeuvres sociales limitée, 1944.

Code social. Montréal: Editions de L'Ecole Sociale Populaire, 1939.

Desrosiers, Jean-Baptiste. *Choisissons la doctrine sociale de l'Eglise ou la ruine.* Montréal: Editions de l'Ecole Sociale Populaire, 1936.

Ducharme, Jacques. *Shadows of the Trees; the story of French Canadians in New England.* New York: Harper and Brothers, 1943.

Dulac, Paul. *Silhouettes d'aujourd'hui.* Montréal: Le Devoir, 1927.

Duncan, Dorothy. *Here's to Canada!* New York: Harper and Brothers Publishers, 1941.

Farley, P. E., and Lamarche, G. *Histoire du Canada.* Montréal: Librairie des Clercs de Saint Viateur, 1937.

Furfey, Paul Hanly. *Fire on the Earth.* New York: The Macmillan Company, 1936.

———. *The Mystery of Iniquity.* Milwaukee: The Bruce Publishing Company, 1944.

Gauthier, Lorenzo. *Pour un ordre social chrétien.* Montréal: Editions de l'Ecole Sociale Populaire, 1941-42.

Gérin, Leon. *Le Type économique et social des canadiens.* Montréal: Editions de l'Action Canadienne Française, Tome I, 1937.

Green, B. M. (ed). *Who's Who in Canada.* Toronto: International Press Limited, 1940-41.

Hémon, Louis. *Maria Chapdelaine, récit du Canada français.* Paris: Bernard Grasset, Editeur, 1921.

Hughes, Everett C. *French Canada in Transition.* Chicago: The University of Chicago Press, 1943.

L'Inventaire du mouvement coopératif. Québec: Ernest Tremblay, 1944.

Lanctot, Gustave. *Les Canadiens français et leurs voisins du sud.* Montréal: Editions Bernard Valiquette, 1941.

Leclair, Sister M. Saint Ida. *Utopias and the Philosophy of Saint Thomas.* Washington, D. C.: The Catholic University Press, 1941.

Lorang, Sister M. Corde. *The Effects of Reading on Moral Conduct and Emotional Experience.* The Catholic University Press, 1945.

MacLean, Donald A. *The Morality of the Strike.* New York: P. J. Kenedy and Sons, 1921.

———. *Christian Industrial Democracy.* Toronto: Catholic Truth Society, 1927.

Magnin, E. *Un demi-siècle de pensée catholique.* Paris: Librairie Blond & Gay, 1937.

Maltais, M.-Ludovic. *Les syndicats catholiques canadiens.* Washington, D. C.: L'Université Catholique d'Amerique, 1925.

Minville, Esdras et al. *L'Agriculture.* Montréal: Editions Fides, 1943.

Minville, Esdras. *Invitation à l'étude.* Montréal: Editions Fides, 1942.

Minville Esdras et al. *Montréal économique.* Montréal: Editions Fides, 1943.
———. *Notre Milieu, aperçu général sur la province de Québec.* Montréal: Editions Fides, 1942.
Montpetit, Edouard. *La Conquête économique. Les Forces essentielles,* Vol. I. Montréal: Editions Bernard Valiquette, 1939.
———. *Etapes,* Vol. II. 1940.
———. *Perspectives,* Vol. III. 1942.
———. *Les Cordons de la bourse.* Montréal: Editions Albert Lévesque, 1935.
———. *Le Front contre la vitre.* Mintréal: Editions Albert Lévesque, 1936.
———. *Pour une doctrine.* Montréal: Librairie d'Action Canadienne-Française Limitée, 1931.
Moore, William Henry. *The Clash! A Study of Nationalities.* New York: E. P. Dutton and Company, 1918.
Ouimet, Raphael. *Biographie canadienne-française.* Montréal, 1920-29.
Roy, Pierre-Georges. *Les Avocats de la région de Québec.* Lévis, 1936.
———. *Les Juges de la Province de Québec.* Québec: Service des Archives du Gouvernement de la Province, 1933.
Rumilly, Robert. *Chefs de file.* Montréal: Les Editions du Zodiaque, 1934.
Saint-Pierre, Arthur. *Le Problème social.* Montréal: Bibliothèque de l'Action Française, 1926.
———. *Questions et oeuvres sociales de chez nous.* Montréal: Ecole Sociale Populaire, 1914.
Siegfried, André. *Le Canada, puissance internationale.* Paris: Librairie Armand Colin, 1937.
Turmann, Max. *Le Developpement du catholicisme social depuis l'encyclique "Rerum novarum."* Paris: Librairies Félix Alcan et Guillaumin Réunis, 1909.
Vattier, Georges. *Esquisse historique de la colonisation de la Province de Québec* (1608-1925). Paris: Librairie Ancienne Honoré Champion, 1928.
———. *Essai sur la mentalité canadienne-française.* Paris: Librairie Ancienne Honoré Champion, 1925.
Walsh, Mary Elizabeth. *The Saints and Social Work.* Silver Spring: The Preservation of the Faith, 1937.
Welton, Sister M. Amadeus. *Monseigneur Paul-Eugène Roy, Archevêque de Québec* (1859-1926). Québec: Les Editions de l'Action Catholique, 1941.

PAMPHLETS

L'aide à la colonisation. Montréal: Ecole Sociale Populaire, 1944.
Anger, F. A., Gouin, L. M., et al. *Vers un ordre nouveau par l'organisation corporative.* Montréal: Ecole Sociale Populaire, 1940.
Archambault, Joseph-Papin. *L'Eglise catholique et les devoirs du chrétien.* Montréal: Ecole Sociale Populaire, 1917.

———. *La Menace communiste au Canada.* Montréal: Ecole Sociale Populaire, 1934.

———. *Pour restaurer la famille.* Montréal: Ecole Sociale Populaire, 1944.

———. *Pour un ordre meilleur.* Montréal: Ecole Sociale Populaire, 1944.

Bellavance, S. *La Formation d'apôtres sociaux par l'A.C.J.C.* Montréal: Ecole Sociale Populaire, 1915.

Caron, Maximilien. *L'Organisation corporative au service de la démocratie.* Montréal: Ecole Sociale Populaire, 1942.

Cercle d'étude, Brève introduction à la coopération des consommateurs. Sainte-Anne-de-la-Pocatière: Fortin et Fils, n. d.

Cloutier, Edmond. *L'Aspect économique du problème industriel.* Montréal: Secrétariat de l'Ecole Sociale Populaire, 1921.

Colombain, Maurice. *Faire des hommes nouveaux.* Québec: Le Conseil supérieur de la Coopération, 1943.

La Confédération des travailleurs catholiques du Canada. Montréal: Secrétariat de l'Ecole Sociale Populaire, 1921.

Cooper, John M. *Temporal Sequence and Marginal Peoples.* Washington, D. C.: The Catholic University of America, 1941.

La Coopérative de consommation. Québec: Imprimerie Ernest Tremblay, n. d.

Desjardins, Alphonse. *La Caisse populaire.* Montréal: Ecole Sociale Populaire, 1912.

Dugré, Adélard. *La jeune fille et les oeuvres de charité.* Montréal: Ecole Sociale Populaire, 1925.

———. *La Paroisse au Canada-français.* Montréal: Ecole Sociale Populaire, 1929.

L'Esprit chrétien dans la famille et dans la société. Extrait de la lettre des Pères du Premier Concile Plénier de Québec. Montréal: Secrétariat de l'Ecole Sociale Populaire, 1916.

Falardeau, Jean-Charles. *Analyse sociale des communautés rurales.* Cahiers de la Faculté des Sciences Sociales de l'Université Laval. Québec: Editions du "Cap Diamant," 1944.

Falardeau, Jean-Charles. *Paroisse de France et de la Nouvelle-France au XVIIe siecle.* Cahiers de l'Ecole des Sciences Sociales Politiques et Economiques de Laval. Québec: Editions du "Cap Diamant," 1943.

Filion, Gérard. *Le Conseil supérieur de la coopération.* Québec: Conseil Supérieur de la Coopération, 1940.

———. *Notions élémentaires de coopération agricole.* Montréal: La Librairie de L'U.C.C., 1939-1940.

———. *La Tenue des assemblées dans une coopérative agricole.* Québec: Imprimerie Ernest Tremblay, n. d.

Gagné, Charles. *Notre problème agricole.* Montréal: Ecole Sociale Populaire, 1924.

Gauthier, Henri. *Le Foyer et ses oeuvres.* Montréal: Secrétariat de l'Ecole Sociale Populaire, 1912.

Gérin-Lajoie, Marie, J. *Le Cercle d'études feminins.* Ecole Sociale Populaire, 1916.

Germain, V. *Les Chroniques de la Crêche.* Québec: Victorin Germain, 1943.

Hannam, H. H. *La Coopération.* Ontario: The United Farmers of Ontario, 1939.

Hébert, Edmour. *L'Organisation ouvrière.* Montréal: Ecole Sociale Populaire, 1919.

———. *Le Problème social et sa solution.* Montréal: Ecole Sociale Populaire, 1919.

Lebel, Léon. *Les Allocations familiales.* Montréal: Ecole Sociale Populaire, 1927.

———. *"Family Allowances" as a Means of Preventing Emigration.* Montréal, 1929.

———. *Le Problème de la famille nombreuse.* Montréal: Le Devoir, 1928.

Lery, Louis C. de. *Ecoles nationales.* Montréal: Ecole Sociale Populaire, 1944.

Lévesque, Georges-Henri. *Service social et charité.* Cahiers de la Faculté des Sciences Sociales de l'Université Laval. Québec: Editions du "Cap Diamant," 1944.

Minville, Esdras. *La Force conquérante de la coopération.* Québec: Le Conseil Supérieur de la Coopération, 1943.

Montpetit, Edouard. *Les Universités et l'enseignement des sciences politiques et sociales.* London: G. Bell and Sons, Ltd., 1922.

Perrault, Antonio. *L'Action sociale.* Montréal: Ecole Sociale Populaire, 1920.

Leo XIII. *On the Condition of Labor.* New York: The Paulist Press, 1939.

Pius XI. *On the Reconstruction of the Social Order.* New York: The American Press, 1938.

Poulin, Gonzalve. *Education populaire et loisirs d'après-guerre.* Cahiers de L'Ecole des Sciences Sociales, Politiques, et Economiques de Laval. Québec: Editions "Cap Diamant," 1943.

Poulin, Gonzalve, et al. *Le Logement à Québec.* Québec: Editions "Cap Diamant," 1944.

Premier Congrès de la Fédération nationale Saint-Jean-Baptiste. Montréal: Paradis, Vincent et Cie, 1907.

Ross, Francis-Xavier. *Circulaire au Clergé.* July 21, 1923.

———. *Education chrétienne et action catholique.* Montréal: Editions Fides, 1943.

———. *Lettre aux Aumoniers, Assistants et Dirigeants de l'Action Catholique et aux Superieurs des Communautés enseignantes dans le diocèse de Gaspé.* September 17, 1942.

———. *Lettre pastorale sur le devoir social.* March 20, 1944.

Sa Grandeur Mgr. Courchesne. Montréal: L'Oeuvre des Tracts, 1928.

Saint-Armand, J. B. *Le Mouvement mutualiste dans la province de Québec.* Société catholique de secours mutuels, 1912.

Saint-Pierre, Arthur. *L'Avenir du Canada-français.* Montréal: Imprimerie du Messager, 1909.

———. *Le Bilan moral d'une grande expérience sociale.* Montréal: Beauchemin, 1924.

———. *L'Organisation professionnelle.* Montréal: Ecole Sociale Populaire, 1913.

———. *La Question ouvrière au Canada.* Montréal, Canada, 1920.

———. *Utopie socialiste.* Montréal: Ecole Sociale Populaire, 1914.

———. *What Are All Those Nuns Good For? An Unusual Answer to an Oft-repeated Query.* Montréal: La Bibliothèque Canadienne Enregistrée, 1928.

Les Semaines sociales. Montréal: Secrétariat de l'Ecole Sociale Populaire, 1920.

Tremblay, Gérard. *L'Organisation ouvrière catholique au Canada.* Montréal: Ecole Sociale Populaire, 1922.

Vanier, Anatole. *Le Comptoir coopératif.* Montréal: Ecole Sociale Populaire, 1916.

Vanier, Guy. *Vers le peuple.* Montréal: Ecole Sociale Populaire, 1920.

Villeneuve, Jean-Marie R. *Spiritualité d'action catholique pour les aumoniers.* Montréal: Editions Fides, 1942.

Newspapers and Periodicals

L'Action Canadienne-française (Montréal), 1928.
L'Action Catholique (Québec), 1920-44.
L'Action Française (Montréal), 1920-28.
L'Action Nationale (Montréal), 1933-40.
L'Action Universitaire (Montréal), 1944.
America (New York), 1942.
La Bonne Parole (Montréal), 1917-23.
Le Canada Français (Québec), 1940-44
The Canadian Register (Toronto and Kingston, Ontario), 1931-43.
La Croix (Paris), 1933.
Culture (Québec), 1944.
Le Devoir (Montréal), 1920-44.
Le Droit (Ottawa), 1920-44.
L'Enseignement primaire (Québec), 1928.
Ensemble! (Québec), 1944.
La Famille (Laprairie), 1945.
Journal of Royal Architectural Institute of Canada (Toronto), 1944.
Laval Médical (Québec), 1944.
Le Messager Canadien (Montréal), 1943.

The Montreal Daily Star, 1920-44.
Montréal-Matin, 1941.
Oblate World (Buffalo), 1939.
L'Ordre Nouveau (Montréal), 1936-40.
Le Patriote (Gravelbourg), 1933.
La Presse (Montréal), 1920-44.
Providence Visitor, 1944.
Relations (Montréal), 1940-44.
Revue Dominicaine (Saint-Hyacinthe), 1928.
Le Richelieu (Saint-Jean), 1942.
Third Order Forum (Chicago), 1928.
The Torch (Somerset, Ohio), 1944.
La Tribune (Sherbrooke), 1920-44.
La Vie des communautés religieuses (Montréal), 1934.
La Vie Nouvelle (Montréal), 1928.

Unpublished Materials

Gaudreau, Sister M. Cécilia de Jésus. "Mexico's Contribution to Rural Indian Education." Unpublished Master's Dissertation, Catholic Teachers' College, Providence, R. I., 1943.

Laramée, Jean-de-Brébeuf. "Suggestions for Promoting Family Life Interest from a French Canadian viewpoint." Paper read at the Family Life Conference, The Catholic University of America, Washington, D. C., February 2, 1945.

INDEX